Explore the South West Coast Path

A GUIDE FOR WALKERS, BACKPACKERS AND TRAIL RUNNERS

Mark Rainsley

 Pesda Press LTD   www.pesdapress.com

First published in Great Britain 2024 by Pesda Press

Tan y Coed Canol

Ceunant

Caernarfon

Gwynedd

LL55 4RN

© Copyright 2024 Mark Rainsley

ISBN: 9781917182003

Maps by Bute Cartographics.
Contains Ordnance Survey data © Crown copyright and database right 2024.

The Author has asserted his rights under the Copyright, Designs and Patents Act, 1988, to be identified as Author of this Work. All rights reserved. No part of this publication may be reproduced, stored in a retrieval system, or transmitted, in any form or by any means, electronic, mechanical, photocopying, recording or otherwise, without the prior written permission of the publisher.

Printed in Poland, www.hussarbooks.pl

About the Author
Mark Rainsley

Mark has lived and worked in the South West for three decades. He has repeatedly walked, backpacked and trail-run the wonderful South West Coast Path and, incidentally, has kayaked around the entire South West peninsula, three times! Mark has authored numerous Pesda Press guidebooks including *South West Trail Running*, *South East Trail Running* and *South West Sea Kayaking*.

Acknowledgements

A huge thanks to the numerous friends and family who joined me in explorations to revisit the entire length of the South West Coast Path, during 'research' for this book! Special thanks to Eurion Brown, Chris Eden, Anne Garnett, Lizzie Garnett and Claire Pinder who gave up more time than most to explore the trails with me. You (usually) brought the good weather with you, and you've all been fantastic company!

Thanks also to the Pesda Press team for their support and guidance; Franco Ferrero for his editing, Vicky Barlow for her great design work, Don Williams of Bute Cartographics for the stunning maps and Andrew Whiting for the proofreading.

Contents

About the Author 3
Acknowledgements 3
Contents 4

INTRODUCTION 7

The South West Coast Path National Trail 7
History of the South West Coast Path 7
What is this book for? 7
Exploring the South West Coast Path 8
    Plan for safety 8
    Navigation and route-finding: follow the acorn! 8
    Trail running 9
    Backpacking and fastpacking 9
    Wild camping 9
The South West Coast Path Association 10
How to use this book 10

SOMERSET AND NORTH DEVON 11

1	Minehead to Porlock Weir 15
2	Porlock Weir to Lynmouth 19
3	Lynmouth to Combe Martin 25
4	Combe Martin to Ilfracombe 29
5	Ilfracombe to Woolacombe 33
6	Woolacombe to Saunton 37
7	Saunton to Barnstaple 41
8	Barnstaple to Bideford 45
9	Bideford to Westward Ho! 49
10	Westward Ho! to Clovelly 53
11	Clovelly to Hartland Quay 57
12	Hartland Quay to Bude 61

NORTH CORNWALL 67

13	Bude to Crackington Haven 69
14	Crackington Haven to Tintagel 73
15	Tintagel to Port Isaac 79
16	Port Isaac to Rock 83
17	Padstow to Porthcothan 87
18	Porthcothan to Newquay 93
19	Newquay to Perranporth 99
20	Perranporth to Porthtowan 105
21	Porthtowan to Godrevy 111
22	Godrevy to St Ives 115
23	St Ives to Pendeen Watch 119
24	Pendeen Watch to Sennen Cove 125

SOUTH CORNWALL **131**

25	Sennen Cove to Porthcurno	133
26	Porthcurno to Penzance	137
27	Penzance to Praa Sands	143
28	Praa Sands to Poldhu Cove	147
29	Poldhu Cove to Lizard Point	151
30	Lizard Point to Coverack	155
31	Coverack to Helford Passage	159
32	Helford Passage to Falmouth	163
33	St Mawes to Pendower Beach	167
34	Pendower Beach to Gorran Haven	171
35	Gorran Haven to Charlestown	175
36	Charlestown to Fowey	181
37	Polruan to Polperro	185
38	Polperro to Seaton	189
39	Seaton to Freathy	193
40	Freathy to Cremyll	197

SOUTH AND EAST DEVON **203**

41	Plymouth (Stonehouse) to Jennycliff Bay	205
42	Jennycliff Bay to Warren Point	209
43	Noss Mayo to Mothecombe	213
44	Mothecombe to Hope Cove	217
45	Hope Cove to Salcombe	223
46	East Portlemouth to Hallsands	227
47	Hallsands to Dartmouth	231
48	Kingswear to Brixham	237
49	Brixham to Torquay	241
50	Torquay to Shaldon	245
51	Teignmouth to Starcross	249
52	Exmouth to Sidmouth	253
53	Sidmouth to Seaton	259
54	Seaton to Lyme Regis	263

DORSET **269**

55	Lyme Regis to West Bay	271
56	West Bay to Abbotsbury	275
57	Abbotsbury to Weymouth	279
58	The Isle of Portland	283
59	Weymouth to Lulworth Cove	287
60	Lulworth Cove to Kimmeridge Bay	293
61	Kimmeridge Bay to Swanage	297
62	Swanage to South Haven Point	303
63	West Bexington to Osmington Mills	307

INDEX 315

Bedruthan Steps (Section 18).

Introduction

Explore, n.
An act of exploring an unfamiliar place; an exploration, an excursion.

Oxford English Dictionary

The South West Coast Path National Trail

The South West Coast Path extends around the fringes of Britain's South West peninsula, from Minehead in Somerset to South Haven Point in Dorset, via Land's End at its westernmost extremity. A continuous 1014km/ 630-mile path, following ever-changing, but regularly breathtakingly beautiful, cliffs, beaches, inlets and headlands. It passes through one National Park, two UNESCO World Heritage Sites and five Areas of Outstanding Natural Beauty. Despite being simple to access with (generally) good public transport links, the SWCP consistently offers challenging adventures, often in surprisingly wild and remote environs. Taking on the SWCP is not just a physical endeavour, the National Trail is far greater than the sum of its parts; exploring it will reveal remarkable and engaging flora and fauna, geology, history and heritage.
There is simply nothing like it!

History of the South West Coast Path

The Coastguard Service was formed in 1822, to combat smuggling. A coastal path was established to allow officers to patrol and inspect every single inlet and landing. One officer was allocated to every half-mile and cottages were established, no more than half a night's march apart. Much of this original path has of course eroded away, but it inspired the South West Coast Path Association, formed 1972-3, to create the National Trail. The SWCP first opened in 1978. The original route followed the South Dorset Ridgeway (section 63) in Dorset, until the Isle of Portland (section 58) was incorporated in 2003.

What is this book for?

There are a number of good guidebooks giving gate-by-gate route descriptions for the SWCP. This book is not intended to describe the route. Instead, it outlines and highlights the actual experience of exploring the SWCP. This book acts as a companion to your SWCP explorations, revealing the many, many engaging landscapes, sites and environs that you will pass through. Its pages are crammed with landmarks and viewpoints, nature and wildlife, history and geology. This book also indicates the physical challenges and potential hurdles which will accompany your explorations.

Should you choose not to carry this book on the trails, you are recommended to read each section's text before setting out, or photograph the pages using your phone; there is so much interest packed along the SWCP, which you might otherwise miss!

Exploring the South West Coast Path

Any fit and competent walker, backpacker or trail runner can explore the SWCP and, ultimately, complete the entire National Trail!

In this book, the SWCP has been divided into sixty-three sections, each of which are achievable within a day (or a morning, if you are a trail runner!).

All approaches to tackling the SWCP are valid …

Many will wish to tackle sections individually, in whichever order suits them, perhaps starting off with shorter or less difficult sections. These people will use cars or public transport to return to each section's start.

Others will wish to tackle multiple sections back-to-back, using booked accommodation or even 'wild camping' along the way. Some will start at Minehead and take on the significant challenge of a continuous 'thru-hike'!

While most choose to tackle the SWCP anti-clockwise, there is no particular reason for this and you can of course explore sections from either direction.

Plan for safety

The SWCP is exposed to all weathers and the route often takes you far from facilities or refreshments. Always set out equipped with appropriate clothing, food and drink. Tell someone where you are going, and have a means to summon help in an emergency. The UK emergency phone number is 999.

NAVIGATION AND ROUTE-FINDING: FOLLOW THE ACORN!

A written route description is not necessary to explore the SWCP. The route is extremely well-signposted, following the 'Acorn' National Trail logo which is regularly marked on signposts, gates, and so forth. The route follows obvious and well-maintained paths; if a path choice appears unkempt or even dangerous, backtrack and check the signs again. Counter-intuitively, towns can be the trickiest places to navigate; the acorn signs are still there, marked on lamp posts, building walls and even pavements, but can be obscured amongst all the urban distractions and clutter.

The 1:40,000 maps accompanying each section in this book provide an overview of the key features and locations encountered along the route. They are adequate to keep track of your position and progress along the SWCP, as are the thirteen Ordnance Survey 1:50,000 Landranger maps covering the SWCP. However, the sixteen Ordnance Survey 1:25,000 Explorer maps show much more detail and are recommended. A cost-effective approach is to subscribe to a phone app such as OS Maps or Outdooractive, giving access to *all* the Ordnance Survey maps along the route. These apps allow you to instantly confirm your location, on screen.

Phone apps which do not use Ordnance Survey mapping are *not appropriate* for use along the SWCP. Google Maps and What3words are however recommended for locating the start and finish points of each section, usually located within towns or villages. Google Maps is invaluable for planning and calculating shuttle journeys back to the start, by car or public transport.

◎ *Penally Hill, Boscastle (Section 14).*

TRAIL RUNNING

The SWCP's rugged trails and innumerable ascents are ideally suited for trail running explorations; simply put, it ranks among the world's finest trail running experiences. Most trail runners will tackle individual sections or, perhaps, link multiple sections with lightweight fastpacking adventures. However, running the entire National Trail, non-stop, is possible! At time of writing (2024), the fastest known time (FKT) for the entire SWCP is 10 days, 8 hours and 24 minutes, achieved by Dave Phillips in 2022. Sarah Perry set the women's FKT of 13 days, 11 hours and 31 minutes, in April 2024.

More information about trail running on the SWCP can be found in the author's book *South West Trail Running*.

BACKPACKING AND FASTPACKING

Those with experience of backpacking or fastpacking (a lightweight trail running approach) can explore multiple sections of the SWCP over several days, or even take on the full 'thru-hike'. A range of approaches are possible; utilising hotels and bed and breakfasts, camping at official sites, and even wild camping. Planning and pre-booking are highly recommended, see the South West Coast Path Association's *Official Guide* for a directory of services.

WILD CAMPING

Wild camping along the SWCP is only appropriate for those with experience of discreet, lightweight, zero-impact expeditioning. There is no legally enshrined right to 'wild camp' along the SWCP, and spots which obviously lend themselves to wild camping are limited. Nevertheless, there is an established tradition of wild camping being tolerated alongside the SWCP, for single small tents and single nights. Choose locations away from dwellings and roads. Pitch your tent at sunset, depart very early. Leave *absolutely no trace*; in particular, this means that lighting fires is *never* appropriate.

If this practice is something that you wish to learn more about, begin by looking up the *Wild Camping Code of Conduct* online.

The South West Coast Path Association

The South West Coast Path Association are the charity which 'look after' the National Trail. Supporting their work by joining (www.southwestcoastpath.org.uk) is strongly recommended; both for its own sake, and because members receive their excellent *Official Guide* which includes an essential, annually updated, directory of food and accommodation options along the route.

How to use this book

Each section's text begins with a summary of the character of the section, along with an indication of whether it is unusually long, challenging or remote from facilities such as food and water. The text then outlines the key points of interest along the route, as they are encountered.

Each section includes the following information, to help plan your adventure;

Distance	The approximate distance in kilometres and miles. Ferry crossings are not included in distances.
Height gain	An estimate of the total amount of ascent, in metres and feet.
Difficulty	A rating out of five for the physical challenge of this section. ●●●●● means flat, surfaced trails, ●●●●● means multiple, rugged ascents. This rating does not take the distance into account.
Maps	The Ordnance Survey 1:50,000 Landranger and 1:25,000 Explorer maps which cover this section.
Start / Finish	The locations where this section starts and finishes.
Parking near start / finish	The locations of car parks close to this section's start and finish, when they are at a separate location.
Public transport	A summary of bus or rail services which can return you to the start, from the finish. Always check details before departing, using Google Maps.

Coverack (Section 31).

Bull Point Lighthouse (Section 5).

Somerset and North Devon

The first 203km / 126 miles does not offer a gentle warm-up for your SWCP exploration! Divided between Somerset and Devon, Exmoor's high moorland plateau forms Britain's highest mainland sea cliffs. There are tremendous views across the Bristol Channel, but such elevation, coupled with the sprawling Atlantic oakwood rainforest, means that the shore is often obscured from sight. Past the serrated headland of Morte Point, the going becomes milder around Bideford Bay's popular surf beaches. A dogleg inland, via the old ports of Barnstaple and Bideford, explores the birdlife havens of the Taw and Torridge estuaries. The trek west to Hartland Point delves back into the Atlantic oakwood, with high cliffs and deep combes once more. Hartland Point marks the literal turning point where the 'north coast' begins, an epic line of Atlantic-facing cliffs.

These shores begin within Exmoor National Park. The Devon part of the SWCP is designated as the North Devon Coast Areas of Outstanding Natural Beauty and is within the UNESCO North Devon Biosphere Reserve.

South West Coast Path Monument, Minehead.

Above Greenaleigh Farm.

1 Minehead to Porlock Weir

Distance 16km / 10 miles	**Height gain** 770m / 2,550ft	**Difficulty** ●●●●○ / ●●●●●
Maps	OS Landranger 181 / OS Explorer OL09	
Start	South West Coast Path Monument, Minehead TA24 5UJ / multiply.roadshow.gender / SS 971 467	
Finish	Porlock Weir car park TA24 8PB / incomes.blast.tastier / SS 864 478	
Parking near start	Quay West car park, Minehead TA24 5UN / vows.whirlpool.causes / SS 969 471	
Public transport	10 bus. Exmoor Coaster bus on Sundays	

There is an oft-repeated myth (e.g. in the best-selling *The Salt Path*), that the reason why the SWCP is usually tackled anti-clockwise is because Somerset offers a milder warm-up. Sadly, this is indeed a myth: the first three sections cross Exmoor! All negotiate high hills and deep combes (Celtic *cym*: valley), and none have refreshments along the route. This first section is indeed a relatively severe introduction, with some significant climbs. However, there is an option to follow the easier 'Old Coast Path Route'.

The South West Coast Path Monument is a giant pair of hands opening a map. Unveiled in 2001, it was designed by local sixth-former Sarah Ward and sculpted in galvanised steel by Owen Cunningham. You are heading west; pick up your rucksack and get going! Minehead's outer limit

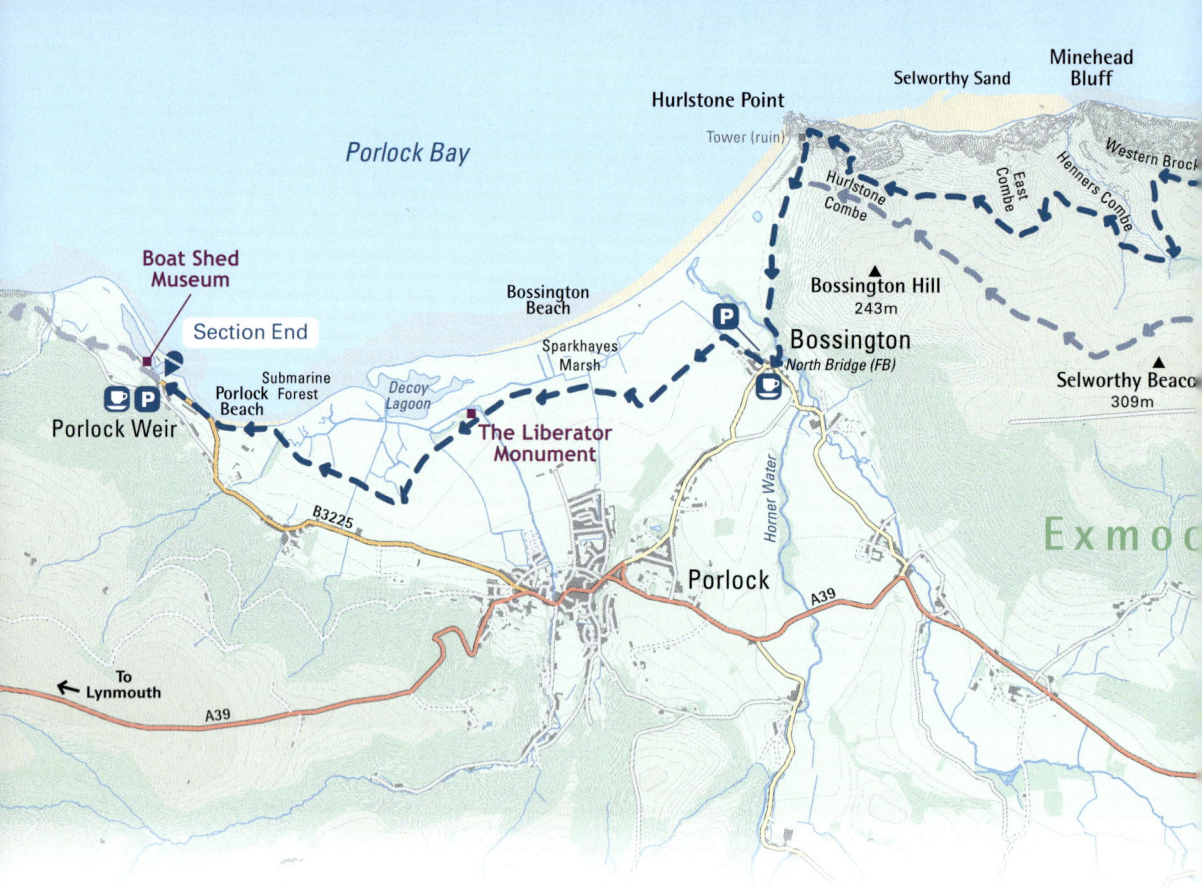

is the once-busy harbour. The path leads alongside meadows backed by wooded hillside. The meadows end, the SWCP enters Exmoor National Park and the first, mild, ascent is encountered above Culver Cliff Sand; like all of the Exmoor coast, the beach is comprised of hefty sandstone boulders, with patches of sand only revealed at the lowest tides.

Greenaleigh Farm's idyllic location overlooks meadows sloping to Greenaleigh Point. The SWCP veers uphill, time to wake up! There will be many big climbs before the SWCP is done, but the first probably hurts the most. A steep zigzag through woods emerges onto moorland covered with bracken, gorse and heather. Around 240m above sea level, the gradient eases. A permissive path branches off on the right, descending a hundred metres to a ruined arch, remains of the fifteenth-century Burgundy Chapel. Only the certifiable will take this side-tour, having just completed the climb.

North Hill's summit plateau extends westwards to Selworthy Beacon. Throughout summer, this high ground is ablaze with colour as the heather flowers, and bilberry bushes alongside the path offer foraging opportunities. Listen and look out for the Dartford Warbler; this tiny bird doesn't migrate and population numbers plummet in winter. The views are tremendous, across the Bristol Channel to South Wales and up the Bristol Channel to the islands of Steep Holm and Flat Holm. Where the path forks, you have a choice; the main route heading off to the right, or the easier 'Old Coast Path Route' leading ahead.

The **Main Route** traverses closer to the coast. Grexy Combe is the first, and most rugged, of three deep combes leading seawards. The hilltop behind is Furzebury Brake, an Iron Age

settlement. A narrower path then traverses the scarp between Eastern Brockholes and Western Brockholes (Middle English *brock*: badger), perched 200m above the beach. Henners Combe is littered with scree slopes, more usually found on mountainsides! Exmoor's coastal scree was formed during the last Ice Age, by freeze-thaw processes: meltwater seeped through the bedrock, before freezing and expanding to shatter it. An arc around East Combe follows, above Selworthy Sand. The SWCP's first big descent follows, a steep zig-zag down to Hurlstone Point, where the 'tower' ruin is a Coastguard station from 1900.

The **Old Coast Path Route** ceased being the official course of the SWCP in 2024, but still offers an easier alternative, being 1.5km shorter with 200m less ascent. It leads along the ridge-top, passing Bronze Age burial mounds dotting the moorland. The 308m summit of Selworthy Beacon is passed after three kilometres. Truly epic views open up ahead, across Porlock Bay to Exmoor's characteristic 'hog's-back' ridges. Incidentally, you are going to climb across all of them. A gradual descent across Bossington Hill leads to a hurtling descent down Hurlstone Combe, crossing scree patches!

The rejoined paths veer inland through woods to Bossington, a picture-postcard thatched village and part of the National Trust's Holnicote Estate.

Porlock Bay's remarkable landscape is quite a contrast. Bossington Beach's four-kilometre pebble barrier formed around 8,000 years ago. After Hurricane Lili breached it in 1996, the sea was

📷 *Porlock Beach.*

allowed to reclaim the farmland. The SWCP threads the hinterland behind the beach, between saltmarsh and fields. High tides or flooding can inundate the route, at which times you'll need to divert inland along footpaths to Porlock and follow the Coleridge Way.

The shingle breach and Decoy Lagoon can be seen at Sparkhayes Marsh. A memorial marks the 1942 crash site of a US Liberator bomber which clipped Bossington Hill, with eleven deaths and one survivor. The dead, bare trees of a drowned copse are possibly the SWCP's strangest sight, a ghostly forest rearing from the saltmarsh.

The coast is joined at Porlock Beach. The tree now enveloped within the shingle ridge was growing freely behind it as recently as 2013, this coast is in flux! Very low tides can reveal 6,000-year-old tree stumps, covered by peat layers containing Mesolithic flints. A pebble trudge leads towards Porlock Weir.

Exmoor National Park

Originally a Medieval Royal Forest (hunting ground), the 692km² National Park was designated in 1954. About 57km / 35 miles of the SWCP traverses Exmoor's 'hog's back'; heather-clad moorland hills, topping Britain's tallest cliffs. Deep combes formed by periglacial floodwaters incise the Devonian sandstone. The Atlantic oakwood, a temperate rainforest, extends down the cliffs to the Bristol Channel's shores, washed by the world's third highest tidal range.

Exmoor is the domain of Britain's largest land animal, the red deer, with a population of around 3,000. They are best spotted around dawn, or during the autumn rut when the stags bellow and wrestle, vying for supremacy.

📷 *St Beuno's Church, Culbone.*

2   Porlock Weir to Lynmouth

Distance 21km / 13 miles	**Height gain** 1,200m / 3,950ft **Difficulty** ●●●●○
Maps	OS Landranger 180, 181 / OS Explorer OL09
Start	Porlock Weir car park TA24 8PB / incomes.blast.tastier / SS 864 478
Finish	Lynmouth EX35 6EF / adopters.exacted.less / SS 722 495
Parking near finish	Lower Lyndale car park, Lynmouth EX35 6ES / bookshop.imported.dragging / SS 723 494
Public transport	Exmoor Coaster and 10 buses, change at Porlock

For much of this long remote outing, the sea is far below and obscured by the dense Atlantic oakwood. In the final third though, truly spectacular views are unveiled …

Picturesque Porlock Weir was a busy working port, until the final shipment of South Wales coal in 1931. To learn more, the Boat Shed Museum is worth a visit. The route follows the shoreline out to pebbly Gore Point, although exceptionally high tides may force an inland diversion following Worthy Toll Road. The Toll Road passes beneath Ashley Combe Lodge, a quirky nineteenth-century Arts and Crafts-style thatched toll house. This was part of the estate of Italianate Ashley Combe House, demolished 1974. The SWCP winds through the former grounds of the house; look out for the culvert and two tunnels, built so that lowly service workers could approach the house unseen.

England's smallest active parish church nestles in isolated Culbone Combe. The churches' nave is tenth century, but Culbone's Celtic name (*kil beun*: Beuno's church) suggests that the

seventh-century Welsh saint may have founded it. The tiny window in the north wall was to allow lepers, banished hereabouts in the sixteenth century, to watch services. Leaving Culbone, there is a choice of routes.

The **Main Route** undulates mildly through Culbone, Embelle and Yenworthy Woods, fording bubbling streams in combes, with occasional glimpses of sea and stony beach. The woodlands are comprised of oaks, sorbus trees and the conifers of a nineteenth-century pinetum. The trees lean precariously on this steep incline; fallen trees usually have to be negotiated. In the thirteenth century, *"disbelievers, the mentally insane, and those practising witchcraft"* lurked in these woods. Nowadays, it's just you; make of that what you will.

Lovelace and Babbage

Ada Lovelace (daughter of poet Lord Byron) lived at Ashley Combe House from 1835. She walked the grounds with fellow mathematician Charles Babbage, discussing his 'Analytical Machine' and 'Difference Engine' inventions: the first computers! Lovelace's notes on how to utilise the latter machine were the first ever computer program.

Exmoor's rainforest

The longest segment of the UK's Atlantic oakwood extends from Porlock Weir to Hartland Point (section 11). The north-facing coast's mild temperatures, shelter from the wind and salty, humid air have, since the Ice Age, nurtured this temperate rainforest. Sessile oak and Scots pine cling to scree-covered slopes and combes. The woodland floor is densely smothered with ferns, lichens and mosses, hence the resident weasels and pine martens are not weasily spotted.

The **Alternative Higher Route** traverses above the treeline, at twice the altitude, following the 300m contour. It's 1.25km longer, but the initial ascent is gradual, so it's not significantly harder. The views are better, back towards Hurlstone Point and Bossington Hill. The often-boggy track links short road interludes at Silcombe and Broomstreet Farms, before a steep descent plunges down Wheatham Combe and re-joins the Main Route at Yenworthy Wood.

The SWCP descends down Yenworthy Combe, towards Glenthorne House. The mansion was built for Reverend Walter Stevenson Halliday in 1829, after he inherited his families' grubby slave plantation wealth. The route arduously climbs and dips, contouring around the half a dozen

combes fanning out above the mansion. The stream trickling down Coscombe Combe is the Somerset-Devon boundary; you've ticked off your first county! The stream emerges 50m higher up the hillside at Sister's Fountain, a cross atop a moss-covered stone alcove. This holy spring was (purportedly) formed when Joseph of Arimathea, bringing the Holy Grail to England, struck the ground with his staff.

Climbing into the Glenthorne Plantations, the coastal scarp grows steeper. The Giant's Rib is an archway formed by wave action, 100m below the path. Garish colour is provided by sprawling rhododendron growths and the views become pretty dramatic when you emerge onto a ridge overlooking Desolation Point. The first significant cliffs seen along the SWCP rear above Sir Robert's Chair, a small stack.

The Battle of Cynuit

Wind Hill is topped by the ramparts of Countisbury Castle, an Iron Age hillfort. This is probably *Arx Cynuit*, described in the *Anglo-Saxon Chronicle* as the site of a major victory for King Alfred's Wessex. Ubba the Viking landed in 878, *"with three and twenty ships, and there was he slain, and eight hundred men with him, and forty of his army. There also was taken the war-flag, which they called the Raven."*

📷 *Lynmouth.*

Chubhill and Gurney's Woods cling to the ever-steepening slope above Countisbury Cove, as the coast arcs towards Foreland Point, Devon and Exmoor's northernmost tip. The SWCP abruptly departs the woods via a track into scree-clad Coddow Combe, a hanging valley leading towards the headland and lighthouse. However, the SWCP shortcuts past, climbing from Coddow Combe. A (non-SWCP) footpath *does* lead around Foreland Point but involves an exhilarating / terrifying scree traverse.

Atop The Foreland hill, you've attained the SWCP's most northerly point ... and one of its most phenomenal views. Soaring 200m cliffs of Devonian Old Red Sandstone curve around Lynmouth Bay to the rocky river delta at Lynmouth. Don't get too close to the airy precipice of Great Red! The exhilarating, extended descent to Lynmouth passes beneath 302m Butter Hill, towards the tower of St John the Evangelist's Church at Countisbury, before zigzagging below Wind Hill and the A39 to two First World War gun emplacements. The gully here marks the geological fault between the Hangman and Lynton Formations; the sandstone ahead is over 400 million years old, Exmoor's most ancient rock.

A roadside interlude and final zigzag above Point Perilous, through garlic-adorned woodland, descend to Lynmouth's manicured promenade; quite a change in character! The East Lyn River wreaked havoc upon Lynmouth in 1952 after nine inches of rain fell, causing thirty-four deaths. A footbridge takes the SWCP across the now-safely canalised river, to tourist shops and cafés.

Lynmouth from Butter Hill.

📷 *The Valley of the Rocks.*

3 Lynmouth to Combe Martin

Distance	22.1km / 13.7 miles
Height gain	1,150m / 3,750ft
Difficulty	●●●●
Maps	OS Landranger 180 / OS Explorer OL09
Start	Lynmouth EX35 6EF / adopters.exacted.less / SS 722 495
Finish	Kiln car park, Combe Martin EX34 0DN / distract.reforming.easygoing / SS 577 472
Parking near start	Lower Lyndale car park, Lynmouth EX35 6ES / bookshop.imported.dragging / SS 723 494
Public transport	301 and 310 buses, change at Barnstaple

This is a long and sometimes gruelling challenge, tackling high and exposed cliff paths and crossing wild moorland. Ever-magnificent scenery culminates with the highest point on the entire SWCP. There are no facilities en route.

Lynmouth Harbour's 'Rhenish' tower (copy of a River Rhine lookout) was reconstructed after the 1952 flood destroyed the c1860 original, which stored bathing saltwater. Opposite the National Park visitor centre, the wire-framed 2017 statue *The Walker* marks where the Coleridge Way and Two Moors Way finish, and where the SWCP departs Lynmouth.

Lynton perches above, accessed by a funicular railway ascending 152.4m up the cliffs, at a dizzying 58% gradient. It has been in use since 1890, powered by water from the West Lyn River. Intended for cargo, it became a tourist mainstay. Is using the railway cheating? The alternatives are, a harsh tarmac zigzag above the tracks, or a woodland footpath commencing past the car park.

The North Walk clings to the cliffs, an exhilarating, exposed path slightly diminished by being tarmacked and popular with tourists. It culminates at The Valley of the Rocks, which eighteenth-century Romantics dubbed 'Little Switzerland'; the poet Robert Southey described, *"the very bones and skeleton of the earth; rock piled upon rock, stone piled upon stone"*. Glacial river flow, possibly a former course of the Lyn rivers, gouged this now-dry cleft into Exmoor's oldest rocks, the slate and sandstone Lynton Formation. Rugged Jack and Castle Rock, crags frequented by feral Cheviot goats introduced in 1976, bristle with strange outcrops; apparently, pagans who danced on the Sabbath.

A toll road plod is slightly dispiriting, although at several points the path diverts away from the tarmac. The surrounds remain impressive, starting with sheer-sided Wringcliff Bay and then Tower Lodge, front gate of Lee Abbey Christian retreat. The abbey originated c1199, but the sprawling neo-gothic mansion dates from the 1850s. Around Lee Bay, Duty Point Tower becomes visible, a nineteenth-century folly. Beach exploration will reveal a natural shower, tumbling from Cuddycleave Wood. The SWCP offers a choice of road past, or path around, Crock Point. Take the path, although the wooded ascent rejoining the road is admittedly tough.

The road, known as Sir Robert's Path, is escaped above Woody Bay; as the name suggests, the route delves into dense oakwood. An optional side-path descends to a waterfall and limekiln, site of a short-lived Victorian resort. True explorers will seek out the beach's tidal bathing pool.

West Woodybay Wood leads to Hollow Brook, forded beneath a cascading waterfall. The trees fall back, unveiling some of the SWCP's grandest surrounds. Looking back, monumental headlands

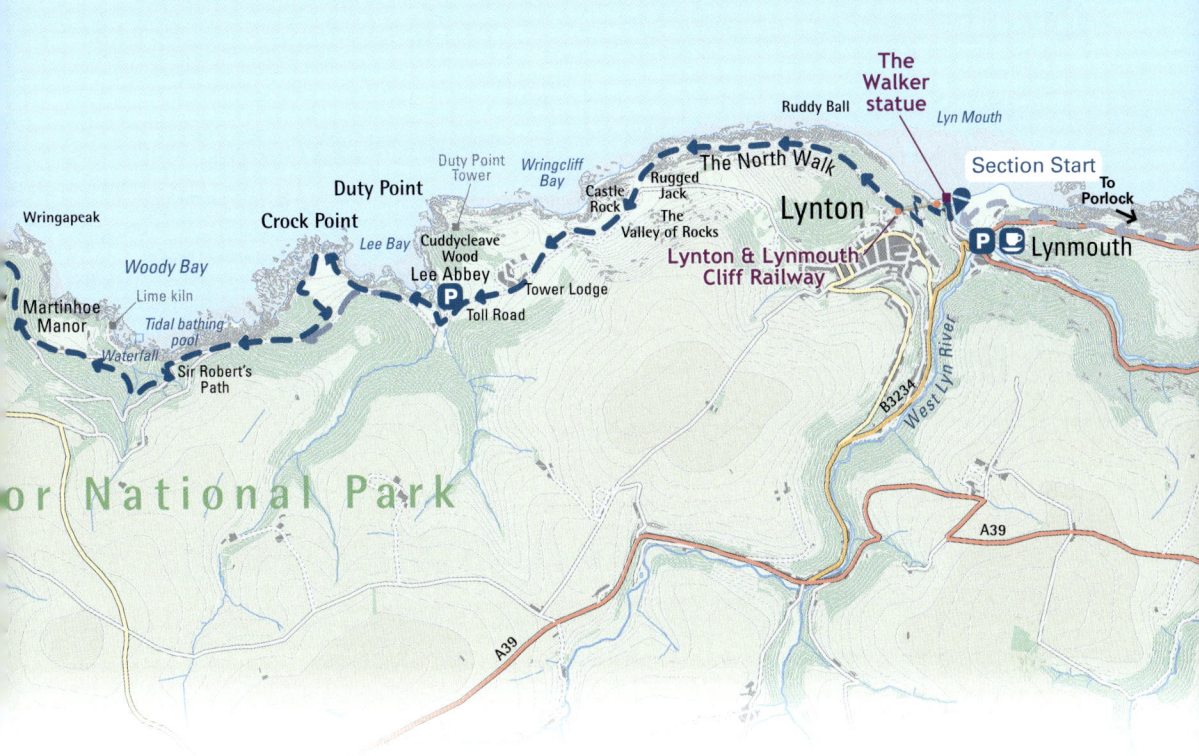

recede into the haze behind Wringapeak archway; the legendary 'Gurt Fish of Wringapeak' lurks beneath, awaiting victims. Below, Great Burland Rocks plunge to The Cow and Calf stacks, supporting nationally important populations of guillemots, razorbills and kittiwakes. Above is The Beacon, site of a Roman fort. Ahead, the best is still to come: Heddon's Mouth.

The path above Highveer Point overlooks the extraordinary Heddon's Mouth Cleave, a V-shaped valley incised by Ice Age flood waters. The scree slopes littering the valley sides were shattered by freeze-thaw. The bubbling River Heddon squeezes through the Cleave (Old English *cleof*: cliff), to percolate through beach pebbles, alongside a restored lime kiln. Second World War U-Boat sailors have claimed that they landed at Heddon's Mouth, to replenish water stocks and stretch legs. Upstream of the woodland stone bridge, the Hunter's Inn is a possible refreshment point.

Enduring the 240m climb from the Cleave, scan the bracken for the High Brown Fritillary butterfly, recognisable by silver spots beneath its wings; this is among its last habitats. Peter Rock is followed by a craggy, exposed path. A stone and earth wall provides an easy guide along High Cliff and above successive wooded clefts, such as North Cleave Gut, plunging 200m into Elwill Bay. The stacks at the base of the dark red cliffs ahead are The Mare and Colt.

This outing now becomes a moorland adventure, negotiating three high hills; Trentishoe, Holdstone and Great Hangman. Passing around Trentishoe Down and Holdstone Hill, circular traces of Bronze Age huts are discernible; the slopes above bristle with prehistoric mounds and megaliths. Before ascending Great Hangman, Sherrycombe rudely bars progress, a deep cleave

accessed by a super-steep, stepless path. The following 160m climb is perhaps punishment for sins committed in this, or a former, life ... but you eventually emerge on top of the world (or the SWCP, at least), at the huge cairn topping 318m / 1043 feet Great Hangman. The gruesome name possibly derives from Celtic; *an maen*: hill of stone.

Great Hangman Gut

Great Hangman is flanked by Britain's highest mainland sea cliff, the 250m Great Hangman Gut. The SWCP and summit are some distance from the coast; for a glimpse of the cliff, explore the path peeling off right during the ascent. This leads to a silver-lead mine adit, beside the immense chasm.

The extended descent to Combe Martin Bay feels like a joyous lap of honour! A rutted gully through heather gives way to grassy trails approaching Little Hangman. Consider a side-tour (just one more climb!) to this 218m pyramid. The summit earthworks are possibly a 6,000-year-old Neolithic tor enclosure. Among Britain's oldest structures, these are found across the South West; little is known about their purpose.

The path along Lester Cliff is an appropriately spectacular finale; high above Wild Pear Beach, overlooked by Little Hangman's distinctive layered flanks. The National Park ends at Lester Point, before entering Combe Martin. You've crossed Exmoor!

Combe Martin.

4 Combe Martin to Ilfracombe

Distance	9.6km / 6 miles	Height gain	400m / 1,300ft	Difficulty	● ● ● ● ●
Maps	OS Landranger 180 / OS Explorer OL09				
Start	Kiln car park, Combe Martin EX34 0DN / distract.reforming.easygoing / SS 577 472				
Finish	Jubilee Gardens car park, Ilfracombe EX34 8AJ / bypassed.careless.twit / SS 518 478				
Public transport	301 bus				

At last, a coast path section adhering close to the coast! This outing is short and never far from the road, nevertheless it is varied and packed with attractive cliffs, coves and inlets, supplying some wonderful views.

Combe Martin excitedly boasts the longest village main street in Britain. The real attraction however is the beach, which extends at low tide to reveal reefs and rockpools, backed by tree-covered slate cliffs and stacks. A long tunnel through Lester Point is a trace of the intensive mining here, from 1292 onwards; the slate contains galena deposits, a mineral yielding lead and silver. Combe Martin silver played a significant role in funding the 116 year-long(!) Hundred Years War (1337-1453) against France.

The climb from Combe Martin is patchy, first passing pleasant Newberry Beach but then following paths, steps and side-lanes on and off the busy A399. Things improve after the Sandy Cove Hotel is reached. Old Coast Road, a lane, becomes a track through woods passing high

above Golden Cove and then Broadsands Beach. The latter is only revealed after you've passed it, a stunning walled-in cove (although, neither broad nor sandy) sheltered by the Inner Stone and Outer Stone stacks. To visit, you'll need to backtrack and descend c240 precarious steps.

Emerging from the trees, the SWCP skirts the edge of a campsite to rejoin the A399. You'll spot the cluster of holiday parks, across narrow Small Mouth cove; until 2013 the next kilometre was pure evil, squeezing dangerously along the A399 between these and 'Watermouth Family Theme Park and Castle'. Thankfully, the route now mostly avoids the road (and the tacky stuff), with a rooty woodland path alongside Water Mouth, a lovely narrow inlet which dries at low tide, leaving moored boats stranded. At the head is Watermouth Harbour, with a quirky café upon a boat. In 1942, PLUTO ('Pipeline under the Ocean') was tested between Water Mouth and Swansea, a prototype fuel pipeline designed to supply the 1944 D-Day landings. The classic view of Water Mouth is from Widmouth Head, where a bench beneath an old Coastguard lookout is reached by steep steps. The inlet is sheltered by a narrow rocky peninsula, topped by a nineteenth-century round tower and surrounded by islets; the placenames of The Warren, Sexton's Burrow and Burrow Nose are unsubtle clues as to what was farmed here.

Broadsands Beach.

The Hunting of the Earl of Rone

Combe Martin maintains an obscure custom, every Spring bank holiday weekend. Uniformed grenadiers pursue and shoot the 'Earl', a creature dressed in sacking, who is repeatedly revived by a hobby horse figure, attended by a 'fool'. Finally, the Earl is thrown into the sea. This *Wicker Man*-esque pageant apparently recalls Ireland's Earl of Tyrone, who challenged Elizabeth I in the 1590s, but is likely to have far older pre-Christian origins.

Rillage Point is 500m west, reached by a clifftop shimmy above sheer-sided Samson's Bay. Enjoy watching the tide surge across this low headland's reefs, because a kilometre alongside the A399 follows, downhill above Hele Bay. Hele is part of Ilfracombe, but the SWCP evades plunging into the town just yet, deviating to Hele Beach. A relentless, zig-zagging 120m climb above Beacon Point is shaded by pleasant woodland. You emerge atop Hillsborough, with a grand view across Ilfracombe. Hillsborough is known as the 'sleeping elephant', on account of its appearance from Ilfracombe Harbour. Descending, two lines of earthen ramparts indicate that this was an Iron Age hillfort.

Rapparee Cove nestles below Hillsborough, surrounded by cliffs. Down a set of steps, a stone memorialises the *London* shipwreck.

Around Ilfracombe Harbour, the SWCP successively passes a skate park, a watersports centre and a lime kiln occupying Larkstone Cove, Marine Drive car park, and the Lifeboat Station. Two contrasting landmarks loom over the harbour, both worth detouring to study closer; *Verity* reaches 20.25m high, a 2012 bronze and steel Damien Hirst statue holding scales and a sword (representing truth and justice); Lantern Hill behind is topped by the Chapel of St Nicholas, patron saint of fishermen, dating from 1321 and adorned with a light claimed to be Britain's oldest working lighthouse.

Ilfracombe from Hillsborough.

Capstone Parade, a tarmac esplanade, leads around Capstone Point to Wildersmouth Beach, where Landmark Theatre's twin towers stand beside the Jubilee Gardens car park. Consider a quick jaunt up Capstone Hill to *Ekaterine*, a surprisingly touching and uplifting statue, given that it commemorates a 14-year-old Russian student who fell from the cliffs in 2000.

The Rapparee Cove grave

In 1796 the merchant ship *London*, sailing from St Lucia to Bristol, was shipwrecked in Rapparee Cove. A mass grave was discovered below the cliffs, in 1997. The archaeological investigation uncovered manacles among the human remains, igniting a fierce and still unresolved controversy: did the grave contain French prisoners of war, enslaved black St Lucians who fought alongside seeking their freedom, captured Irish 'rapparee' rebels from a 1690 wreck (which gave the cove its name), or simply Devon locals? St Lucian officials have called for the remains to be repatriated.

◉ *Torrs Park viewpoint.*

5 Ilfracombe to Woolacombe

Distance 12.9km / 8 miles	**Height gain** 625m / 2,050ft	**Difficulty** ●●●●○
Maps	OS Landranger 180 / OS Explorer 139	
Start	Jubilee Gardens car park, Ilfracombe EX34 8AJ / bypassed.careless.twit / SS 518 478	
Finish	The Esplanade car park, Woolacombe EX34 7DJ / dusters.dabbling.magazines / SS 457 437	
Public transport	31 bus	

This is the last of the SWCP's tough westward yomps alongside the Bristol Channel. Spiky cliffs of Devonian slate, overlooking small inaccessible coves, lead to Morte Point and into Bideford Bay, where the SWCP's first large sandy beaches face west, exposed to the Atlantic's full force.

Firstly, Ilfracombe must be escaped. Jubilee Gardens car park fronts the Landmark Theatre, built in 1997 and certainly a landmark due to its idiosyncratic 'cooling towers'. Steps lead behind the theatre to a clifftop path ascending to Granville Road, which looks down upon the seemingly inaccessible Tunnels Beaches.

Torrs Walk Avenue winds uphill to the Torrs Walk, constructed in 1888 to give sightseers access to Torrs Park, the Seven Hills area overlooking Ilfracombe. The path contours high along the cliff, through woodland, then ramps up several gears with an extended zigzagging ascent (look out for a lime kiln on a side path) to the 137m high summit. The reward is a superb vista, including Lundy Island to the far west. The summit plinth's toposcope was added in 2012, designed by Ilfracombe Arts College students. Far below, Brandy Cove's name references its smuggling heritage.

The SWCP undulates through Torrs Park to Langleigh Lane, a sunken track ascending from Ilfracombe. The bedrock is scored with grooves, which allowed carts to grip on the steep incline. After a delightfully old-school 'Public path' sign, the SWCP passes through fields above Flat Point and Freshwater Bay (named for its freshwater springs), to a lane descending steeply into Lee Bay.

Lee Bay, a smattering of houses behind a sea wall, is notable for the phenomenal reef and rockpools exposed at low tide; go explore, search for blennies and gobies hiding in the crevices of the sawtooth slate and intruded pink quartz. A lane and path ascent onto Damage Cliffs is directly followed by a descent to steps accessing Sandy Cove (not sandy!), where Lee Bay smuggler Hannibal Richards (1764-1849) kept a lookout posted, helping him to evade capture whenever customs men came.

The stretch to Bull Point lighthouse is fairly strenuous, descending to two successive secluded valleys and footbridges, almost at sea level. First is Hilly Mouth; the tough climb out crosses a hill adorned by three prehistoric megaliths (on private land). The second, Bennett's Mouth, is accessed and departed via steep zigzags. Take time (and a few breaths) to enjoy the coastal wildflowers thriving and providing colour among the coastal rocks; reddish English stonecrop, pink rock sea-spurrey and white sea campion.

The Tunnels Beaches

In 1823-4, Welsh miners bored six tunnels (five survive) through the cliffs, allowing tourists to access the beaches and three constructed tidal pools. Until 1905, bathing was strictly segregated; a bugler sounded the alarm if a man attempted to spy on female bathers. The beaches can be visited (for a fee) from the tunnel entrance on Runnacleave Road. The colonnaded bathhouse here was built in 1836 by the Ilfracombe Sea Bathing Company, offering therapeutic hot and cold baths of pumped seawater.

Bull Point Lighthouse is perched fifty-four metres above the waves. Its unusual Modernist design, including four oval concrete 'foghorns' (one is a window), is explained by its history. The original light was completed in 1879 and functioned until September 1972, when the keeper reported cracks appearing in the walls. Six days later, the cliffs collapsed and subsided up to thirty metres from the edge, taking much of the lighthouse complex with it! The new lighthouse was completed in 1975.

The path ahead arcs around Rockham Bay towards Morte Point. Above Rockham Beach, a boardwalk crosses the valley floor. The beach is a sandy expanse at low tide but is currently inaccessible, as the steps have collapsed. Nevertheless, you should spot the boiler of the *SS Collier* on the reef; this was wrecked in 1914, fortunately the entire ship's company (seven men, a dog, a cat and a caged goldfinch) safely escaped by dinghy. Approaching Morte Point, the path becomes dramatically rugged and rocky as it traverses the steep heather-covered scarp. Below, the reef is incised with tiny inlets like Oreweed and Whiting Coves, used in the past for smuggling.

📷 *Morte Point.*

Morte Point means … well, how is your French? Here, the underlying geology is laid bare, to spectacular effect. Immense pressures have tilted the 380-million-year-old Morte Slate rock onto the vertical plane and formed streaks of white quartz. Rows of severely jagged slabs stab skywards, reminiscent of a stegosaurus herd. Seaward, a tidal race (rapid) pours across the razor-sharp rocks around Morte Stone; this wrecked five ships in 1852 alone. Morte Point was, *"the place God made last and the Devil will take first"* and there are (fanciful) tales of the 'Mortemen Wreckers', who lit lights to lure ships onto the Point.

A mild grassy amble leads from Morte Point. Three small beaches, Grunta (supposedly named after a cargo of pigs was wrecked!), Combesgate and Barricane, lead to the finish at Woolacombe village. It's not quite so easy, however! Above Grunta, the SWCP is directed inland and sharply uphill past Mortehoe village, to contour high (120m high, to be precise) above the beaches. Enjoy the fine view of Morte Point from the bracken-covered slopes, before the path descends through Combesgate Valley and returns to the seafront grassland alongside The Esplanade. Approaching the car park, the Woolacombe Memorial overlooks Woolacombe Sand's wide span; two megaliths commemorating the US soldiers stationed here during the Second World War.

📷 *Putsborough Sand and Woolacombe Sand.*

6 Woolacombe to Saunton

Distance 14km / 8.7 miles	**Height gain** 100m / 300ft	**Difficulty** • • ○ ○ ○

Maps	OS Landranger 180 / OS Explorer 139
Start	The Esplanade car park, Woolacombe EX34 7DJ / dusters.dabbling.magazines / SS 457 437
Finish	Saunton Beach car park EX33 1LG / extent.neckline.wrenching / SS 447 376
Public transport	21C, 21 and 31 buses, change at Braunton and Mullacott Cross. Not Sundays

This section boasts the SWCP's first large sandy beaches and also its first sand dunes! Woolacombe Sand, Putsborough Sand, Croyde Sand and Saunton Sands all face west into the Atlantic Ocean, picking up any groundswell as surf. The beaches are understandably popular, but there is room enough to find solitude. The going is much easier than so far encountered along the SWCP, although be prepared for sand in your shoes.

Challacombe Hill Road departs Woolacombe. A path meanders and undulates for two kilometres through Woolacombe Warren, a dunescape of marram grass and actively shifting sands; the soft grains underfoot make for slow progress. In 1909, Woolacombe Sand was given to the National Trust by Rosalie Chichester of Arlington Court, whose family had owned it since 1133. When the beach is in sight, you may be surprised by how far the shoreline recedes at low tide.

An escape route from the dunes eventually appears; steep steps, alongside a sign warning about Second World War beach defences (they occasionally resurface at very low tides). The steps grind through gorse and trees, emerging thirty metres higher on Marine Drive. This track contours the

◉ *Approaching Baggy Point.*

slopes of Woolacombe Down, the higher elevation providing perspective; Morte Bay is hemmed in to the north by Morte Point's sloping headland, and to the south by Baggy Point's cliffs, the sands describing a mild arc between the two. The SWCP shimmies high above the beach's southern third, Putsborough Sand, briefly following the beach access lane before taking a path onto Napps Cliff, start of Baggy Point headland.

Baggy Point is a hundred-metre-high ridge of Devonian slate and sandstone, extending three kilometres oceanward. The path above the north cliffs passes alongside grassy fields, before turning south at a ninety-four-metre triangulation point, overgrown and obscured behind a wall. A clifftop meadow is adorned with a wooden 'ship's mast'; this is a 'rocket post', previously used by the coastguard for training with shipwreck rescue equipment. The nearby wall is adorned with a Second World War pillbox, not to repel Nazis but instead one of ten dummies built on the headland to train US soldiers for the D-Day landings. Steps descend to the tip of Baggy Point, where, dawn and dusk, Manx shearwaters glide past en route to their burrows in Pembrokeshire. An (optional!) exposed path extends to the very end, above steeply dipping sandstone strata. Below is Baggy Leap reef, which wrecked *HMS Weazle* during a 1799 gale; of 106 crew, only the purser survived.

A wide, easy path leads along Baggy Point's southern side into Croyde Bay, at lower elevation but with precipitous interludes. Should you fall off, a rather solid landing awaits on the wave-cut platform below, a product of changing sea levels. Pencil Rock is so-named as the sandstone thereabouts crumbles, pencil-lead-like, into shards. The National Trust employ black Hebridean sheep to manage the gorse, however a more severe clearance occurred in 2022 when a major wildfire (started by a disposable barbeque) ravaged the undergrowth. Passing through a wooden gate, note a plaque commemorating Henry Williamson, the author of 1927 novel *Tarka the Otter*: 'BAGGY POINT INSPIRED HIS WRITING'. A side-path beside a bench offers a precarious descent to the 'Baggy Erratic', a 50-tonne gneiss boulder on the reef. This is the largest of numerous incongruous 'erratics' dotted around the headland, transported from Scotland by glaciers.

📷 *Croyde Bay.*

Baggy House, a large white Art Deco-style home built in 1995, indicates that you are approaching Croyde. Just past, a huge lichen-covered whalebone is a remnant of a 1915 stranding in the bay. The SWCP does not continue into Croyde village, instead it splendidly leads across Croyde Sand beach (no dogs, May to September), backed by the dunes of Croyde Burrows. Take some time to watch the surfers, then climb the steps to Down End, near where the wave-cut platform recommences.

The SWCP leads around the headland below Saunton Down, above the low cliffs overlooking the reef. This coast is an SSSI (Site of Special Scientific Interest), due to its importance in understanding Pleistocene (Ice Age) sea level fluctuations. A series of ancient 'raised beaches', up to thirteen metres above the current sea level, reflect both isostatic (land rebound) and eustatic (sea level) changes resulting from melting ice during warmer 'inter-glacial' periods. The two effects counter each other, with the isostatic effect being greater; hence the raised beaches.

The SWCP ascends steps to cross Croyde Road, passing between a ruined Coastguard lookout and Chesil Cliff House, an enormous lighthouse-style Art Deco mansion. Probably the most spectacular modern residence along the SWCP, the decade-long travails of constructing it were documented on the TV show *Grand Designs*. As well as dividing local opinion, it led to debt and divorce for the creators. At time of writing, it has never been lived in and can be yours for the discounted price of £5.25 million.

The SWCP climbs steeply onto Saunton Down. The approach to Saunton makes for a glorious finale; a gorse-lined path elevated above the road, which is mostly hidden from view. Soak up the vista of surf waves breaking along the five-kilometre length of Saunton Sands, backed by the enormous dunes of the expansive Braunton Burrows. When the path descends to the road, the steps uphill are the 'Alternative route' to Saunton (see section 7). Saunton Sands car park is across the road and down the steps.

River Taw around Penhill Point.

7 Saunton to Barnstaple

Distance	18.9km / 11.7 miles **Height gain** 275m / 900ft **Difficulty** • ◦ ◦ ◦ ◦ / • • ◦ ◦ ◦
Maps	OS Landranger 180 / OS Explorer 139
Start	Saunton Beach car park EX33 1LG / extent.neckline.wrenching / SS 447 376
Finish	Barnstaple Long Bridge EX31 1HB / cubs.basin.jets / SS 557 328
Parking near finish	Seven Brethren car park, Barnstaple EX31 2AP / influencing.papers.tend / SS 558 326
Public transport	21C bus

Some choose to skip or bypass sections 7 and 8, as there is a high percentage of tarmac along former railway routes, and perhaps also because the SWCP deviates inland, around the estuaries of the Taw and Torridge Rivers. Really … don't skip them. Approach these flat but varied landscapes with an open mind, there is plenty here to engage and maybe even awe.

This section commences with a choice of routes departing Saunton Beach car park. The standard first kilometre takes the track uphill from the car park and leads 350m along the un-pavemented B3231 to a lane on the right, directly after Saunton Golf Club's entrance. The **Alternative route** avoids the B3231, adding a * to this section's difficulty; to reach it, backtrack a short distance along the SWCP by climbing the steps from the car park. This route steeply claws a hundred metres up onto Saunton Down. The descent passes Saunton Court, a fifteenth-century manor house remodelled by Edwin Lutyens in 1932, to rejoin the 'standard' route at the aforementioned lane.

A third, unofficial, alternative is to stick to the coast by following Saunton Sands around to Crow Point car park; potentially awkward around high tide.

For six kilometres, the SWCP skirts the eastern fringes of Braunton Burrows, a vast area of sand dunes. The coastal dunes peak at over thirty metres in height, but the path meanders across the golf course's low dunes, winding through woods to emerge at Sandy Lane car park, where the 'American Road' is joined. This gravel track is so-named as the US military widened it during the Second World War.

The American Road is left, on the left, at a dusty crossroads. A path through dunes reaches Crow Point car park, then Broad Sands beach leads to Crow Beach House, also known as 'the White House'. This 'coast' is actually the River Taw, which meets the River Torridge just 800m downstream at Crow Point. Across the water, Instow Barton Marsh is just a kilometre away, and Appledore 1.6km; however, they are, respectively, twenty-two and thirty-five kilometres further along the SWCP!

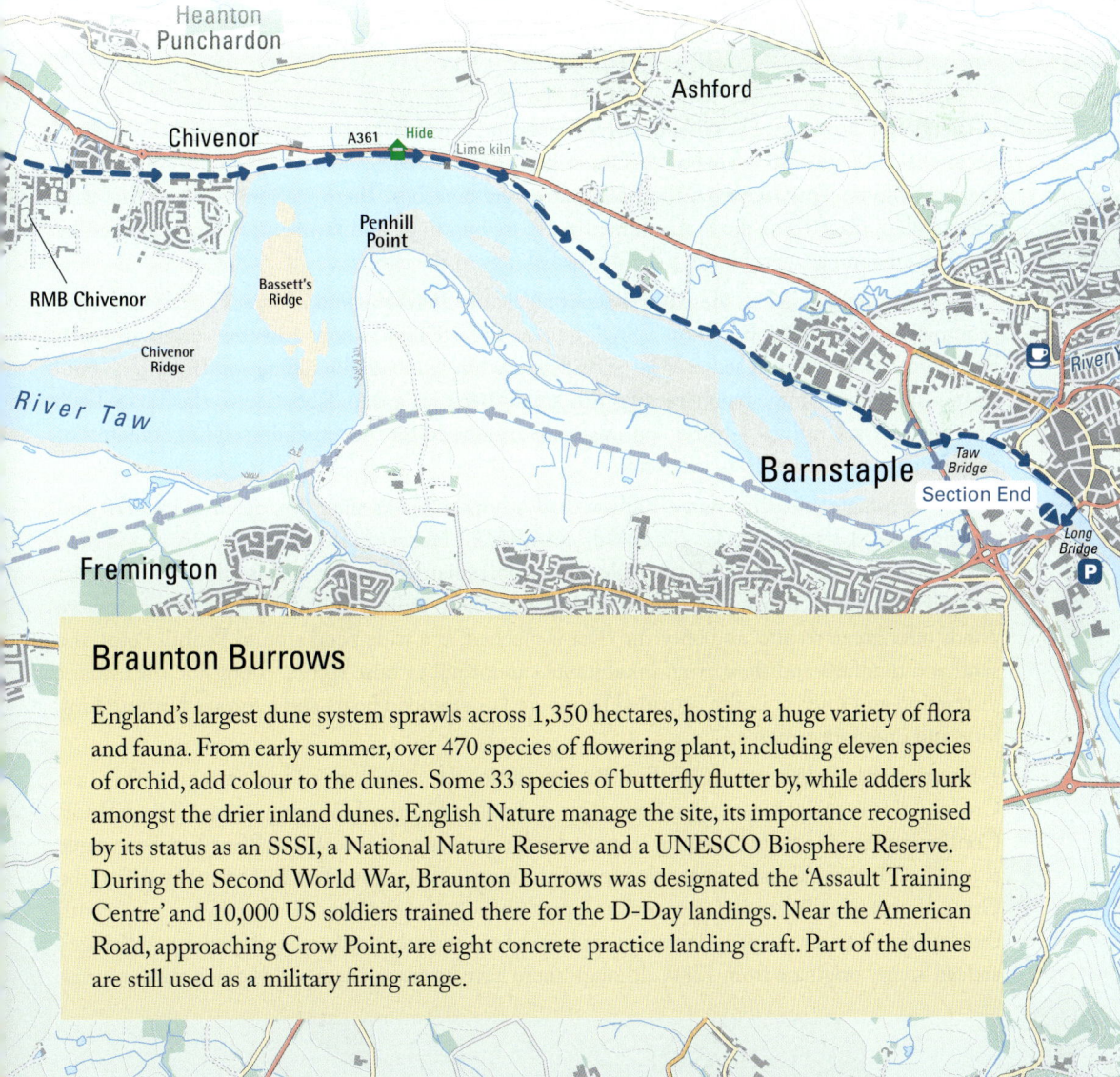

Braunton Burrows

England's largest dune system sprawls across 1,350 hectares, hosting a huge variety of flora and fauna. From early summer, over 470 species of flowering plant, including eleven species of orchid, add colour to the dunes. Some 33 species of butterfly flutter by, while adders lurk amongst the drier inland dunes. English Nature manage the site, its importance recognised by its status as an SSSI, a National Nature Reserve and a UNESCO Biosphere Reserve. During the Second World War, Braunton Burrows was designated the 'Assault Training Centre' and 10,000 US soldiers trained there for the D-Day landings. Near the American Road, approaching Crow Point, are eight concrete practice landing craft. Part of the dunes are still used as a military firing range.

Saunton Sands and Braunton Burrows.

The SWCP now veers back inland to Horsey Island. Until 2016, the route followed this eighty-hectare island's seaward edge, however, breached coastal defences diverted it to the 'inland' side. Devon Wildlife Trust acquired the island, after the breaches. There are fine views of this wild and desolate place from the embankment path, its buildings and farmland being reclaimed by successive flooding tides. Horsey Island now belongs to the egrets.

Sea walls run parallel to the River Caen, to Velator Quay. This muddy creek's final kilometre is actually the artificial Braunton Canal, dug in the 1850s to allow 130-ton vessels to reach Braunton. The river is crossed at Velator Bridge, reaching industrial buildings on Braunton's outskirts. The SWCP immediately escapes this small town, via a roundabout, onto the Tarka Trail. This tarmac track utilises a disused railway course, followed for the remaining eight kilometres of this section and also much of section 8.

The Barnstaple and Ilfracombe Railway had a hundred-year shelf life, opening in 1870 and closing in 1970. Its course takes the SWCP past *RMB Chivenor* (a Royal Marines base) and then alongside the River Taw, into Barnstaple. The wide, billiard-table-flat trail is effectively a cyclist motorway; however, nature and some beautiful views keep tedium at bay. Early on, nature reserve ponds offer green respite, and once the river is reached, at a wide bend around Penhill Point, the sand and mudflats and their avian inhabitants cannot fail to raise spirits. Alongside the estuary, distraction and interest is also provided by moored or stranded boats and barges, a birdwatching hide and lime kiln remains.

Entering Barnstaple, the 2007 Taw Bridge carries the A361 in a high arc above the Taw. Crossing this is an option, missing Barnstaple and rather pointlessly shaving 800m off the SWCP. Continuing into the town's bustling centre, a bridge crosses a side creek, the River Yeo. Barnstaple is over 1,000 years old, having been developed as a *burh* (Old English: fortified town) by Alfred the Great. Barnstaple's regional dominance as a port ended when the Taw silted up in the nineteenth century; the riverside quays and warehouses have been sympathetically redeveloped. Long Bridge's sixteen arches originate from 1280, although there have been various rebuilds down the centuries.

River Taw at Instow Barton Marsh.

8 Barnstaple to Bideford

Distance 16.8km / 10.4 miles	**Height gain** 10m / 30ft **Difficulty** • • • •
Maps	OS Landranger 180 / OS Explorer 139
Start	Barnstaple Long Bridge EX31 1HB / cubs.basin.jets / SS 557 328
Finish	Riverbank car park, Bideford EX39 2QS / assume.freezers.holds / SS 455 269
Parking near start	Seven Brethren car park, Barnstaple EX31 2AP / influencing.papers.tend / SS 558 326
Public transport	21 or 21A bus

Much of this section follows a disused railway. The main appeal is the strangely compelling, but bleak, estuarine tideland. Sightings of barn owls and birds of prey such as peregrine falcons and merlin are common, but this is really the kingdom of the wading bird; 20,000 overwinter here.

Enjoy the fine view from thirteenth-century Long Bridge, before a grim trudge past retail parks alongside the A3125. Tunnels beneath the A361 reach a Tarka Trail information board; you have escaped the conurbation.

The tarmac trail that the SWCP now follows was part of the London and South Western Railway, until closure in 1982. The rail route leads through Anchor Wood; a footpath on the left, where the woods end, leads 200m off the SWCP to the Dripping Well, a reputed holy spring framed by a nineteenth-century brick arch. Following the railway course, the SWCP is near-straight for 2.5km, with farmland to the left and the River Taw and marshland to the right. Two quirky shelters are passed, the first constructed in mid-trail from railway remains and looking not unlike a bus stop.

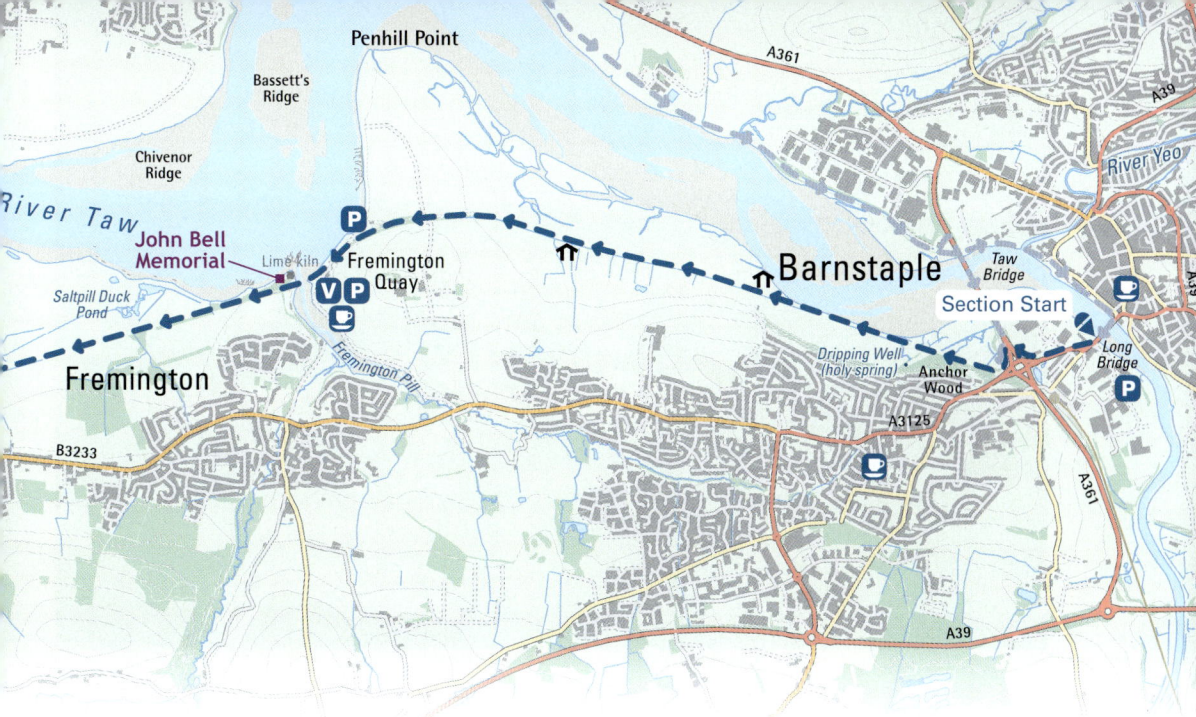

The Taw arcs around Penhill Point, but the railway line cuts across this peninsula via a deep wooded cutting, spanned by a brick bridge. The river is rejoined at splendid Fremington Quay; here, the high wooden quayside, with a rusting ship or two usually moored, overlooks the silted foreshore. Inside the heritage centre and café, occupying the site of the former railway station, displays reveal that this quiet backwater was once the busiest port between Land's End and Bristol! Scale the lookout tower for a view along the estuary.

Muddy Fremington Pill creek is crossed by the former rail bridge; note the lime kiln remains on the right, and also a memorial to John "Dinger" Bell, *'local fisherman and character'*, who drowned in 1986. Two kilometres of straight-line tarmac follow, sometimes sheltered by trees, sometimes open to the estuary. The reeds of Saltpill Duck Pond and then Home Farm Marsh are passed on the right, the latter a dairy farm which has seen huge increases in biodiversity since being run by The Gaia Trust. A shelter in the form of an upturned boat marks the start of Isley Marsh, an RSPB Nature Reserve where the mudflats and saltmarsh creeks come close to the trail. In winter, spoonbills can sometimes be spotted here.

Where Isley Marsh ends, the embankment leading off perpendicularly to the right is your escape route from the tarmac. The SWCP winds above East Yelland Marsh to reach the estuary shore. A wire fence and jetty are traces of Yelland Power Station, closed in 1984 and demolished. Controversial plans have been mooted to redevelop the site by building 200 homes.

A sandy path along the embankment leads past a second jetty at Instow Barton Marsh, where abandoned and graffiti-ed ships are berthed. Crow Point (section 7), marked by a navigation beacon, is 600m across the water. Here, the Taw ends its solo project and merges with the River Torridge. Between them, the two rivers drain around 2,000km² of Devon.

An amble amongst orchid-colonised dunes is perhaps this section's most pleasant part. The SWCP comes back close to the railway route at a series of huts, some converted from rail carriages.

📷 *Bideford.*

Instow Sandhills car park leads to a road along Instow's seafront. Instow is a quiet village locked in a permanent staring match with Appledore, the similarly attractive village across the estuary. Instow Sands were used for D-Day rehearsals; at low tide, they almost span the Torridge to reach Appledore. Instow's stone pier is the departure point for the Appledore ferry, operating two hours either side of high tide. The ferry cuts out ten kilometres of the SWCP, fast-forwarding into section 9. But why would you?

The 1874 signal box at Instow railway station has been restored and is occasionally opened to the public. Four kilometres of tarmac rail route closely follow the Torridge, punctuated by a lime kiln, a red metal sculpture (I have no clue) and a military jetty. The concrete spans of Torridge Bridge loom overhead; it was completed in 1987, after traffic pressure caused two arches of Bideford Long Bridge to collapse.

East-the-Water is Bideford's less affluent (i.e. scruffy) half. The rail route passes under the B3233 road to Bideford Railway Heritage Centre, with an interpretative centre housed inside a rail carriage. Bideford Long Bridge (206m long, to be precise) dates from c1280. Its twenty-four irregularly spaced arches possibly recall an earlier wooden bridge's dimensions. Bideford gained its town charter in 1272 and was established as a port by Sir Richard Grenville, in 1575. It's impossible to lose your way here*, metal footprints mark the SWCP. A statue of Tarka the Otter (eponymous subject of Henry Williamson's 1927 novel) sits on the quayside near the bridge. Further along where the Lundy Island ferry departs, the Quay Fountain jets 24 spouts of water at high tide, one for each bridge arch.

Riverbank car park's entrance is overlooked by a statue of Victorian author Charles Kingsley, who wrote *Westward Ho!* in Bideford in 1855. Commemorating Kingsley is problematic; even his famous children's novel *The Water-Babies* (1862-3) contains remarkably offensive anti-Catholic, antisemitic and racist sentiments.

* Usual disclaimers apply.

📷 *Westward Ho! Beach.*

9 Bideford to Westward Ho!

Distance 13km / 8.1 miles	**Height gain** 150m / 500ft	**Difficulty** ● ● ○ ○ ○
Maps	OS Landranger 180 / OS Explorer 139	
Start	Riverbank car park, Bideford EX39 2QS / assume.freezers.holds / SS 455 269	
Finish	Main car park, Westward Ho! EX39 1LH / home.force.jeeps / SS 432 291	
Public transport	21 bus	

This untaxing but engaging estuarine exploration loops around the peninsula which inhibits the River Torridge's arrival at Bideford Bay, finishing less than three kilometres from the start point.

The quayside path fronting the car park is known as the Landivisau Walk, after Bideford's French twin town. Various interesting vessels are moored here, including *SS Freshspring*, a former Royal Fleet Auxiliary water carrier launched in 1946 and now on the National Register of Historic Vessels.

The escape from Bideford is a bit patchy, variously routed through a bland housing estate, lanes and alleyways; keep following the metal 'footprint' symbols embedded in the pavements. Twice, the SWCP offers choices of high or low tide routes; these are only minor deviations. Torridge Bridge's concrete spans loom overhead; note waterfront house The Old Kiln, built in 1933 on top of a lime kiln. After Cleave Quay, the SWCP veers inland; the peculiar concrete obstructions on the tree-shrouded path are 'dragon's teeth', Second World War tank traps. Signs indicate that you are passing through the National Trust's Burrough Farm property. Emerging at a small cove, an optional boardwalk crosses the saltmarsh, low tide only.

📷 *Northam Burrows Country Park.*

An embankment, raised above reclaimed marshland, leads past more wrecks towards Appledore Shipyard's hulking workshops and cranes. Among Britain's few remaining shipbuilders, the yard has built over 300 vessels since being founded in 1855, including sections of Britain's two *Queen Elizabeth*-class aircraft carriers. After a period of closure, it reopened in 2020 under Harland and Wolff ownership. Boardwalk paths bypass the yard inland; a lane-trudge passes the entrance and then dilapidated industrial units at Newquay Dock.

Richmond dry dock marks the start of Appledore's waterfront. Built in 1856, this fitted out around fifty-five ships built at Richmond, on Canada's Prince Edward Island. It was acquired by The Wheatcroft Collection in 2020 and is being refurbished to store their historic vessels including *S130*, the last surviving German E-boat. Further history and heritage are available at North Devon Maritime Museum, 250m from the waterfront.

Appledore is an attractive town, with rows of houses stretching around the promontory where the Rivers Taw and Torridge merge. The Quay has fine views of Instow, across the Torridge. The narrow thoroughfare of Irsha Street, with colourful eighteenth- and nineteenth-century houses, is Appledore's oldest part, once notorious for prostitution and witchcraft*. This ends where Appledore Lifeboat Station looks out across the Skern, an embayment of tidal mudflats, frequented by Brent geese in winter. The SWCP follows low cliff and beach, with high tides forcing a short diversion inland along lanes.

The two routes reconverge at the toll booth entrance to Northam Burrows Country Park. The remainder of this section is a pleasant perambulation of this 253-hectare SSSI. Burrows Lane crosses stone Appledore Bridge and leads north across grassy coastal plain, passing between the Skern and a seasonal brackish lagoon. Grey Sand Hill spit is crossed, reaching the Rivers Taw and Torridge where they reach the sea. Enjoy grand views across to Braunton Burrows and Crow Point, also out to treacherous Zulu Bank, a challenge to incoming vessels. In 1791

---

* Witches and magic: not actually a thing.

Appledore, from Instow.

the *Abeona* was grounded here, proving to contain £5,000 worth of smuggled silk and china! Reaching Bideford Bay, the path winds south among small dunes, alongside the fairways of Royal North Devon Golf Club.

Northam Burrows Country Park is protected from the Atlantic by Pebble Ridge, a three-kilometre-long high barrier which is retreating one metre annually. Local legend suggested, 'when Charles III reigns, the sea will reach Northam'; recent events proved this prediction wrong by 1700 years! A visitor centre and café stand alongside Sandymere, a seasonal pool used as a car park when dry.

Northam Burrows Road, a dusty gravel track lined by parked cars, leads towards the resort of Westward Ho!, with Pebble Ridge barring sea views you may prefer to cross onto the beach. Reaching Westward Ho!, the SWCP oddly deviates inland via backroads; most will simply follow the boardwalk from the Country Park entrance to the seafront amusements.

Bideford Bay from Sloo Wood.

10 Westward Ho! to Clovelly

Distance 18km / 11.2 miles	**Height gain** 900m / 2,950ft	**Difficulty** ● ● ● ●
Maps	OS Landranger 180, 190 / OS Explorer 126, 139	
Start	Main car cark, Westward Ho! EX39 1LH / home.force.jeeps / SS 432 291	
Finish	Mount Pleasant, Clovelly EX39 5TL / glare.upholding.promotion / SS 316 249	
Parking near finish	Clovelly car park EX39 5RW / discloses.craftsmen.shallower / SS 314 248	
Public transport	319 and 21 buses, change at Bideford. Not Sundays	

The SWCP's long arc around Bideford Bay is bookended by flat sections; a disused railway from Westward Ho! and the Hobby Drive track, approaching Clovelly. Don't be lulled into complacency; hidden between, a relentless succession of small ascents is cumulatively pretty challenging. The second half passes through especially attractive woodland.

Westward Ho! originated in 1864, named after Charles Kingsley's 1855 novel. Rudyard Kipling attended college here, describing it as, *'Twelve bleak houses by the shore'* in his novel *Stalky and Co*. It's still unprepossessing; the SWCP passes Marbella-style apartments and serried ranks of chalets and caravans. The view seaward is better; the Rock Pool tidal swimming pool was cut into the reef over 140 years ago.

Westward Ho! ends at Seafield House, an 1885 'Gothic coastal'-style property known, for obvious reasons, as Spooky House. The course of the Bideford, Westward Ho! and Appledore

Railway is followed; this only operated 1901-17 and was never connected to the rail network. Above, gorse-covered Kipling Tors is topped by 'The Wuzzy', an abandoned coastguard lookout.

Mermaid's Pool, a natural swim spot in the reef, marks the start of a geological SSSI covering the six kilometres to Rowden Gut. The Bideford Formation is fully sequenced in this near-straight coast's cliffs and wave-cut platform: mudstone, sandstone and siltstone laid down by river deltas, 319 million years ago in the Carboniferous period. The railway is departed at Cornborough Cliff; the SWCP now undulates along Abbotsham Cliff and Green Cliff, between pebble beaches and low grassy eminences. A lime kiln survives at Green Cliff, alongside trickling waterfalls. You'll already have lost count of the ups and downs before they expand in scale, negotiating flights of steps across Cockington Cliff, Westacott Cliff and Babbacombe Cliff. Between the first two, the route emerges from a deep cleft onto the driftwood-strewn beach.

The SSSI's end is marked by a wooded valley (Barrel Copse, leading from nearby Portledge Manor) above sandy beaches and a surprising interlude of vividly red cliffs; this Permian sandstone is not encountered again until South Devon! The path veers up the wooded Peppercombe valley, a National Trust estate but owned from the twelfth century by the Pine-Coffins. They built Castle Bungalow, the 1920s wooden chalet in distinctive Great Western Railway colours. Its name references Peppercombe Castle, an Iron Age hillfort of which little remains. Shelter and rest can be had in the Coach House building, beside the bridge crossing Peppercombe Water.

The second half of this section is also characterised by an SSSI, this time biological; Hobby to Peppercombe SSSI encompasses a swathe of the remarkable Atlantic oakwood (page 21), extending across six kilometres of high coastal scarp (ten kilometres of the SWCP!). Gnarled or coppiced sessile oaks strewn with liverworts, funguses and lichen (over 250 species!) offer shade to bilberries, ferns and mosses on the forest floor. The path within this temperate rainforest is frequently narrow, stony and rooty, becoming muddy or even treacherous in the wet. Despite (or possibly because of) this challenging 'Mirkwood' experience, this rates amongst the SWCP's finest woodland stretches.

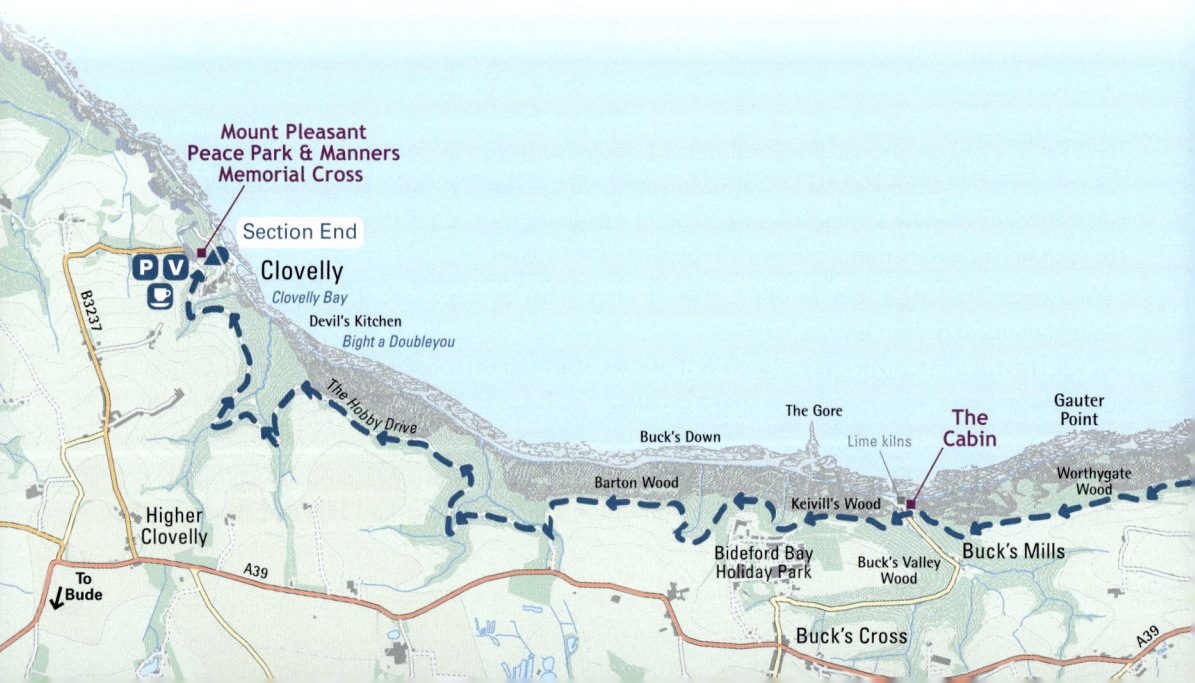

Clovelly

The whitewashed fishing village is justly famous. The cobbled High Street, known as 'Up-along', descends improbably steeply from the 1901 Queen Victoria fountain, with well-preserved buildings stacked alongside. Goods are lowered by sled and, until their retirement in 2023, donkeys lugged lazy visitors. A fourteenth-century quay protects the harbour; four bollards are made from cannons, reputedly from the Spanish Armada. Charles Kingsley lived here 1831-36, when his father was rector. The Hamlyn family have owned Clovelly Village since 1738. An entrance fee is included in the hefty car park cost.

📷 *Clovelly.*

Buck's Mills

The steep track to the beach passes overgrown limekilns and The Cabin, a nineteenth-century fisherman's hut used, from the 1920s until 1971, by painters Judith Ackland and Mary Stella Edwards; it is listed by Historic England as one of their, 'Places with Queer Histories'. A waterfall tumbles onto the beach, site of a sixteenth-century harbour built by Richard Cole (allegedly of *Old King Cole* nursery rhyme fame), which did not survive. The Gore boulder spit extends seaward at low tide, created by an ancient landslip but supposedly the Devil's attempt at a causeway to Lundy Island. Into the twentieth century, whenever the fishing declined, local men would sail there daily, to work in the quarries.

The sharp climb from Peppercombe accesses Sloo Wood and then Worthygate Wood, notable for their uneven 'undercliff' terrain, formed by ancient landslips. A super-steep rocky descent emerges at the tiny community of Buck's Mills. Across the road, the path immediately climbs back into the woods.

Wider paths dip into and out of the upper rim of, successively, Buck's Valley Wood, Keivill's Wood and Barton Wood. Little differentiates them, beyond Woodland Trust signage, and glimpses of Bideford Bay Holiday Park above Barton Wood.

This section finishes along Hobby Drive, a wide cobbly track through dense beech woodland. This five-kilometre carriage ride to Clovelly Court mansion was originally constructed, using Napoleonic prisoners, for James Hamlyn. Hobby Drive proceeds tortuously, with tight bends engineered around steep combes. Towards the end, a series of benches offer views of Clovelly's harbour, 160m below; one bench commemorates an 833-yard extension, opened in 1901. On the right, High Street track leads down into Clovelly Village. When Hobby Drive ends at a wooden gate, Clovelly's Visitor Centre (a shopping complex resembling a motorway services) is uphill on the left.

📷 *Blegberry Cliff.*

11 Clovelly to Hartland Quay

Distance	16.6km / 10.3 miles
Height gain	725m / 2,400ft
Difficulty	● ● ● ● ○
Maps	OS Landranger 190 / OS Explorer 126
Start	Mount Pleasant, Clovelly EX39 5TL / glare.upholding.promotion / SS 316 249
Finish	Hartland Quay car park EX39 6DB / nobody.threaded.thousands / SS 222 247
Parking near start	Clovelly car park EX39 5RW / discloses.craftsmen.shallower / SS 314 248
Public transport	319 bus, from Hartland village

The Hartland Peninsula is practically a SWCP rite of passage, with its extraordinary transition from sheltered woods clinging to north-facing cliffs, to the salt-lashed and wreck-strewn 'Iron Coast'. This eclectic outing commences with tough climbs traversing park- and woodland, eases along lofty meadows to Hartland Point, with a demanding finale negotiating cleaved Atlantic ramparts.

Mount Pleasant Peace Park and the Manners Memorial Cross commemorate Clovelly men who lost their lives in the First World War. Lieutenant John Manners was the nephew of Christine Hamlyn, who donated the site to the National Trust in 1921. Through a black gate, the SWCP edges around landscaped parkland. The Cabin is a woodland shelter, built in the early nineteenth century for Sir James Hamlyn. Clovelly Court mansion, briefly in view, originated in the thirteenth century, but was rebuilt several times after the Hamlyns took ownership in 1738; they still own the estate.

The Atlantic oakwood swathes the coast to Mouth Mill. The trees part at The Angel's Wings, an ornate bench with pagoda-style roof, carved in 1826 by the Hamlyn's butler. The next clearing

is Gallantry Bower's 120m heathland summit, topped by a Bronze Age 'bowl barrow' burial mound. The name either cheerily refers to gallows, or to lovers who jumped to their deaths. Fulmars nest below.

A steep descent reaches the well-preserved nineteenth-century lime kiln overlooking Mouth Mill's stony beach, which supposedly inspired Charles Kingsley's *The Water-Babies*. Blackchurch Rock is named for its spire-like profile and the sunlight blazing through two 'windows', where mudstone has eroded between harder sandstone strata. To the west, a waterfall plunges thirty metres. Ships delivered South Wales coal and limestone along this harsh coast by doing 'beach work'; running aground and awaiting the next tide.

A demanding stretch follows: a zigzagging 120m ascent clears the treeline onto Brownsham Cliff, before zigzagging back down, through bracken, into a hanging valley crossed by a foot-bridge and (you guessed) zigzagging up again, onto 142m Windbury Head, an Iron Age hillfort. A memorial names the crew of a Wellington bomber which crashed into the cliffs in 1942; the engine is in Hartland Quay's museum.

The geology relents, making the seven kilometres to Hartland Point easier, along wildflower-margined field boundaries, with occasional woodland and steps into small clefts. Hedges obscure the cliff edge, but near Exmansworthy Cliff's 152m trig point there are great views back to Blackchurch Rock. Eldern Point has another memorial; ten US servicemen died in 1943 when their B-24 Liberator impacted below. The smuggler's path accessing Shipload Bay's sandy beach is long gone. Passing East Titchberry Farm, a working National Trust property, a garish radar 'golf ball' (radome) hogs the view. Operated by the Civil Aviation Authority since 1987, this was an MOD site. Concrete footings supported a Second World War radar.

    A small café above Barley Bay heralds Hartland Point, the 'Promontory of Hercules' in Ptolemy's *Geography*. Brochures dub it, '*Furthest from the railways*'; England's remotest point from the rail network. You're still in Devon, but Cornwall's epic north coast effectively commences here; wave-battered cliffs confront the Atlantic for over 200km, to Land's End.

    A side-path leads behind Coastguard buildings to a viewpoint. Hartland Point Lighthouse stands beneath the headland, elevated thirty metres above tidal rapids extending offshore to Lundy Island. Trinity House's James Douglass completed the lighthouse in 1874. Wave erosion undermined it, so sections of cliff were deliberately collapsed until the present sea wall was constructed in 1925. Rusting pieces of the *MV Johanna*, wrecked on the last day of 1982, are strewn across the rocks.

    Dawn and dusk, April to September, Hartland Point hosts a wildlife spectacle. Manx shearwaters (so-named as their wingtips almost graze the water) fly past, en route to their Lundy and Pembrokeshire burrows. The record is 15,000 in one morning!

    The Bristol Channel ends here. Southwards, the coast undergoes a change in character ... this is the Iron Coast.

    Blagdon Cliff is topped by a memorial to 153 '*officers, crew and medical staff*' who died in 1918, when a U-boat torpedoed hospital ship *Glenart Castle*.

    Upright Cliff is descended to a footbridge spanning Titchberry Water's deep cleft and waterfall, backdropped by Smoothlands' smooth slabs. The dry valley behind this pointed hill once carried Titchberry Water. Damehole Point can be accessed by a precarious footpath.

    The rough climb onto Blegberry Cliff reveals a jaw-dropping landscape best described as; Mordor meets the Atlantic. Sawtooth reefs perpetuate horizon-ward. *Two* waterfalls plunge onto

Blackchurch Rock from Brownsham Cliff.

Blegberry Beach, where traces of the *SS Hoche*, an 1882 shipwreck, survive. Blegberry Water's V-shaped cleft is immediately followed by the Abbey River valley; twelfth-century Hartland Abbey is 1.5km upstream. The SWCP veers up-valley around Blackpool Mill, a fifteenth-century cottage, before the final climb: past Dyer's Lookout onto Warren Cliff.

Atop Warren Cliff, a ruinous arch perfectly frames St Nectan's Church, the 'Cathedral of North Devon'. The arch survives from 'The Pleasure House' folly, which originated in the sixteenth century as a rabbit warrener's house. The Rocket House cottage follows, built to store rescue equipment after the steamship *Uppingham* was wrecked at Longpeak in 1890.

Hartland Quay has mislaid its quay; commissioned by Drake and Raleigh, it was destroyed by a storm in 1896. Harbour buildings, now a hotel and museum, line The Street down to Warren Beach. Note Bear Rock, the tall, isolated stack behind Warren Beach.

The Iron Coast

The savagely serrated reefs from Hartland Point to Bude have been dubbed 'The Iron Coast', on account of its high number of shipwrecks. A wave-cut platform extends 250m seaward, its skyward-jutting profile continuing the cliffs' zigzag strata. The 'zigzags' (accurately, anticlines and synclines) were generated 290 million years ago, when supercontinent Pangea was formed from the 'Variscan Orogeny' collision of continents Laurasia and Gondwana. Encroaching seas eroded mudstone layers and harder sandstone 'ribs' remain. Charles Kingsley in his 1855 novel *Westward Ho!*: 'Each cove has its black field of jagged shark's tooth rock which paves the cove from side to side … To landward, all richness, softness and peace; to seaward, a waste and howling wilderness of rock and roller.'

Speke's Mill Mouth and St Catherine's Tor.

12 Hartland Quay to Bude

Distance	23.8km / 14.8 miles	Height gain	1,275m / 4,150ft	Difficulty •••••
Maps	OS Landranger 190 / OS Explorer 126			
Start	Hartland Quay car park EX39 6DB / nobody.threaded.thousands / SS 222 247			
Finish	Summerleaze car park, Bude EX23 8JP / irony.elaborate.covertly / SS 207 064			
Public transport	219 bus, to Hartland village			

The 'Iron Coast' (page 60) is among the South West's scenic highlights; dark forbidding cliffs confront the ocean, fronted by expanses of sandstone fangs jutting skyward. Rushing streams have incised deep gullies into the folded strata, abruptly ending as waterfalls tumbling onto the reefs. This lengthy challenge, starting in Devon and ending in Cornwall, is also extraordinary for its solitude and for at least ten notable ascents; it's a contender for the SWCP's toughest section.

Ascending from Hartland Quay, note the stranded yacht wreck, a prop from the 2020 film of Daphne Du Maurier's *Rebecca*.

The first of innumerable dramatic landscapes is encountered at St Catherine's Tor, an isolated conical hill rearing eighty-four metres above the beach. The name may refer to a now-lost medieval summit chapel, although nineteenth century accounts allude to Roman remains. Wargery Water flows behind the hill and cascades onto the reef; note traces of the medieval dam, which formed Hartland Abbey's swannery. The valley was actually carved by 'Spekes River', before coastal erosion claimed its course north from the Milford Water valley to Warren Beach.

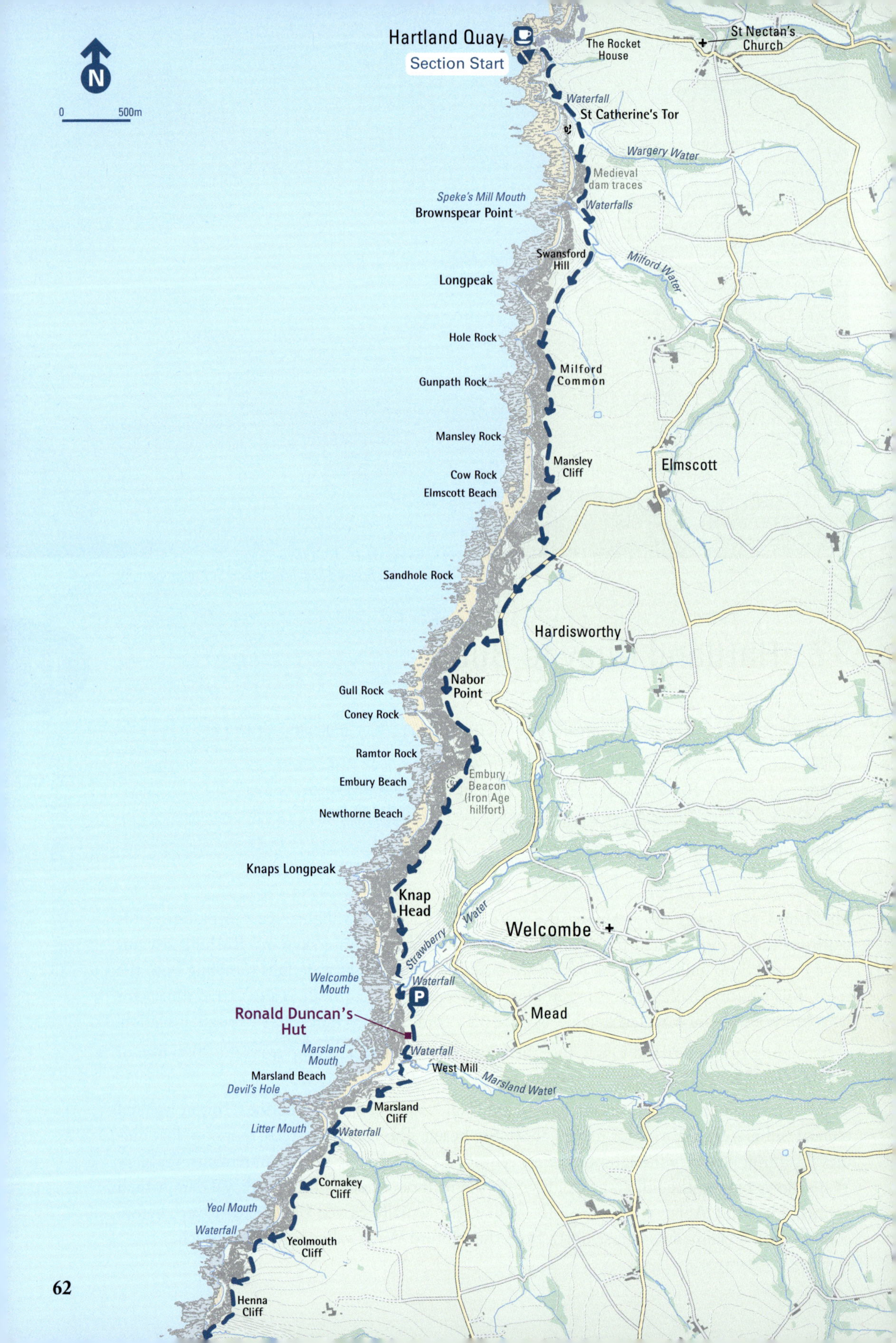

0 500m
Hartland Quay
Section Start
The Rocket House
St Nectan's Church
Waterfall
St Catherine's Tor
Wargery Water
Medieval dam traces
Speke's Mill Mouth
Brownspear Point
Waterfalls
Swansford Hill
Milford Water
Longpeak
Hole Rock
Milford Common
Gunpath Rock
Mansley Rock
Mansley Cliff
Elmscott
Cow Rock
Elmscott Beach
Sandhole Rock
Hardisworthy
Nabor Point
Gull Rock
Coney Rock
Ramtor Rock
Embury Beach
Embury Beacon (Iron Age hillfort)
Newthorne Beach
Knaps Longpeak
Knap Head
Strawberry Water
Welcombe
Welcombe Mouth
Waterfall
Ronald Duncan's Hut
Mead
Marsland Mouth
Waterfall
West Mill
Marsland Water
Marsland Beach
Devil's Hole
Marsland Cliff
Litter Mouth
Waterfall
Cornakey Cliff
Yeol Mouth
Waterfall
Yeolmouth Cliff
Henna Cliff

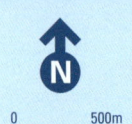

Higher Sharpnose Point from Hawker's Hut.

At Speke's Mill Mouth, Milford Water plunges sixteen metres, then a further thirty metres in four successive cascades: the SWCP's finest waterfall! Across the footbridge, a side-stream leads behind Swansford Hill. Longpeak's cliffs only come into view after you've ascended onto Milford Common, commencing four kilometres of easier clifftop trails. 'Easier' is subjective, an intense squall blew the author off his feet here.

In 1962, Gunpath Rock wrecked the tanker *RFA Green Ranger*. Traces are visible at low tide and its portholes decorate the 'Wrecker's Retreat Bar' at Hartland Quay. After passing above Elmscott Beach, the SWCP veers inland for 800m of lane (hopefully the path will soon be be restored), returning to the eroding precipice around Nabor Point, marked by a picnic table. Embury Beacon, at 157m this section's highest point, hosts an Iron Age hillfort. The SWCP skirts the earthen ramparts, the interior is crumbling into the void.

Knap Head gazes down upon Welcombe Mouth and Marsland Mouth, twin valleys whose waterfalls meet the reef just 500m apart, yet are separated by a tall cliff colonised by cackling fulmars. It's clear that the easier interlude has finished! Down at Welcombe Mouth, stepping stones cross Strawberry Water. The gruelling climb and descent to Marsland Mouth is ameliorated by shelter and seating in Ronald Duncan's Hut. This was the poet and playwright's writing studio, built in 1962 from a Coastguard lookout. Until his death in 1982, Duncan lived at West Mill, which according to Charles Kingsley in *Westward Ho!* was, 'the abode of the White Witch, Lucy Passmore'. Crossing the footbridge spanning Marsland Water is a significant moment; a sign announces your arrival at '*Kernow*': Cornwall! The SWCP has covered about 185km / 115 miles so far, and it's another 478km / 297 miles before you re-enter Devon, at Plymouth.

The pattern is repeated: – steep descents into hanging valleys abruptly ending at waterfalls, followed by steep climbs out. The steps into Litter Mouth practically freefall! Back on top at Cornakey Cliff, note Gull Rock, pierced by Devil's Hole. Yeol Mouth's footbridge is overshadowed by Yeolmouth Cliff's intimidating vertical slabs. At Henna Cliff, Morwenstow village comes briefly into view, before you dip and climb again. Ordnance Survey maps locate St Morwenna's Well in

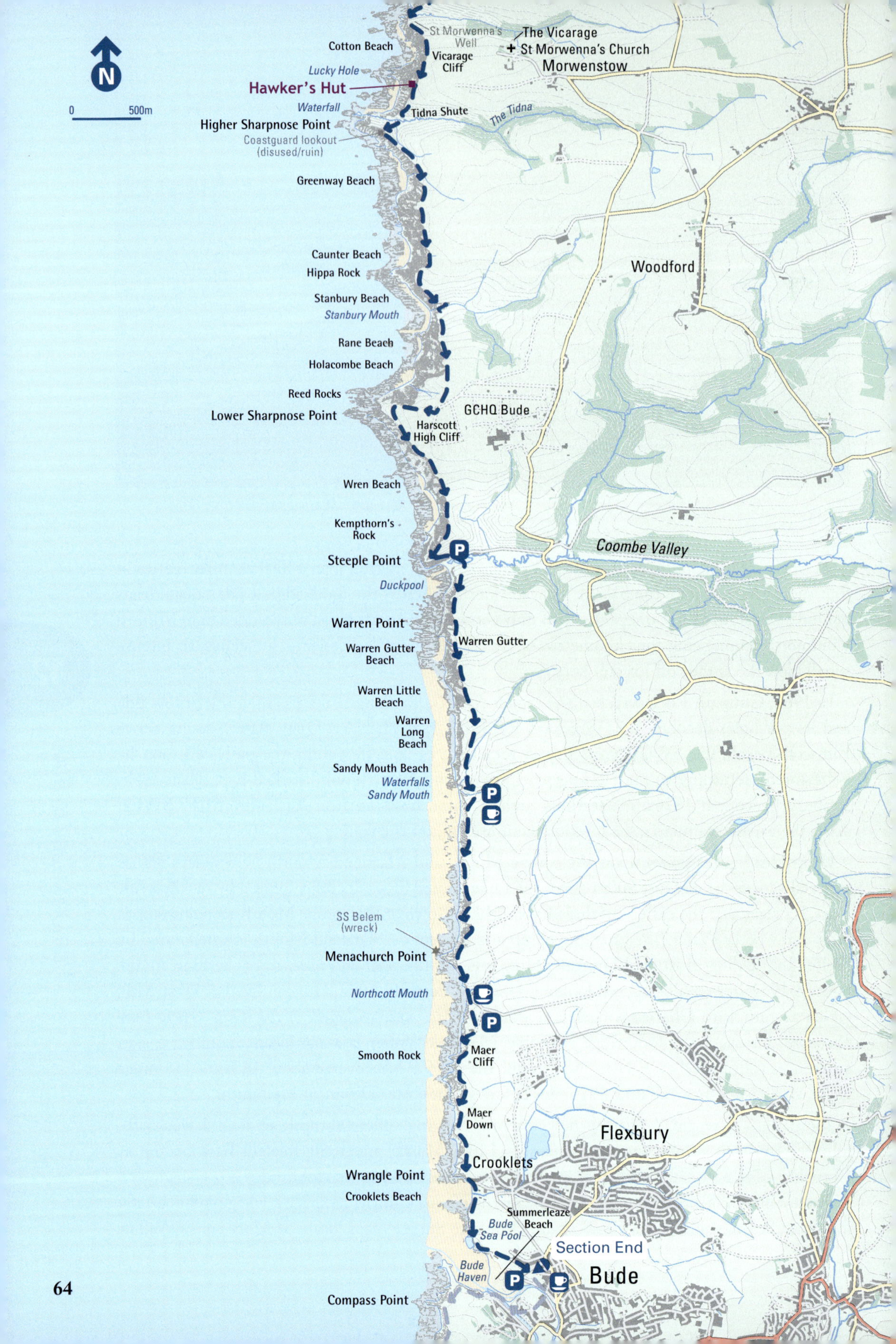
N
0
500m
Cotton Beach
St Morwenna's Well
The Vicarage
St Morwenna's Church
Morwenstow
Vicarage Cliff
Lucky Hole
Hawker's Hut
Waterfall
Tidna Shute
The Tidna
Higher Sharpnose Point
Coastguard lookout (disused/ruin)
Greenway Beach
Caunter Beach
Hippa Rock
Woodford
Stanbury Beach
Stanbury Mouth
Rane Beach
Holacombe Beach
Reed Rocks
Lower Sharpnose Point
GCHQ Bude
Harscott High Cliff
Wren Beach
Kempthorn's Rock
Steeple Point
Coombe Valley
Duckpool
Warren Point
Warren Gutter Beach
Warren Gutter
Warren Little Beach
Warren Long Beach
Sandy Mouth Beach
Waterfalls
Sandy Mouth
SS Belem (wreck)
Menachurch Point
Northcott Mouth
Smooth Rock
Maer Cliff
Maer Down
Flexbury
Crooklets
Wrangle Point
Crooklets Beach
Summerleaze Beach
Bude Sea Pool
Section End
Bude Haven
Bude
Compass Point

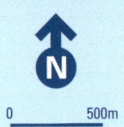

this cleft; actually, this gabled medieval shrine is located on Vicarage Cliff, inaccessible without significant danger! It is however depicted in a stained-glass window at St Morwenna's Church.

A gate above Vicarage Cliff leads to the National Trust's smallest property. Hawker's Hut is a ramshackle turf-roofed shack built into the cliff using shipwreck timbers.

This section's highlight comes after clambering from Tidna Shute valley to a crumbling lookout hut. An exposed footpath onto Higher Sharpnose Point rewards those who brave this side-tour with a 360° panorama.

Stanbury Mouth's winding gorge, spanned by a high footbridge, guards the array of radar dishes and 'golf balls' dominating the skyline. Formerly Second World War airfield *RAF Cleave*, this is now *GCHQ Bude*, part of the 'Five Eyes' international surveillance network. Twenty-five per cent of the UK's internet traffic is intercepted behind the chain fence. Allegedly.

Lower Sharpnose Point's name is explained by sandstone slivers slicing skyward. Coombe Valley comes into view, leading to Duckpool beach, reached via a dramatic zigzagging traverse around Steeple Point. This section's easier remainder is visible, stretching south; the reef continues, but the cliffs lower and a low tide sandy beach extends to Bude. A footbridge crosses a rocky stream near Duckpool's car park and toilets.

A final notable climb leads over Warren Point, crossing the cleft of Warren Gutter above arrays of pointed stacks; Bude Bay's answer to the Alps! Below Sandy Mouth's café, two separate waterfalls reach the beach.

Parson Hawker

Hawker's Hut was built by Robert Hawker, Morwenstow's eccentric vicar from 1835 to 1875. Known locally as 'Parson Hawker', he excommunicated his cat and rarely washed. He used the hut to smoke opium (joined on occasion by Alfred, Lord Tennyson and Charles Kingsley) and compose verse, including *The Song of the Western Men*, Cornwall's unofficial anthem. Hawker also created the harvest festival.

Hawker's vicarage and church can be spotted from the SWCP, 600m inland along a footpath from Vicarage Cliff. The Vicarage, built 1837, has six chimney stacks modelled on Hawker's previous churches' towers. Outside St Morwenna's Church, the *Caledonia's* figurehead (shipwrecked 1843) stands alongside a granite cross inscribed, *'Unknown Yet Well Known'*. Hawker gave Christian burials to around forty drowned sailors here, also leading rescue attempts.

Given earlier challenges, the trail to Northcott Mouth barely registers! Traces of the *SS Belem*, wrecked in 1917, lurk below Menachurch Point. 'Dragon's teeth' tank traps guard Northcott Mouth from Nazi invasion. Fossil-hunters here search the Bude Formation's 319-million-year-old shales for *Cornuboniscus budensis*, the unique 'Bude fish'.

Undulating open fields wind their way down to Bude. Note Smooth Rock, an isolated slab below Maer Cliff, and bomb craters dotting Maer Down, a Second World War target range. Crooklets Beach is always busy; Bude is among Cornwall's most popular resorts. The SWCP leads above the 1930 Bude Sea Pool (chilly!) and along Summerleaze Beach to the car park.

Godrevy Island (Section 21).

North Cornwall

The north coast: an epic wall of wave-battered cliffs adorned with caves, reefs and stacks, fully exposed to the prevailing weather and Atlantic swells. Exploring the 210km / 130 miles to Sennen Cove is a hugely rewarding, but often arduous, experience. The only notable interlude is the dunes of St Ives Bay, before the extremely rugged Penwith Peninsula recommences the cliffscape.

North Cornwall's grand scenery is inextricably intertwined with its heritage. Even in the wildest places, human activity can be read in the landscape; Iron Age cliff castles (also called promontory forts), fishing harbours, lighthouses, and mining ruins.

Much of this magnificent coast is within the Cornwall Area of Outstanding Natural Beauty. The remarkable post-industrial landscapes have been recognised as being of international importance, designated as the Cornish Mining World Heritage Site by UNESCO.

Scrade and Chipman Point.

📷 *Castle Point.*

13 Bude to Crackington Haven

Distance	16.6km / 10.3 miles **Height gain** 750m / 2,450ft **Difficulty** ● ● ● ● ○
Maps	OS Landranger 190 / OS Explorer 111
Start	Summerleaze car park, Bude EX23 8JP / irony.elaborate.covertly / SS 207 064
Finish	Crackington Haven car park EX23 0JG / wink.workbench.recipient / SX 143 968
Public transport	95 bus

The SWCP's sweep around Bude Bay starts easy, but when the coast swings south-west, the gradients ramp up significantly, as does the scenery.

From Summerleaze car park, the SWCP crosses the River Neet via Nanny Moore's Bridge, a three-arched eighteenth-century packhorse bridge. Nanny Moore was a 'dipper', an escort for women bathers.

The SWCP passes the Bude Light, a multi-coloured needle erected in 2000 to commemorate nineteenth-century inventor Sir Goldsworthy Gurney. Bude Castle stands behind, built by Gurney in 1830 and now a Heritage Centre. Gurney defied naysayers by constructing the castle on dunes using a concrete 'raft'. He pioneered oxygen-boosted oil lamps which illuminated the Houses of Parliament, and steam-powered road carriages.

Bude Canal is followed to the restored sea lock, which is crossed to Efford Cottage. This was Sir Thomas Acland's summer residence, built in 1823. Acland commissioned the Storm Tower

on Compass Point, an octagonal homage to Athen's Tower of the Winds. Known locally as 'The Pepperpot', it was rebuilt further from the cliffs in 1881, with a second move currently planned! It isn't quite vertical, and has drifted seven degrees out of compass alignment since erection in 1835.

Efford Beacon offers a fine view back across Bude. Grassy paths lead south, after Upton you're never far from road. The remarkable folded cliff strata and sawtooth wavecut platforms of the 'Iron Coast' continue (page 60), however the cliffs are often unstable, slumping seaward along the lines of fault and bedding planes; numerous past landslides can be discerned. As the SWCP gradually lowers in height towards Widemouth Bay, it passes Phillip's Point Nature Reserve (among the Cornish Wildlife Trust's smallest) and the promontories of Higher and Lower Longbeak, both topped by Bronze Age burial mounds.

Widemouth Sand's wide mouth encompasses expanses of both sand and reef. The car park at the village of Widemouth Bay is followed by a sojourn amongst dunes to a second car park, at Black Rock beach; Black Rock is the lone stack rising from the reef.

Across Wanson Water stream the difficulty increases, commencing with a calf-burning road ascent from Wanson Mouth, to the viewpoint parking area at Penhalt Cliff's hundred-metre summit. An even steeper path zigzags downhill through heather, joining the lane into Millook. Millook Water, which bubbles through coppiced ancient woodlands in the valley upstream, has carved a miniature canyon to the sea at Millook Haven.

The zigzag road climb from Millook is irritating, but thankfully tarmac is finally left behind. From Raven's Beak the SWCP follows fields atop broad slopes, densely overgrown with trees and scrub, formed by ancient landslides. The path dips into a wooded cleave above Sharnhole Point to ford a rocky stream, then re-emerges onto fields to a wonky trig point 164m above Dizzard Point. Scraggy, stunted oaks cling to the escarpment; rather delightfully, the path deviates through this wind-gnarled woodland.

The Battle of Millook Haven

In 1820, armed Customs men landed at Millook Haven from the Boscastle Preventive Boat and seized 500 barrels of rum. A cutter subsequently arrived and offloaded two boatloads of armed men. The Customs men were outgunned by the smugglers, who reclaimed the rum and also stole the Preventive Boat! This 'battle' indicates the strength of the 'free trading' industry, as does the fact that an offered £200 reward failed to retrieve the Customs vessel.

After a small dip to cross a stream, Chipman Point is marked by a curved wooden bench, inscribed at either end with mileages: *'Minehead 132 Poole 500'*. This fine viewpoint offers a quick geology lesson; this section's multiple headlands and promontories are formed from (more resistant) sandstone, whilst the coves and inlets eroded along faults in (less resistant) slate and shale.

Chipman Cliff rears above the bay of Scrade, where a stream tumbles onto the beach from a gorge at the base of the steep-sided valley, backed by a pinnacled promontory pierced by Mot's Hole cave. Just *how* steep-sided is the valley? A zigzag descent is followed by probably the SWCP's steepest climb, an unrelentingly remorseless staircase of dizzying vertiginousness. Marvel and enjoy!

A less severe climb and dip above Cleave Strand leads to further scenic wonders. The landscape ahead is complex and unconventional, you'll be puzzling where the path will take you! Castle Point is a ridge extending westward, its northern slope to Thorn's Beach bearing the traces of ancient slumps and landslides, sheared along the line of the bedding planes. The SWCP spectacularly follows the ridge's airy crest, enveloped by gorse and heather but once an Iron Age cliff castle.

A descent from Castle Point into the valley forming its southern flank is inevitably followed by another zigzag climb, blessedly the last of this section. Looking back, you'll see Aller Shoot waterfall cascading from the valley onto the reef. Atop Pencannow Point, Crackington Haven and its sandy beach are revealed, but you'll be absorbed by the overlapping headlands that await towards the south-west, from Cambeak in the foreground to Trevose Head Lighthouse, thirty-five kilometres distant and almost twice as far along the SWCP! Before descending into Crackington Haven, consider a side-tour uphill along a footpath to St Gennys Church; the graveyard is the resting place of sailors from three different shipwrecks.

Bossiney Haven.

14 Crackington Haven to Tintagel

Distance 18.5km / 11.5 miles	**Height gain** 1,075m / 3,550ft **Difficulty** ● ● ● ● ○
Maps	OS Landranger 190 / 200 OS Explorer 111
Start	Crackington Haven car park EX23 0JG / wink.workbench.recipient / SX 143 968
Finish	Tintagel Castle Shop and Exhibition, Tintagel PL34 0DQ / swelling.doted.unheated / SX 052 889
Parking near finish	King Arthur's car park, Tintagel PL34 0DB / rollers.cloud.conspire / SX 056 884
Public transport	95 bus

A wild coast of lofty cliffs and soaring stacks, punctuated by the dramatic harbour at Boscastle. This adventure, culminating with The Island at Tintagel (by legend, King Arthur's Camelot), cannot fail to blow your mind.

Crackington Haven's sandy beach is hemmed in by dark reefs and cliffs. This is the world-famous Crackington Formation, striated shale and sandstone formed 328-318 million years ago and concertinaed by inconceivable heat and pressure into 'zigzags' which were subsequently warped horizontally, forming 'recumbent folds'.

Streams tumble onto the reef from the cliffs around Tremoutha Haven. In 1836, a harbour and new town, 'Port Victoria', was planned to be established here. Had this not come to nothing, sleepy Crackington Haven would look very different. A deep cleft and a zigzag climb access the sheer, exposed cliffs overlooking Cambeak, the imposing pyramidal headland guarding Crackington Haven.

Veering south, the SWCP perches atop severely folded cliffs, negotiating a cleft high above Little Strand beach. This is bookended by the Northern Door, a vast arch formed by recumbent folds, and Samphire Rock, a tapered stack. This and the following sandy beach, The Strangles, are remote and inaccessible. The Strangles' ominous name is appropriate; twenty vessels were reputedly wrecked here in a single 1820s year, although it may simply mean, 'strange hills'.

High Cliff is the highest point on Cornwall's coast, at 223m; the clue was in the name! The views are predictably grand. The SWCP departs the coastal scarp and descends steeply among ancient landslides, where feral goats subsist and peregrine falcons patrol vigilantly. This heather- and gorse-strewn undercliff is as wild a SWCP landscape as any; perched far above Rusey Beach's reefs yet overshadowed by High Cliff's dark portentous wall. The stiff climb out attains Rusey Cliff's summit, only a few metres lower than High Cliff. It also crosses the geological boundary between the Crackington and Boscastle Formations; the rocks become older (formed 347-323 mya), with even darker shale, veined with silvery quartz.

Somehow, the path becomes even more dramatic! Boardwalk and stepping stones negotiate a route past the 170m sheer wall at Buckator, looming alongside Gull Rock stack. A sharp descent at Fire Beacon Point deposits you onto the steep incline above the vertical Beeny Cliff. Far below, Atlantic grey seals haul ashore at the Beeny Sisters rocks to snooze or 'cottle' (sleep submerged, with their snouts visible). Seals Hole is the largest of dozens of caves, tunnels and blowholes

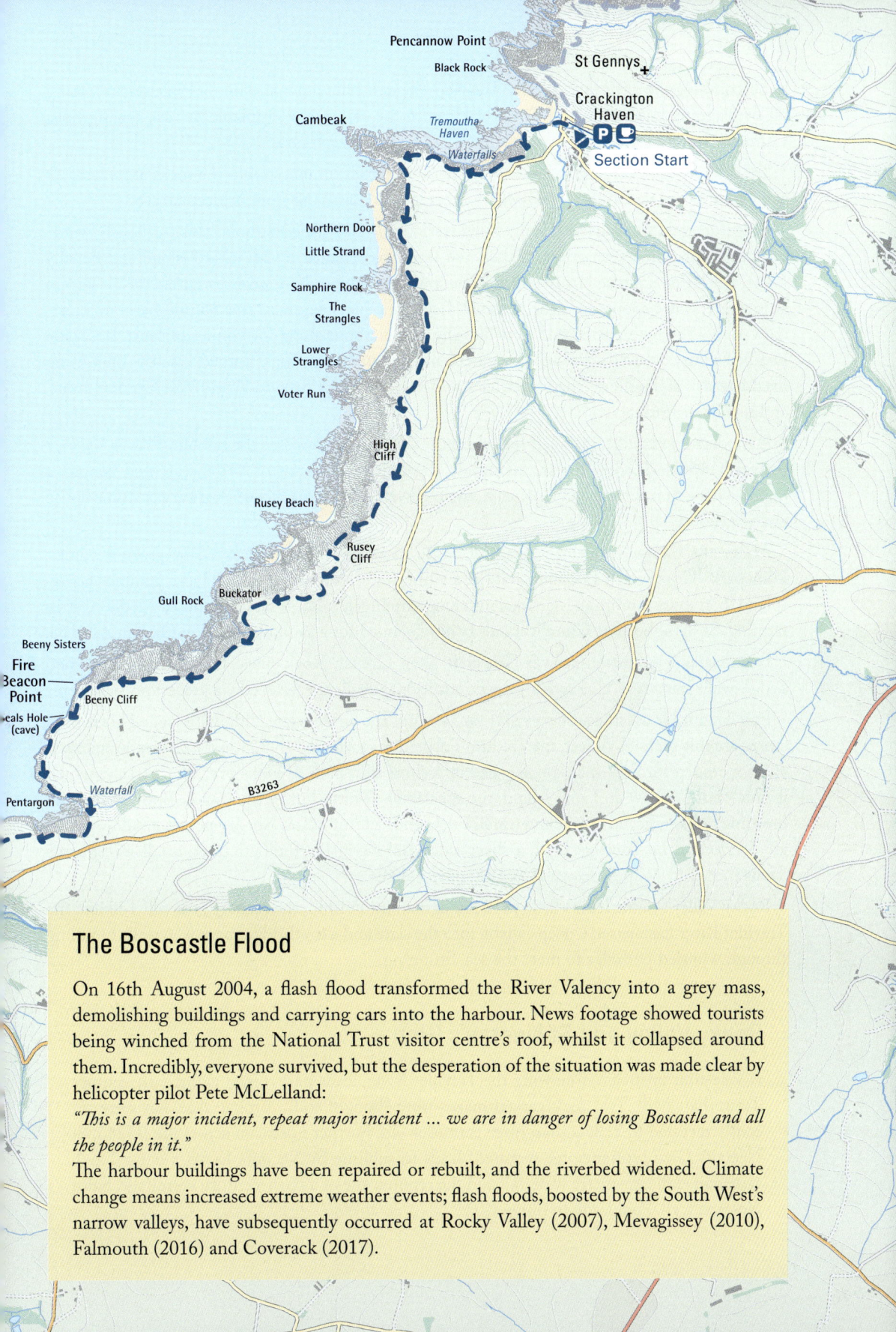

The Boscastle Flood

On 16th August 2004, a flash flood transformed the River Valency into a grey mass, demolishing buildings and carrying cars into the harbour. News footage showed tourists being winched from the National Trust visitor centre's roof, whilst it collapsed around them. Incredibly, everyone survived, but the desperation of the situation was made clear by helicopter pilot Pete McLelland:

"This is a major incident, repeat major incident ... we are in danger of losing Boscastle and all the people in it."

The harbour buildings have been repaired or rebuilt, and the riverbed widened. Climate change means increased extreme weather events; flash floods, boosted by the South West's narrow valleys, have subsequently occurred at Rocky Valley (2007), Mevagissey (2010), Falmouth (2016) and Coverack (2017).

honeycombing the cliffs to Boscastle. The view ahead is phenomenal, with multiple stacks rearing off overlapping headlands, and Tintagel Head in the distance, identifiable by vast, incongruous Camelot Castle Hotel.

The long inlet of Pentargon has a forty-metre waterfall tumbling onto the rocks at its head. It is most safely viewed after crossing the footbridge and climbing from its deep cleave.

Ridgetop ambling leads to Penally Hill, overlooking Boscastle Harbour. This tortuously winding inlet, a drowned river gorge, is sheltered from the Atlantic by Meachard island and Penally Point. The latter is pierced by the 'Devil's Bellows' blowhole; when waves compress the air within at low tide, water spouts into the harbour. Two stone piers augment this natural harbour, originally built 1584 by Sir Richard Grenville. The only harbour along forty miles of coast, Boscastle handled a busy ore trade through the nineteenth century, with ships 'warped' into the inlet using fixed hawsers and pulleys. The Outer Jetty was destroyed by a Second World War German mine, and rebuilt in 1962.

A modern footbridge, installed following the 2004 floods, crosses the bubbling River Valency (Cornish *Melin-chi*: mill-house), alongside the quirky Museum of Witchcraft and Magic, a popular attraction since 1960. Upstream, the Cobweb Inn was a sixteenth-century customs house and warehouse.

Above the harbour, the Iron Age cliff castle of Willapark is frequented by grazing ponies. Willapark's Coastwatch Lookout Station, a white tower, originated in 1823 as a summer house. Inland, Forrabury Common is divided into long 'stitchmeal' plots, a rare example of Medieval strip farming. St Symphorian's Church stands behind, named for a saint beheaded in Gaul in AD 178.

Boardwalks lead above Grower Gut cleft, then Grower Rock stack. Herringbone-patterned hedge-walls known as 'curzyways' provide additional challenge, crossed via precarious slab steps.

Past Manor House, the scenery *really* ratchets up. The lighter slate cliffs, with jagged horizontal strata, are this section's oldest, the Tredorn Formation (formed 347-323 mya). Ladies' Window is an arch eroded through the slate, reached by a short side-path. It looks over Short Island, which is only 'short' relative to Long Island, the spectacular Matterhorn-esque stack. Both stacks host breeding guillemots, razorbills and (on Short Island) a few puffins. Needle-pointed Saddle Rocks are overlooked by Trevalga Cliff, a sheer-sided hill alongside the path, then a tall wall guards Trewethet Gut, a gaping 'zawn' (Cornish: deep cleft).

Rocky Valley's name leaves little to the imagination! Within, the scenery goes full Tolkien; the Trevillet River has incised a deep canyon into the slate and a footbridge spans waterfalls tumbling through whorled potholes to meet the sea. Stunning.

Rocky Valley and St Nectan's Glen

A side-tour upstream, following the Trevillet River, leads past ruined eighteenth-century Trewethett Mill. Two rock-carved mazes were thought to be Bronze Age, but were recently revealed to be less than three centuries old. Further upstream across the B3263, St Nectan's Glen (entrance fee required) leads to sublime St Nectan's Kieve, a natural arch across an eighteen-metre waterfall and the reputed site of a sixth-century hermitage, Saint Nectan's Cell. Popular with hippies.

◉ *Beeny Cliff.*

A bench on Bossiney Common takes in the grand sweep of bay around to Lye Rock, a promontory almost severed from the mainland. Lye Rock wrecked Italian barque *Iota* in 1893; cabin boy Domenico Catanese is buried at St Materiana's Church (section 15). Within the bay are Benoath Cove and Bossiney Haven, joined at low tide and among Cornwall's most beautiful secluded beaches.

Within Bossiney Haven's cleft, look for Elephant Rock, resembling a 'trunk' dipping into the water. Bossiney Castle, a motte and bailey, is 500m inland along a footpath; reputedly, King Arthur's Round Table arises from the mound on midsummer night. Purely to cause confusion, the headland behind Lye Rock is another Willapark, also an Iron Age cliff castle. Exploring it rewards with views of The Sisters, sheer-faced islets frequented by auks.

In 1897, Barras Nose became the National Trust's first English coastal acquisition. A verse by Thomas Hardy is inscribed on a stone, *'Hard by was great Tintagel's table round ...'.* The promontory was purchased as a memorial to the poet Tennyson, specifically to rescue it from encroaching development such as the vast and awful King Arthur's Castle Hotel (built 1896, now Camelot Castle Hotel). The NT own around 40% of Cornwall's coast and have acquired about 500km of the SWCP since 1965, via their Project Neptune.

The Island looms ahead, a hulking plateau adorned with the walls of Tintagel Castle. It isn't quite an island, being connected by a crumbling ridge. English Heritage's £4 million cantilever footbridge, unveiled in 2019, spans the void (with a central 40mm gap!).

Tintagel Haven, also known as Merlin's Cove, was a quarry port in the nineteenth century, with slate lowered via a 'Heath Robinson' system of pulleys and derricks, alongside the waterfall. Steps descend to the beach, where Merlin's Cave passes clean through the headland, alongside a sleeping Merlin carved into the cliff; in Tennyson's *Idylls of the King*, the magician discovers the boy Arthur here.

The path leads above Tintagel Haven to English Heritage's café and gift shop.

📷 *Tintagel Haven.*

The Island at Tintagel

Access to The Island requires a hefty entrance fee. English Heritage have been 'reimagining' the site, with additions such as the bridge and the ghostly Gallos (Cornish: power) bronze statue of King Arthur, atop Tintagel Head's epic cliffs.

This easily-defended headland was, inevitably, an Iron Age cliff castle. The association with King Arthur began c1136, when Geoffrey of Monmouth invented most of the Arthurian legends in his *Historia Regum Britanniae* (History of the Kings of Britain), claiming that Tintagel was Arthur's birthplace. Tintagel Castle, built in the 1230s, was deliberately located here by Richard, Earl of Cornwall, to associate himself with the legends.

Traces of over seventy buildings, from a fifth- and sixth-century settlement, perch on terraces above Tintagel Haven. Archaeologists have unearthed Mediterranean pottery and, intriguingly, the 'Arthur Stone' inscribed with the name *Artognou*. The Ordnance Survey still mark the site as a monastery, but this theory is long-discounted.

◎ *Jacket's Point.*

15   Tintagel to Port Isaac

Distance 14km / 8.7 miles	**Height gain** 800m / 2,600ft	**Difficulty** •••••
Maps	OS Landranger 200 / OS Explorer 111, 106	
Start	Tintagel Castle Shop and Exhibition, Tintagel PL34 0DQ / swelling.doted.unheated / SX 052 889	
Finish	New Road car park, Port Isaac PL29 3SB / forge.passport.germinate / SW 999 809	
Parking near start	King Arthur's car park, Tintagel PL34 0DB / rollers.cloud.conspire / SX 056 884	
Public transport	96 and 95 buses, change at Camelford Station. 95 bus on Sundays	

How to follow up the magnificent scenery to Tintagel? The answer is, Port Isaac Bay; one of the National Trail's toughest and remotest stretches. A mild clifftop warm-up to Trebarwith Strand is followed by six demanding climbs in close succession, as the route slices across the grain of steep-sided valleys descending to the shore. There are zero facilities after Trebarwith Strand.

King Arthur's car park is 700m inland from the SWCP, in Tintagel village. Note the quirky Old Post Office opposite the car park, with its wonky roof. It is actually a fourteenth-century farmhouse owned by the National Trust and is pretty much the only genuinely old thing in Tintagel, despite all the Arthurian nonsense. Join the SWCP at the English Heritage buildings above Tintagel Haven, where you can shop for Arthurian tat.

Slate cliffs upwards of ninety metres in height are the order of the day. Glebe Cliff offers fine views of The Island and castle (useful if you couldn't afford the entrance fee).

Backways Cove.

St Materiana's Church likely originated in the sixth century (there is an inscribed Roman stone inside and Materiana was a fifth-century princess) but the current building is Norman, restored in the nineteenth century. Tintagel Youth Hostel is located in a former quarry building, amidst slate spoil on Dunderhole Point.

The path clings, at a dizzying height above the waves, to the slopes around Higher and Lower Penhallic Point. Trebarwith Strand comes into view, a long sandy beach flooded at high tide. Gull Rock rears offshore, a tall stack from this perspective resembling a blancmange! Quarries have eaten into the cliffs above the strand, operating into the twentieth century. 'Curzyway' hedge-walls of quarried slate line the trail.

Hole Beach was the site of Caroline Quarry and is so-named for the quarried-out cave, fifteen metres above the sand. The stone platform, perched on the cliff above, seated a gantry for lowering slate. Lanterdan and West Quarries follow shortly after; the SWCP passes above an isolated twenty-five-metre pinnacle and other spires and thin walls of unworked slate. These were left in situ because they were lower quality, but also to support winching mechanisms. Cutting the slate and lowering it onto boats was harsh work; in 1889 three men vanished into sea when the face that they were boring sheared off.

The SWCP descends to the narrow valley accessing Trebarwith Strand. The Prince of Wales Engine House, with its tall chimney, can be spotted up the valley; these ghostly mining ruins are common along the SWCP around Cornwall, but this is the first encountered. A track was incised through rock to the beach for donkeys to extract sand and seaweed, used as fertiliser. Trebarwith Strand's pubs and café are the last civilisation before the ten arduous kilometres to Port Gaverne: buckle up!

The SWCP ascends behind the Port William Inn, very steeply, onto Dennis Point. Port William is the sheer-walled amphitheatre a hundred metres below, where slate was loaded. The trail then zigzags down again, into Backways Cove. A stream bubbles through a rocky chasm at the base of this steep-sided cleft (they are *all* steep-sided clefts, from here on), which is dotted with mining ruins. The cove is fronted by the glistening slate cliff of Start Point.

Above Barrett's Zawn.

After crossing the footbridge and zigzagging out of the valley, the path smooths along Treligga Cliff, passing Bronze Age burial mounds. A relatively mild descent and ascent above Tregardock Beach passes behind a distinctive isolated peak known as The Mountain. A crossroads beside a footbridge gives the option of a side-tour to the beach, where at low tide a waterfall freefalls onto the sand; worth considering, if you haven't showered for days! This was the site of a Tudor silver mine, but the mine shaft atop Tregardock Cliff is nineteenth century. Tregardock Cliff's scree-like slopes descend to wave-lapped slate slabs.

This was all the calm before the storm! Four back-to-back valleys follow, all characterised by intense gradients and limited steps; nightmarish when muddy. Only the first valley has a footbridge, the streams are tiny but could be awkward in severely wet conditions.

The first valley is accessed via a dramatic ridge descending to Jacket's Point. Enjoy the cress beds beneath the footbridge, then climb alongside a sheer-walled inlet to the cliff above Crookmoyle Rock.

Dropping into the second valley, note the huge gash in the slope, to seaward of the path; this dauntingly steep tunnel was bored to access the beach.

The third valley, at Delabole Point, is escaped up a path teetering above the partially collapsed cliffs of Barrett's Zawn. Look for the entrance of the 'Donkey Hole', a long dark tunnel through which slate was hauled to the beach, now unstable and inadvisable.

By now, you may be suspecting that you've strayed into an Escher artwork. The fourth valley leads, via possibly the steepest and most rugged climb of all, above Ranie Point onto 130m Bounds Cliff, animated by a screeching kittiwake colony. The path levels off (praise be!) but is interrupted by hefty stone walls, crossed via jutting steps.

A final valley barely registers, a mild ridge descent to a boardwalk footbridge above St Illickswell Gug. A path leads above precipitous sheer cliffs, around Tresungers Point. A road is crossed at Cartway Cove, to a steep track into Port Gaverne: you are back in civilisation. Former fish cellars line the waterfront, known as 'Pilchard Palaces' (Cornish *palas*: dig). A final steep climb, along the road, leads to the car park.

📷 *Epphaven Cove.*

16 Port Isaac to Rock

Distance	19.6km / 12.2 miles
Height gain	900m / 2,950ft
Difficulty	● ● ● ● ○
Maps	OS Landranger 200 / OS Explorer 106
Start	New Road car park, Port Isaac PL29 3SB / forge.passport.germinate / SW 999 809
Finish	Rock Quarry car park, Rock PL29 6FD / shopping.resettle.makes / SW 928 757
Public transport	96 bus, from Rock Clock Garage. 95 bus on Sundays

This section is initially almost as tough as the previous, however the going eases around the wonderful Pentire headland, and the River Camel estuary is a mild delight.

From the car park, a clifftop path brings you to Fore Street, leading downhill into The Haven inlet, Port Isaac's heart. This whitewashed fishing village is instantly recognisable from TV Drama *Doc Martin*. The narrow thoroughfares behind the waterfront include Squeezy Belly Alley! Port Isaac is home to sea shanty singers *Fishermen's Friends*, who started out performing beside the lobster pots on the Platt, Port Isaac's narrow waterfront. This is surrounded by nineteenth-century 'Pilchard Palace' fish cellars, one housing the lifeboat.

Roscarrock Hill ascends from the Platt (passing Fern Cottage, Doc Martin's 'house') to steep steps onto Lobber Point, overlooking the 1920s breakwaters; the earliest pier, from Henry VIII's reign, is visible at low tide.

The SWCP arcs down to the reefs of Pine Haven, then immediately ascends eighty metres up unrelenting steps. The fenced-off path crosses the neck of Varley Head; on the far side, sheer

Rock to Padstow ferry

The ferry operates daily from 8 am to 4.45 pm from late October to April, with the final departure gradually extending to 7.45 pm through the warmer months. Card payments only are accepted, the cost was £3 in 2024. At low tides, the ferry goes to St Saviour's Point, 400m north of Padstow. Check details with the Padstow Harbour Commissioners www.padstow-harbour.co.uk; their office number is 01841 532239.

cliffs soar above Greengarden Cove and lead below Bronze Age burial mounds on Scarnor Point to the memorable Reedy Cliff. Here, the path zigzags down precarious steps towards bouldery Downgate Cove, wiggles across the coastal scarp, then scales fifty metres onto Kellan Head via winding switchbacks. The path clings to the precipice around Kellan Head, eventually relenting as it enters the inlet of Port Quin.

Just a smattering of cottages and Pilchard Palaces (and a useful water tap) remain of Port Quin, the 'village that died'. By Victorian legend, the menfolk perished in an unspecified fishing disaster, depicted in Frank Bramley's 1888 painting *The Hopeless Dawn*, displayed in London's Tate Gallery. More likely, Port Quin was depopulated gradually after the pilchards died out and the local mines failed. Port Quin is the reputed site of a Viking longship burial, however there is no archaeology to back this tale up.

Doyden Castle marks Doyden Point. Samuel Symons built this Gothic folly in 1839, for hedonistic partying; boringly, it's now a holiday rental. Gilson's Cove Mine extracted silver-rich antimony; the path passes between its shafts, resembling prehistoric stone circles. Trevan Point's crags offer a viewpoint around Port Quin Bay towards the looming Pentire headland.

Following the descent to the beaches at Epphaven Cove and Lundy Bay, the going becomes notably easier. Lundy Hole is a deep chasm, supposedly created when St Menefrida flung a comb at the Devil, with such force that the earth opened up. A more prosaic explanation is that Lundy Hole is a sea-eroded cave, whose roof has collapsed.

The path undulates over Carnweather Point and Com Head to The Rumps, Cornwall's best-preserved Iron Age cliff castle. The SWCP turns away at the entrance, apparently deterred by the three thrift-covered ramparts and rock-cut ditches scored across the neck of Rumps Point, protecting its twin headlands. The eastern high point is the spot to scan The Mouls, the pyramidal island just 300m offshore, for nesting puffins.

Continuing towards Pentire Point, look back to Rumps Point; it has a distinctive 'dragon's tail' profile caused by a volcanically-intruded dolerite sill. Look also for a memorial plaque alongside a bench; here in September 1914, Laurence Binyon was inspired to compose the poem *For the Fallen* ('*They shall grow not old…*'), which was to become the Ode of Remembrance recited at memorial services.

Rump's Point.

St Enodoc's Church

A slightly crooked thirteenth-century spire is visible from Daymer Bay; this is the lovely St Enodoc's Church, reached by a 400m side-tour. It was restored in the nineteenth century, after three centuries buried in the dunes, with churchgoers entering via the roof! This is the resting place of Poet Laureate John Betjeman, who died at Trebetherick in 1984.

Pentire Point's rocky apex might be Cornwall's finest viewpoint, with 360^0 vistas along the coast across Padstow Bay and inland up the River Camel estuary. A kilometre offshore, Newland island rears above the tides.

The SWCP gradually descends, above a wide rock-cut reef, towards the sands of Hayle Bay, backed by the conurbation of Polzeath. Two side-coves and an eroded beachside path delay arrival at the resort, which is characterised by surf shops and eateries. Unless you need to surf or eat, continue out of Polzeath via The Greenaway, a wide track above reefs of green-purple banded slate. These extend to Trebetherick Point, site of a lifeboat disaster in 1900 (page 91) and entrance to the River Camel (Cornish *kamm*: crooked and *heyl*: estuary).

At low tide, Daymer Bay's beach becomes part of a continuous sandy expanse extending up-river past Rock. The SWCP offers the choice of either walking across the beach, or atop the dunes behind.

Brea Hill is a distinctive mound-shaped hill, itself topped by Bronze Age burial mounds. The SWCP climbs onto and contours around its flanks, giving an overview of this section's final stretch; a sandy path winding through a dune system, above the low cliffs of a raised beach. The largest dune is fifty-metre-high Cassock Hill, marking the entrance to Rock.

Rock, 'the Saint-Tropez of Cornwall', is an exclusive enclave, with foodie restaurants and boutique shops. Unless you're a hedge-fund manager seeking a holiday home (average 2024 property price: £1.2 million), head to Rock Quarry car park, or if continuing to Padstow, the ferry slipway just after. At low tide you'll have to trudge some distance across the sands to reach the ferry.

Trevose Head Lighthouse.

17 Padstow to Porthcothan

Distance	21.8km / 13.5 miles	Height gain	475m / 1550ft	Difficulty	●●●●
Maps	OS Landranger 200 / OS Explorer 106
Start	North Quay, Padstow PL28 8AF / audible.land.radiating / SW 920 755
Finish	Porthcothan Bay car park PL28 8LW / coats.equity.dogs / SW 858 719
Parking near start	Harbour car park, Padstow PL28 8BN / hostels.setting.lilac / SW 919 753
Public transport	56 bus

A wonderful medley of North Cornwall's 'greatest hits'; lighthouses and towers atop airy headlands jutting into the Celtic Sea, seabird-thronged cliffs, thrift-covered maritime heath and wave-pounded beaches.

The Rock ferry lands at North Quay, beside Padstow's bustling inner harbour. North Cornwall's largest port received its first stone pier in 1536, its subsequent growth restricted by the Doom Bar which bars large ships. Padstow derives from *Petrocstow*, 'Petroc's spot'; the Welsh saint founded a monastery here, cAD500. The saint would disapprove of Padstow's pagan-inspired 'Obby 'Oss Festival, which takes place every May 1st.

Tarmac paths lead from town. The Rock ferry lands at St Saviour's Point during low tides. Padstow War Memorial, a tall Celtic cross, overlooks the stunning expanses of the River Camel's estuarine sands. St George's Cove is a wooded inlet sheltering St George's Well, a tiny holy

Mother Ivey

Mother Ivey was a sixteenth-century witch or soothsayer. She cursed a merchant who ploughed a surplus boatload of pilchards into fields, rather than share with locals; his eldest son died soon after. Supposedly, the land behind Mother Ivey's Bay is still cursed.

spring. Gun Point Battery's concrete is Second World War, but its stone walls date from the American War of Independence!

Boardwalks lead behind the dunes and brackish marshes of Harbour Cove, where, at low tide, a vast sandy beach is exposed; the Doom Bar. In 2007, a *Time Team* archaeological dig on cliffs at Lellizzick uncovered Romano-British roundhouses, with evidence of trading links to Byzantium. The cluster of buildings surrounding tiny Hawker's Cove include the old lifeboat station and pilot's cottages.

Stepper Point guards the entrance to the Camel. Its tip has been quarried away; in 1829, capstans were fixed onto the quarry levels, allowing men and mules to haul ropes and 'warp' ships into the estuary against the prevailing south-westerlies. The SWCP ascends above the quarries, passing a Coastwatch lookout station to the 1830 daymark tower at the summit. This a grand viewpoint, with vistas far along the north coast and back up-estuary to Bodmin Moor.

Pepper Hole, a collapsed cave, and Butter Hole, a vertiginous cove, are just the warm-up acts for a spectacular stretch of coast. From Gunver Head, the path descends steeply alongside the three Merope Islands (Higher, Middle and Lower), separated from the mainland by the wafer-thin

📷 *Mother Ivey's Bay.*

Tregudda Gorge. Longcarrow Cove leads to Porthmissen Bridge, a slender outcrop perforated by archways. Opposite, Marble Cliff is unmistakeable by its white limestone striped through dark mudstone and by its raucous seabird colonies; fulmars, guillemots, kittiwakes and razorbills. On Roundhole Point, don't fall down Round Hole: another collapsed cave, forming a spectacular blowhole in big swells.

Cliffs lead from Trevone Bay to Harlyn Bay, amongst Cornwall's few north-facing beaches; surfers head here when everywhere else is too big. Past Harlyn Bridge, the SWCP follows the beach and can be briefly blocked by high tides. Behind the beach is a Bronze Age burial ground, where gold lunulae necklaces have been unearthed.

Cataclews Point has been heavily quarried for a volcanic sill of 'Blue Elvan', greenstone used for St Paul's Cathedral's steps. The path squeezes past Harlyn Sands and Mother Ivey's Bay holiday parks, above Mother Ivey's Bay.

Padstow Lifeboat Station, relocated from Hawker's Cove in 1967, is a dramatic sight. An enormous shed, completed in 2006, extends on stilts into Mother Ivey's Bay, sheltered by the Merope Rocks behind. Here, the SWCP ascends onto Trevose Head. Trevose Head Lighthouse is a twenty-seven-metre white tower, built 1847; the SWCP passes behind and it is best viewed across Stinking Cove from the quarry at Dinas Head, where there is a 'rocket post', used for coastguard training. Out in the Celtic Sea, dolerite stacks resist the incessant swells; The Bull and, further offshore, the Quies. Descending from Trevose Head, a second Round Hole is passed: a gaping forty-metre chasm.

The reefs and sands of conjoined Booby's Bay and Constantine Bay are popular with surfers. The *SV Carl* is revealed at low tide in Booby's Bay, a First World War shipwreck. The SWCP leads along Constantine Bay's beach, in front of a dune system. Sixth-century Saint Constantine was a king who converted after meeting St Petroc. Treyarnon Point hides Treyarnon Bay, overlooked by a Youth Hostel and requiring a mild stream crossing.

📷 *Pepper Cove.*

This section's final two kilometres do not disappoint. A narrow gully separates Trethias Island from the SWCP. Wine, Pepper, Warren and Fox Coves are successive narrow inlets, with the ramparts of an Iron Age cliff castle amazingly extending across the promontories between; over two millennia, the sea has eroded the inlets into the fort. Wine and Pepper are named on account of smuggled shipments landed there. Fox Cove contains the remains of the *SS Hemsley I*, an oil tanker wrecked in 1969.

A final medley of stacks lead into the long inlet of Porthcothan Bay; the Minnows Islands, a ridgebacked loner in Rowan Cove and lastly Will's Rock, outside Long Cove. 'Will' was a lucky / unlucky Customs Officer who somehow survived after being left by smugglers to drown in the rising tide.

The Doom Bar

This ominously-named shifting sandbank was apparently created when a local man shot The Mermaid of Padstow, mistaking her for a seal. The dying mermaid, who had been in love with him, cursed the town and summoned a sandstorm.

The Doom Bar has caused over 600 vessels to come to grief and has extracted a heavy price from Padstow Lifeboat Station, previously based at Hawker's Cove; in 1867, five lifeboatmen drowned when their lifeboat capsized attempting to rescue the grounded *Georgiana* and in 1900, two lifeboats and eight lifeboatmen were lost in a single night while aiding the *Peace and Plenty*, wrecked on Trebetherick Point.

Park Head.

📷 *Porth Mear.*

18 Porthcothan to Newquay

Distance	19km / 11.8 miles **Height gain** 450m / 1,450ft **Difficulty** ● ● ○ ○ ○
Maps	OS Landranger 200 / OS Explorer 106
Start	Porthcothan Bay car park PL28 8LW / coats.equity.dogs / SW 858 719
Finish	Towan Headland car park, Newquay TR7 1HN / immediate.sprain.smug / SW 800 627
Public transport	56 or Atlantic Coaster bus, from Newquay Bus Station

Mostly easy paths lead above dramatically indented cliffs of Devonian slate, into the sizeable resort of Newquay. The towering stacks at the popular beauty spot of Bedruthan Steps are far from the only points of interest.

   Houses line Porthcothan Bay's southern rim to this sandy inlet's entrance, where the daunting chasm alongside the path is a collapsed cave. Three wave-lashed rocks directly offshore, connected at low tide, are the Trescore Islands. Grand views northwards encompass Will's Rock and the Minnow Islands, backdropped in the distance by Trevose Head and the Quies rocks.

   Porth Mear is a small cove fronted by a pebble beach and, at low tide, extensive reefs and rockpools. The cliffs gradually increase in stature, overlooked by Bronze Age burial mounds. Totty Cove is followed by Lower Butter Cove, a sheer-sided cleft with a huge arch leading through to High Cove.

Park Head scythes westwards, site of an Iron Age cliff castle. Its clean ridges and sharp-edged precipices are explained by numerous cliff falls; the SWCP short cuts across this unstable headland. Stacks line Park Head's southern flanks, as far as the beach of Pentire Steps, where a slate wall and line of trees offer shelter.

Magnificent Bedruthan Steps is among the SWCP's most visited spots. A succession of tall isolated stacks litter the beach for over a kilometre, with colourful names; Diggory's Island, Queen Bess Rock (named due to past likeness to the Tudor monarch), Samaritan Island (named after a ship wrecked here in 1846), Redcove Island, Pendarves Island, and finally Carnewas Island. According to one version of the truth, these were the stepping stones of the giant Bedruthan (Cornish *Bos Rudhen*: red-one's dwelling). However, the placename originated with the Victorians, likely describing miners' stairways. The stacks post-date the last Ice Age, formed as softer Devonian slates were eroded by the waves' incessant pounding. Iron Age Redcliff Castle's two ramparts precede Pendarves Point, the classic stacks viewpoint. Since 2019, cliff falls have closed the steps to the beach. Just uphill, a National Trust visitor centre and café occupies Carnewas Mine's former 'count house'.

Bedruthan Steps.

Bedruthan Steps are a hard act to follow, but the following kilometre does not disappoint. Trerathick Cove is pretty vertiginous, High Cove even more so! The descent around Trenance Point overlooks Mawgan Porth beach, backed by the conjoined villages of Trenance and Mawgan Porth. The SWCP crosses traces of the St Columb Canal on the cliffs, an eccentric project commenced in the 1770s and never completed.

Sand is crossed to the road bridge spanning the wide, braided River Menalhyl. Back atop the cliffs, vertically-walled Beacon Cove sits between Berryl's Point and Griffin's Point, the latter incised by valleys which delineate yet another Iron Age cliff castle, this one boasting sizeable ramparts.

From Stem Point, Watergate Beach (also known as Tregurrian) is unveiled, three kilometres of sand extending around Watergate Bay. Note the arch at the base of the seventy-metre cliffs. A level path atop the cliffs is only interrupted by the descent to the Watergate Bay Hotel, below Trevarrian Hill, and immediate ascent up again onto Tinner's Point. Newquay Airport is close inland, evidenced by the regular aircraft buzz. Metal barriers line fields alongside the path, protecting endangered corn buntings' nests.

Watergate Beach ends at Zacry's Islands, twin islets. Twin burial mounds offer a sweeping preview of Trevelgue Head and Towan Head, encompassing Newquay Bay and Newquay's sprawling conurbation. Whipsiderry Beach follows, where the tallest stack is Black Humphrey Rock or Flory Island; the first name refers to a notorious smuggler and wrecker who lurked in the mine tunnels perforating this rock.

Trevelgue Head is actually on Porth Island, connected to the mainland by an airy bridge overlooking Dollar Rock stack. Cliff falls currently force the SWCP to bypass this Iron Age cliff castle by road. Nevertheless, its impressive seven ramparts, Bronze Age burial mounds and blowhole can be explored via a side-tour. Vast caverns line the beaches below Trevelgue Head; 'Banqueting Hall' cave, since collapsed, hosted concert audiences in the 1930s. The Gannel Marine Conservation Zone starts here: it protects Newquay's coastal waters, as far as Kelsey Head (section 19).

Newquay

Newquay was first called *Towan Blystra* (Cornish: 'boat cove in sandy hills'). A sixteenth-century 'new quay' established it as a port, until the railway arrived in 1846 and with that, tourists. Newquay sees around six million visitors annually, being especially popular with young people seeking surf and hedonistic nightlife.

📷 *Newquay.*

From here on, the route passes through Newquay. Roads lead past Porth Beach and across to Lusty Glaze, where the vertical gash in the cliff was an incline for the never-completed St Columb Canal. Barrowfields park is dotted with Bronze Age burial mounds, before more road around Tolcarne Beach and past Newquay railway station. The Old Tramway and public parks lead to Towan Beach, where The Island is a 1930s holiday home connected to the mainland by a suspension bridge. Across Beach Road, a park and bowling green reach Fore Street's surf shops.

If you need respite from the tourists, side-tour down South Quay Hill to the harbour. The isolated pier, dating from 1870, was linked to the rail network via a tunnel. Urbanised Atlantic grey seals frequent the harbour; they surf alongside the boardies and subsist on chips!

North Quay Hill lane overlooks the harbour and ends at Fly Cellar, a stone platform used to barrel pilchards. Up the steps, the unique Huer's House is a circular, whitewashed eighteenth-century hut, topped by a miniature lookout tower, all possibly built atop a fourteenth-century chapel. It was manned by a 'huer' who shouted, *"Hevva, hevva!"* whenever pilchard shoals were spotted. Beneath the path to Towan Headland car park are the Tea Caverns, utilised by smugglers.

Fistral Beach, Newquay.

📷 *The Gannel.*

19 Newquay to Perranporth

Distance	18.1km / 11.2 miles	Height gain	575m / 1,900ft	Difficulty	● ● ● ● ●
Maps	OS Landranger 200 / OS Explorer 104
Start	Towan Headland car park, Newquay TR7 1HN / immediate.sprain.smug / SW 800 627
Finish	Droskyn car park, Perranporth TR6 0DR / zoomed.zooms.depths / SW 754 544
Public transport	U1 / U1A Coast to Coast bus, to Newquay Bus Station

Between the popular resorts of Newquay and Perranporth, the SWCP traverses a coast indented with fine beaches and sprawling dune systems; add a star to the difficulty rating if you dread trudging through soft sand! Firstly, escaping Newquay is surprisingly complicated; check low and high tide times before departing, as this will determine your route choice.

The Old Lifeboat House (operated 1899-1934) stands beside the car park. The unmistakeable gothic-spired Headland Hotel (1898) overlooks Fistral Beach, home to surfing competitions and a contender for Britain's premier big wave spot. A fenced path leads behind the dunes, passing Newquay Golf Club. Alternatively, stick to the beach. Both options attain Esplanade Road, where there is a choice of routes, determined by your timings and need to cross The Gannel, the River Gannel's shallow estuary.

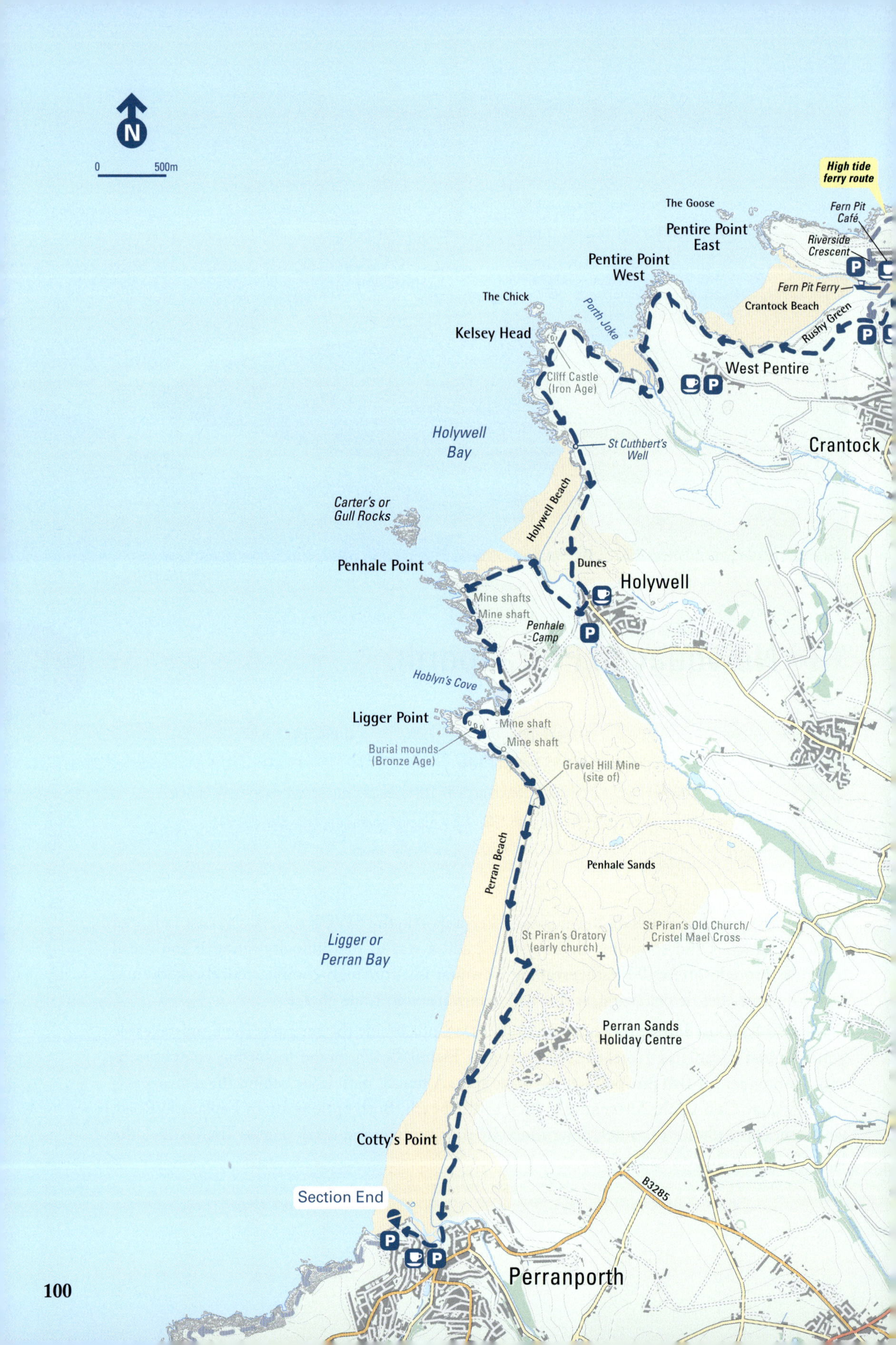
N
0
500m
High tide ferry route
The Goose
Pentire Point East
Fern Pit Café
Riverside Crescent
Pentire Point West
Fern Pit Ferry
Crantock Beach
The Chick
Porth Joke
Rushy Green
Kelsey Head
West Pentire
Cliff Castle (Iron Age)
Crantock
Holywell Bay
St Cuthbert's Well
Holywell Beach
Carter's or Gull Rocks
Dunes
Penhale Point
Holywell
Mine shafts
Mine shaft
Penhale Camp
Hoblyn's Cove
Ligger Point
Mine shaft
Mine shaft
Burial mounds (Bronze Age)
Gravel Hill Mine (site of)
Perran Beach
Penhale Sands
Ligger or Perran Bay
St Piran's Oratory (early church)
St Piran's Old Church/ Cristel Mael Cross
Perran Sands Holiday Centre
Cotty's Point
B3285
Section End
Perranporth

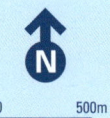

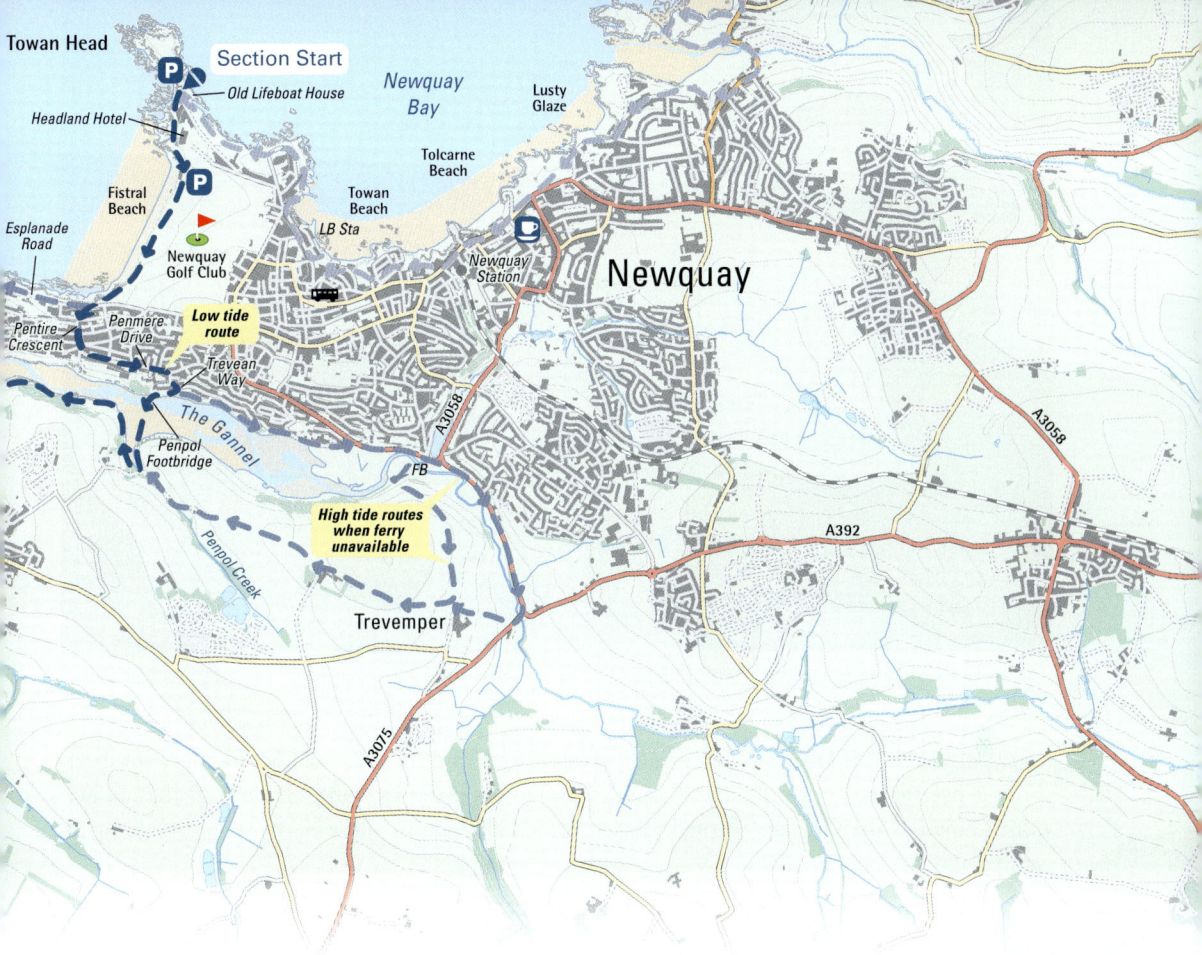

Fern Pit Ferry

The ferry operates daily from 9 am to 6 pm, three hours either side of high tide, from late May to mid-September. The cost was £1.40 in 2024. Check details with the Fern Pit Cafe www.fernpit.co.uk; their phone number is 01637 873181.

Low tide route: Possible for at least three hours either side of low tide. Dreary suburban roads (Pentire Crescent, Penmere Drive, Trevean Way) lead directly to The Gannel, crossed by Penpol Footbridge, a delightful boardwalk. The route continues across the sands and up Penpol Creek.

High tide ferry route: Esplanade Road and Riverside Crescent bend around the headland of Pentire Point East to the Fern Pit Café, where privately owned steps lead down to the Fern Pit Ferry. There is also a footbridge which is usable at low tide, for free, when the café is open. On the far bank, the SWCP is re-joined near Crantock Beach car park.

High tide route when ferry unavailable: This longest option leads up The Gannel from Penpol Footbridge and briefly follows the A392 before a footbridge across the River Gannel. A track leads uphill past Trevemper, before descending to Penpol Creek. In exceptional high tides, the footbridge is submerged and Trevemper is reached past two further roundabouts on the A392.

📷 *Crantock Beach.*

Penpol Creek is a lovely secluded inlet, crossed by a ford at its head. The Gannel's southern shore is overlooked by a millionaire's row of homes, atop the far bank. Be advised that an evil spirit known as the Craake (Cornish dialect for 'croak') haunts the estuary, recognisable by its wailing shriek.

The Gannel opens onto Crantock Beach, the first in a succession of stunning strands. St Carantoc was a sixth-century missionary who sailed an altar to the beach. Rushy Green, the dunes and heathland backing the beach, is crossed to low cliffs lining the beach's southern edge.

Porth Joke, also known as Polly Joke, is the secluded inlet squeezed between the headlands of Pentire Point West and Kelsey Head; a footbridge crosses the stream bubbling across the sands. 'Joke' derives from 'chough', Cornwall's 'national' bird. Kelsey Head's grasslands are strewn with wild flowers in spring and an Iron Age cliff castle overlooks The Chick, a rugged islet.

A pair of tall pyramidal islands dominate Holywell Bay: the stunning Carter's Rocks, also called Gull Rocks. The dunes behind the bay are huge and the path is heavy-going! It leads past a seasonal lagoon, to briefly enter Holywell village.

St Cuthbert's Well

Despite being a two-kilometre side-tour along the beach from Holywell village, this remarkable cave is well worth seeking out. Tucked beneath Kelsey Head and only accessible at low tide, the cave is adorned with multi-coloured stalactites and basins of calcium bicarbonate ('flowstone'). By legend, the cave formed when the saint's body was brought ashore; pre-NHS, sick children were brought here for healing.

Holywell Bay.

Penhale Point, overlooking Carter's Rocks, is frequented by choughs who breed hereabouts. The path squeezes between clifftop mine shafts and the fence of Penhale Army Camp, which closed in 2010; the Nissen huts were built in 1943 for American soldiers preparing for D-Day. Proposals have been submitted to redevelop the site into a resort. At Hoblyn's Cove, the path edges above sheer-sided clefts.

From the Bronze Age burial mounds on Ligger Point, grazed by wild ponies, a breathtaking vista unfolds; Perran Beach, three kilometres of glistening strand backed by Penhale Sands, Cornwall's largest (650 hectares) and highest (ninety metres) dune system. The SWCP passes around the site of Gravel Hill Mine (closed 1880s) and descends a steep track to the beach, formerly a steam-powered incline serving the mine.

The beach (named after St Piran) is first followed. Cliffs bar the way at high tide and the SWCP is signposted up a sandy gorge into Penhale Sands. The amount of ascent is surprising; the dunes were formed during higher sea levels. Grinding uphill on soft sand, try to appreciate the kidney vetch, pyramidal orchids and meadowsweet thriving here. The route reaches its highest point at around seventy metres and veers back seaward; St Piran's Oratory, an important early Christian site, is 500m further inland.

Past Perran Sands Holiday Centre, the going becomes firmer underfoot as the SWCP descends onto the clifftop approaching Perranporth. Unless high tides force you into the dunes, the town centre is reached via a beach short cut.

Perran Beach and Penhale Sands.

St Piran's Oratory

Sixth-century monk St Piran became patron saint of tin miners and latterly, Cornwall! The chapel which he (purportedly) built where he came ashore survives, to an impressive degree; it was uncovered in 1835, after seven centuries buried in the dunes. Until 2015, a hideous concrete bunker smothered the chapel; now, the stone walls and roofless interior are viewable.

Further inland are traces of St Piran's Old Church and the three-holed *cristel mael* Celtic cross, amongst the county's oldest.

St Agnes Head from Chapel Porth.

20 Perranporth to Porthtowan

Distance 13.2km / 8.2 miles	**Height gain** 500m / 1,650ft **Difficulty** ●●●●○
Maps	OS Landranger 203 / OS Explorer 104
Start	Droskyn car park, Perranporth TR6 0DR / zoomed.zooms.depths / SW 754 544
Finish	Porthtowan Beach car park TR4 8AA / offstage.bolt.lemons / SW 692 480
Public transport	304 and U1 / U1A Coast to Coast buses, change at Three Spires

This coast is scarred and littered by the traces of centuries of mining activity; this is the Cornish Mining World Heritage Site's 'St Agnes Mining District'. Don't be put off! The ruins add to, rather than detract from, the stunning scenery and tall impressive cliffs.

Perranzabuloe Millennium Sundial is outside Droskyn car park. Local artist Stuart Thorn designed this granite stone circle surrounding a six-metre steel gnomon, quirkily set to 'Cornish time': twenty minutes before Greenwich Mean Time.

Cliff Road and Tregundy Lane lead from Perranporth. A track continues onto Droskyn Point, the site of Droskyn Mine, now occupied by a gloriously-located Youth Hostel. The cliff edge path leading towards Cligga Head becomes increasingly rough-surfaced from mine spoil. Mine adits are passed and the first of many conical cages is encountered; don't investigate too closely as they cover open mine shafts! The shafts are unsealed, as they house bat colonies; about twelve of the UK's seventeen species breed in Cornwall.

Geologists get excited about Cligga Head (Cornish *klegar*: cliff), the first granite cliffs along the SWCP. Around 290 million years ago, during the Permian period, the 'Cligga Head Intrusion' rudely intruded into the surrounding sedimentary Devonian slates, the heat mineralising the slates into what Cornish miners call 'killas'. Killas contains the rich tin and copper lodes which are the source of Cornwall's mineral wealth and is encountered wherever granite intrudes along the coast.

The SWCP winds uphill through small quarries and spoil heaps onto Cligga Head, covered by graffitied concrete remains of a Second World War wolframite mine. Wolframite contains

tungsten, used for armour plating and bullets. The 'British and Colonial Explosives Company' manufactured explosives here from 1889 until 1905 and during the First World War.

Cliffs stained red and green by copper ore and perforated by mine adits, lead to rocky Hanover Cove, a protected wreck site. The Falmouth Packet *Hanover* foundered here in 1763, having overshot Land's End. Only three survived from sixty-seven onboard.

Rounding Pen a Gader, there are arresting views of Green Island and numerous jagged stacks rising from a rock-cut reef at Trevellas Porth. The drone of small aeroplanes and helicopters indicates that Perranporth Airfield is nearby, previously a Second World War fighter base. Alongside the SWCP are concrete and earth 'dispersal pens', built for Spitfires.

The SWCP dips into and out of steep-sided Trevellas Coombe, crossing a bubbling stream at a road bridge. Known as the Jericho Valley, the waste tips, chimneys and overgrown ruins are traces of Blue Hills Mine, which closed in 1897.

Trevaunance Cove and Newdowns Head.

Trevaunance Cove is this section's only settlement. Coal was landed at the cove (raised up-cliff by horse-powered winding gear) and ore shipped out. Granite blocks become visible at low tide, traces of five successive piers swept away since 1632! The village of St Agnes is a side-tour uphill, past the eighteenth-century Stippy Stappy ('steep steps') terraced cottages.

The climb from Trevaunance Cove passes around an overgrown gorge, honeycombed with mine entrances, arriving atop vertiginous hundred-metre cliffs. A level path among mine waste, overlooking vast caves and arches around Polberro Cove, leads past Newdowns Head.

St Agnes Head, marked by a Coastwatch lookout station, is a dramatic spot. Far below, through the swirling fulmars and kittiwakes, the tide surges around the Crams rocks. The two offshore rocks, where guillemots, puffins and razorbills breed, are called Bawden Rocks or Man and his man. Reputedly, a child-munching giant named Bolster tossed them there.

A precipitous crag-lined path skirts Carn Gowla, where peregrine falcons nest, to Tubby's Head, an Iron Age cliff castle. The SWCP descends towards an iconic landmark, Towanroath engine house. Part of Wheal Coates mine (Cornish *wheal*: working) which operated between 1802 and 1913, this pumped out a 180m shaft. Just uphill are Old Whim and New Whim engine houses. These evocative ruins are a perennial favourite of photographers.

Descending into the narrow inlet of Chapel Porth, look for traces of a medieval chapel to the right of the path, alongside a holy well in the gully. This possibly dates from the tenth century. According to legend, St Piran landed at Chapel Porth, having sailed from Ireland on a millstone.

At low tide, a long strand extends from Chapel Porth to Porth Towan; with care, this beach can be followed. The official route crosses the stream beside the National Trust car park and follows the valley upstream. This section's final ascent grinds up Mulgram Hill to cross Wheal Charlotte Moor, a lunar landscape of mine spoil which is being attractively re-colonised by colourful heather.

A gradual descent leads to Porthtowan. The beach, Porth Towan, is popular as it receives sun almost all day. Low tide exploration will reveal a wonderful tidal pool tucked beneath the northern cliffs.

◎ *Wheal Coates Mine.*

The Cornish Mining World Heritage Site

The Cornish Mining World Heritage Site (properly, the 'Cornwall and West Devon Mining Landscape WHS') was designated by UNESCO in 2006, to preserve and showcase the region's unique heritage.

The combination of Cornwall's rich ore lodes and the introduction of steam pumps led to astounding expansion during the eighteenth and early nineteenth centuries; Cornwall became the world's largest tin and copper producer, with over 2,000 mines. The mines became unprofitable after foreign lodes were opened up and most closed in the early twentieth century. Cornish miners emigrated to work in the Americas, Australia and South Africa, a diaspora of at least 250,000.

This post-industrial wasteland of spoil heaps, scarred hillsides, crumbling chimneys and gutted engine houses is not an enticing prospect, on paper! In practice, this heritage legacy, gradually being reclaimed by nature, is interwoven into the fabric of the landscape, augmenting rather than detracting from its beauty.

Porth-cadjack Cove and Samphire Island.

Horse Rock and the Pepperpot, Portreath.

21 Porthtowan to Godrevy

Distance 14.8km / 9.2 miles	**Height gain** 375m / 1250ft **Difficulty** ● ● ● ● ○
Maps	OS Landranger 203 / OS Explorer 102, 104
Start	Porthtowan Beach car park TR4 8AA / offstage.bolt.lemons / SW 692 480
Finish	Godrevy National Trust car park TR27 5ED / increased.budgeted.locals / SW 584 422
Public transport	3km walk to Bar Lane, T2 The Tinner and 304 buses, change at Threemilestone

Although there are a number of harsh climbs, the majority of this section follows a level plateau. The stand-out features are the numerous spectacular islets and stacks, tucked beneath ninety-metre cliffs of Devonian sandstone and, later, slate. Only the seabirds can access these harsh and isolated environments; consider carrying binoculars.

A lane and then byway track ascend onto the heathland plateau above Porth Towan. There are views inland to Carn Brea, topped by a twenty-seven-metre Celtic cross erected in 1836 to commemorate mining magnate Francis Basset; his estate encompassed most of this section. The clifftop is rejoined above the pyramidal Tobban Horse, the first of numerous stacks. Pink thrift thrives amongst mining waste and capped shafts; an unusual square chimney stands alone beside the path, then a pillbox-like 'batcastle' is encountered, capping Kite's Shaft. Eerie sounds emanate from the shaft; it connects with a sea cave at the base.

Sally's Bottom, where the World Heritage Site (page 109) ends, is a dramatic cliff-rimmed amphitheatre. Concrete mining remains line its eastern edge, with views of Gullyn Rock and

Sheep Rock (more stacks, colonised by auks, herring gulls and shags). Stone steps plummet downhill, following a wire fence. At the bottom, a stone marks Bottom Shaft, then the ascent out immediately commences. The reward for the climb is the view of a fine waterfall, plunging to the beach. A second, adjacent, cove offers further views of Gullyn Rock.

Along Nancekuke Common, the wire fence closely lines the path past a concrete hut, Diamond (a distinctively pointy stack), another intense down-and-up cleft and finally, a blockhouse structure currently daubed with *'Will You Marry Me?'*. The *'MOD Property Keep Out'* signs and the briefly-glimpsed fibreglass 'golf ball' are clues that this is *RRH (Remote Radar Head) Portreath*, an RAF station and Second World War fighter base.

Gooden Heane Cove is another amphitheatre, enclosed by Gooden Heane Point. Lighthouse Hill road descends into Portreath. An optional side-path leads to the Pepperpot, an eight-metre 1846 daymark tower topped by a weather vane, overlooking Horse Rock. A plaque recites Laurence Binyon's poem *For the Fallen*, claiming that it was composed here. Pentire Point in section 16 makes the same claim: whom to believe?

A road leads around Portreath's sinuous pier and harbour basins. From 1815, these were served by Cornwall's first railway, the horse-drawn Portreath Tramroad; 100,000 tons of copper were exported yearly. Portreath Beach is bookended by tidal pools; Portreath Rock Pool is

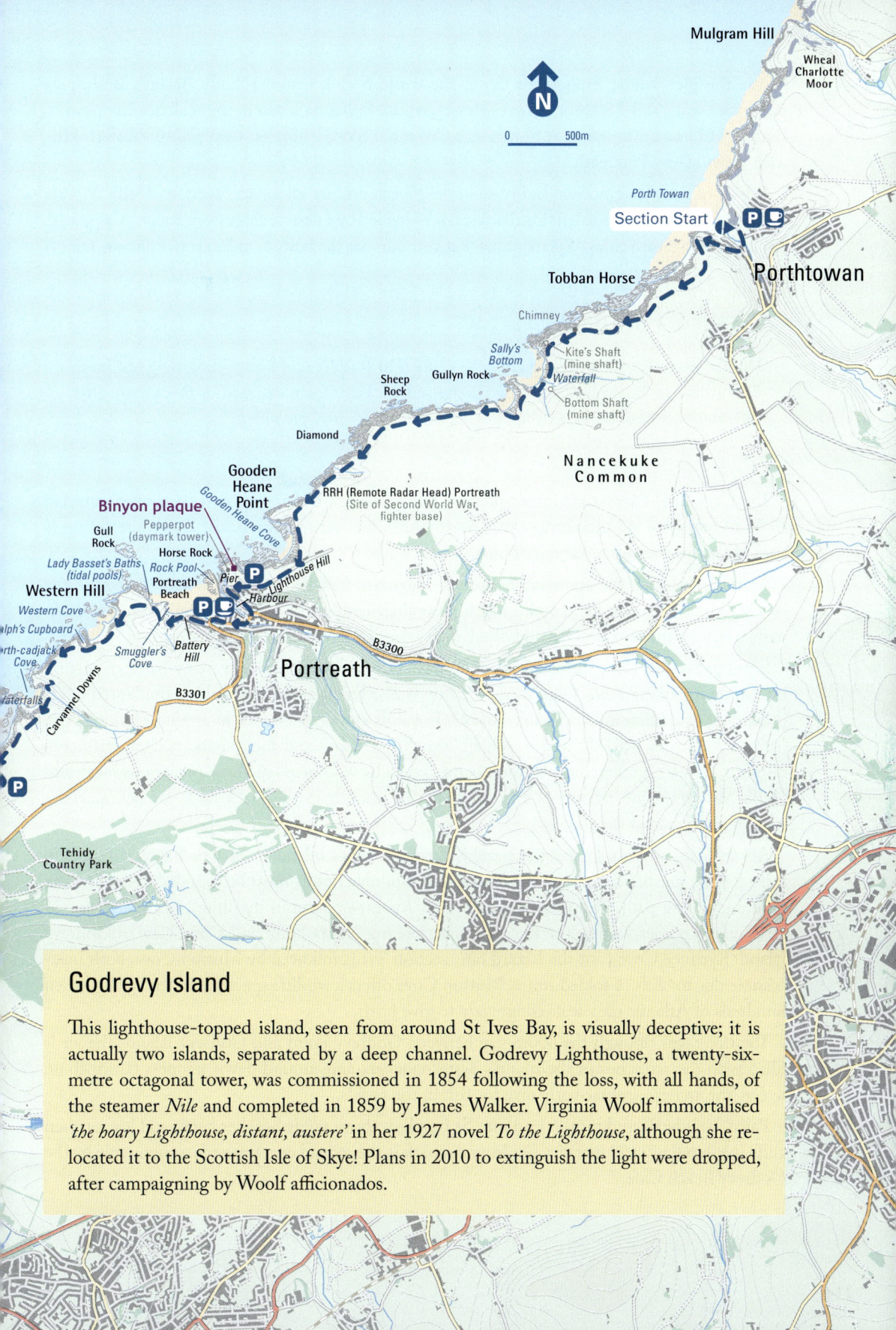

Godrevy Island

This lighthouse-topped island, seen from around St Ives Bay, is visually deceptive; it is actually two islands, separated by a deep channel. Godrevy Lighthouse, a twenty-six-metre octagonal tower, was commissioned in 1854 following the loss, with all hands, of the steamer *Nile* and completed in 1859 by James Walker. Virginia Woolf immortalised *'the hoary Lighthouse, distant, austere'* in her 1927 novel *To the Lighthouse*, although she relocated it to the Scottish Isle of Skye! Plans in 2010 to extinguish the light were dropped, after campaigning by Woolf afficionados.

beside the pier, whilst Smuggler's Cove, the western end, features 'Lady Basset's Baths', six pools rock-cut 1780-1800 for Frances Basset, whose father believed in the sea's healing powers. Battery Hill road terminates at Smuggler's Cove; the SWCP climbs steeply onto Western Hill, with views across Portreath.

A wall of truly magnificent eighty-metre cliffs extends six kilometres west, to Hell's Mouth. Western Cove, with its isolated ridgeback stack, is divided by a narrow ridge from Ralph's Cupboard, a collapsed cave with sides so precipitous that you can't see the bottom unless you're already falling.

Wrath of Portreath

Wrath ('Ralph') was a nasty giant who resided in Ralph's Cupboard, flinging giant boulders at fishing boats and snacking on the sailors. Fishermen claimed of this chasm that, *"Nothing ever came out of it which was unfortunate enough to get into it."*

The Carvannel Downs are interrupted by Porth-cadjack Cove, with two successive waterfall clefts to negotiate via the zigzag path, overlooking two vertiginous stacks; Samphire Island is named for the plant once harvested here.

At Basset's Cove, the eponymous mining magnates installed a winched cage to access the beach. Tehidy Country Park, 300m inland, was their family seat. Crane Castle's Iron Age ramparts overlook the cove and beyond, the Crane Islands: yet more impressive stacks.

Level paths lead along the Reskajeage Downs (Cornish: heathland of many battles), passing intermittent parking areas. Gaps in the clifftop wall offer stunning views along the North Cliffs (including two different Deadman's Coves!). The cliffs and imposing stacks around Hudder Cove (site in 2011 of a 100,000 tonne rockfall: search YouTube) and Hell's Mouth teem with cormorants, fulmars, guillemots, kittiwakes and razorbills who breed at these precarious locations. Hell's Mouth's name references a portentous cave mouth in the black rock, far below. Hell's Mouth café is across the road.

Above Fishing Cove (a naturist beach), there are views inland to St Ives Bay and Godrevy, this section's finish. Firstly however, Navax and Godrevy Points must be rounded, following the now-undulating path. The Knavocks (Cornish *Kynyavos*: autumn dwelling), heathland grazed by Shetland ponies, lead to the trig point overlooking Navax Point and a first view of Godrevy Island. Kynance Cove (not the Lizard one, section 29) is followed by Mutton Cove, both inaccessible due to cliffs of folded strata. Mutton Cove offers a wildlife spectacle in the spring, when hundreds of Atlantic grey seals congregate to give birth.

The tide rages through the 400m gap between Godrevy Point and Godrevy Island. The air is filled with the screeches of the island's oyster-catchers and, around dawn, gannets (Cornish *an sethor*: 'the archer') spectacularly dive for fish in the rapids.

Paths, boardwalk and tarmac lead into St Ives Bay, above sandy beaches, reefs, and low earthen cliffs inhabited by sand martins. Godrevy car park is the second encountered, recognisable by the Godrevy Beach Café.

📷 *Upton Towans and St Ives Bay.*

22 Godrevy to St Ives

Distance 18.7km / 11.6 miles	**Height gain** 325m / 1050ft	**Difficulty** • • • • •
Maps	OS Landranger 203 / OS Explorer 102	
Start	Godrevy National Trust car park TR27 5ED / increased.budgeted.locals / SW 584 422	
Finish	Island car park, St Ives TR26 1SY / version.venues.comply / SW 520 410	
Public transport	T2 The Tinner bus to Bar Lane, then 3km walk	

St Ives Bay's glorious sandy beaches are backed by Cornwall's second largest dune complex, The Towans (Cornish *tewyn*: dune). North Cornwall's cliffs are, for once, conspicuous by their absence! The central part of this outing trudges along roads, but estuaries and their birdlife maintain interest. St Ives is possibly Cornwall's most attractive town and is something of a Mecca for art enthusiasts.

Godrevy car park is exited via a boardwalk, passing a Second World War pillbox. Steps descend to a footbridge crossing the Red River, so-named for tin waste staining, until the last mine closed in 1998. The engine house chimney and scarred landscape indicate an industrial past; Gwithian Sandpit annually extracted 25,000 tonnes of sand and gravel. In 2005 it became St Gothian Sands Local Nature Reserve. Tracks and paths wind through the nature reserve, with the beach only occasionally glimpsed beyond the slowly recovering dunes, reedbeds and seasonal lagoons. Stone slab waymarkers are encountered from the Red River onwards and crop up through the following five kilometres.

The coast is re-joined at a lifeguard hut. It's possible to descend onto Gwithian Beach and follow the shoreline for nearly four kilometres to Black Cliff, scanning St Ives Bay for bottlenose dolphins, but the official route is recommended. This explores 'The Towans', 400 hectares of dunes, reaching up to seventy-two metres in height. Those wary of wading through sand will be pleased to find that the going is easy, with much of the path grassed over.

Gwithian Towans is followed by Upton Towans, owned by the Cornwall Wildlife Trust. Known as 'Dynamite Towans', from 1888 to 1920 this was the vast National Explosives Company factory. The roofless ruins originate from the 1890s, the earliest surviving concrete magazines. An accidental explosion in 1904 killed four workers and broke windows in distant St Ives. Phillack Towans and Common Towans follow, the SWCP passing in front of St Ives Bay Chalet and Caravan Park and then Beachside Leisure Park. Mexico Towans, where the dunes are particularly densely covered with marram grass, is the final part of The Towans.

Black Cliff, overlooking wide Porth Kidney Sands, marks the entrance to the River Hayle's estuary (Cornish *heyl*: estuary). Lifeguard stations and pillboxes are passed, before wending upriver past Hayle Towans via lanes, tracks and car parks. Hayle is entered along the recently redeveloped North Quay.

Hayle burgeoned from the eighteenth century as a shipbuilding and mine engineering centre. This growth was fuelled by bitter rivalry between two foundries over waterfront access. The Cornish Copper Company constructed East Quay, overlooking a tidal sluice and bridges across

Gwithian to Mexico Towans SSSI

The SSSI encompasses all of 'The Towans'. The fertile calcareous soil (i.e., rich in calcium, from crushed shells) provides a habitat for over 300 species of vascular plant; a fifth of all species in Cornwall. The rare silver-studded blue butterfly and six-spot burnet moth flit among pink pyramidal orchids and yellow bird's-foot trefoil, whilst tall marram grass shades cantankerous adders from the sun and provides cover for the ground-nests of the skylarks chirruping overhead.

📷 *St Ives.*

Copperhouse Pool, crossed by the SWCP. Harvey & Co developed South Quay at the head of Penpol Creek, where the SWCP passes between a railway viaduct and an angular Asda building.

Carnsew Road is followed out of town until a path heads right, to re-join the waterfront at Carnsew Pool (constructed in 1834 to flush silt from the quays). The busy B3301 ('The Causeway') leads to the head of the estuary at Griggs Quay, a grim pavement trek redeemed by the RSPB's Hayle Estuary Nature Reserve; curlew, egrets and oystercatchers inhabit the lagoons and islets of Ryan's Field on the left, and the estuarine mudflats of Lelant Water on the right.

From the Old Quay House pub, the SWCP passes beneath a railway before following it, past Lelant's two stations, towards the sea. Quiet lanes and paths are lined by pleasant gardens, uninspiring until the imposing granite tower of St Uny's Church is reached. A track leads beneath the pillbox-guarded railway to the estuary's entrance. Porth Kidney Sands recede 1.5km, with Godrevy Island in the distance; a wonderful vista. 18,000 bar-tailed godwits, curlews, egret, herons, oystercatchers and shelducks overwinter here, at Britain's south-westernmost estuary.

The SWCP negotiates the clifftop beneath the railway, steps climbing around Carrack Gladden headland to Carbis Bay. Note Carbis Bay Hotel's luxury beach 'huts'; the 2021 G7 Summit was hosted here, with controversial environment impact.

St Ives is entered via lanes between villas, crossing the railway twice. Note the 'Baulking House', an early nineteenth century huer's hut above Porthminster Point. Past St Ives' railway station at Porthminster Beach, the harbour is reached.

St Ives is an attractive place to explore, its narrow, whitewashed streets perched on a headland surrounded by beaches. Fifteenth-century St Ia's Church is named for St Ia, who supposedly arrived on a leaf. The 'fishermen's aisle' has windows for checking on boats during services! The harbour is guarded by John Smeaton's 1770 pier, the Old Lighthouse upon it (1820s) and also aggressive herring gulls, who steal food from your hand. A working fishing fleet survives, although St Ives peaked as a fishing station in the 1830s, landing 22 million pilchards annually. Downalong, formerly sail lofts, now studios and holiday lets, leads to The Island car park.

Carnelloe Mine and Gurnard's Head.

23 St Ives to Pendeen Watch

Distance	20.8km / 12.9 miles	**Height gain** 150m / 3,450ft	**Difficulty** ● ● ● ● ●
Maps	OS Landranger 203 / OS Explorer 102		
Start	The Island car park, St Ives TR26 1SY / version.venues.comply / SW 520 410		
Finish	Pendeen Lighthouse car park TR19 7ED / blogging.ketchup.cork / SW 379 358		
Public transport	Land's End Coaster bus from Pendeen village		

England's wildest coastline! The Penwith peninsula's northern side makes for one of the SWCP's most strenuous sections, with numerous ascents and plentiful bog and boulder underfoot. There are no settlements or facilities, although villages with pubs can be retreated to, inland, at a couple of points. The reward is immersion in truly breath-taking environs. Inland of the SWCP, moorland hills loom behind a patchwork system of stone walls, originating from the Neolithic period and amongst the oldest structures still in use, worldwide. Seaward, the empty Atlantic is fronted by lonely headlands, inaccessible coves and cliffs lacerated by deep zawns. The geology veers between pale 270-million-year-old granite, and dark slates and hornsfels, laid as sediment 400 million years ago and mineralised by the heat and pressure of the granite's intrusion. Nature is in the ascendant: samphire, sea beet, sea campion, sedge and thrift thrive along the clifftops; the bogs are brightened by tall purple loosestrife; adders lurk in stone walls; far below, seals haul ashore and sunfish and basking sharks are commonly sighted in the deep inshore waters.

Firstly, loop around 'The Island', St Ives Head, also known as Pendinas (Cornish: headland fort). Squeezed onto the promontory are Iron Age ramparts and a Coastwatch lookout station, located within Lamprock Battery's gun emplacements (1859). The summit is occupied by the fifteenth-century granite chapel of St Nicholas, patron saint of fishermen, originally a beacon light.

Porthmeor Beach arcs towards the low headland of Carrick Du, marked by a distinctive greenstone stack. Commencing with an ascent from Clodgy Point, the terrain underfoot becomes notably rougher; rock-strewn paths climb and dip through maritime heath above small coves and inlets, linking minor headlands. Clodgy Point is followed by Hor Point, then a traverse above pristine sands to cross Pen Enys Point, then boardwalks above Trevalgan Cliff (with an 'ancient' stone circle), then the trig point on Carn Naun Point and finally a descent to a slab footbridge and waterfall above River Cove.

That exhausting stretch was just the warm-up! The Carracks, offshore rocks hosting a population of Atlantic grey seals, mark where this remote coast veers west-south-west, absorbing the ocean's full force; from this point on the headlands jut further seaward, and the cliffs are increasingly indented by narrow coves and sheer-walled zawns.

The St Ives School

Artists appreciate St Ives' (apparently) unique light; seemingly, every second building is a gallery or studio! This originated in 1928, when local fisherman Alfred Wallis's 'naïve' sea paintings inspired the 'St Ives School of Art'; examples can be seen at the Tate St Ives gallery on Porthmeor Beach. This was opened in 1993 and sees a quarter of a million visitors a year. The Tate also administer the Barbara Hepworth Museum and Sculpture Museum, located close to the harbour in the twentieth-century sculptor's former home.

Wicca Pool is notable for its fine granite castellations, veined through dark slate. Stepping stones across the stream at Wicca Cliff lead onto Tregerthen Cliff, where the path descends to Gala Rocks' wide reef. The going here becomes as rugged as the SWCP gets, the path temporarily replaced by clambering amongst angular boulders! An ascent, crossing a stream, leads above sandy Porthzennor Cove onto Zennor Head; note the lone rock perched atop a cleft between boulders.

At a junction, the SWCP zigzags steeply downhill to a waterfall-filled cleft above Pendour Cove. The rustic hamlet of Zennor is 700m up the valley, should you wish for a diversion or escape.

After climbing from Pendour Cove and around Carnelloe cliff above Veor Cove, Carnelloe headland is passed around, above the stack of Carnelloe Long Rock. Traces of Carnelloe Mine are passed, including an overgrown wheelpit ruin. At Porthglaze Cove, a footbridge perches above another waterfall stream.

The long promontory of Gurnard's Head, so-named for the fish it resembles, dominates the view. Before it is reached, Boswednack Cliff, Rose-an Hale Cove and Treen Cove must first be negotiated. Between the coves, this section's sole house stands on Lean Point; Treen village is

Porthmeor Cove.

only 700m inland, accessed via a steep footpath. Sandy Treen Cove is also overlooked by the crumbling engine house of Gurnard's Head Mine and the remains of medieval Chapel Jane; to locate the chapel, look for steps down from the SWCP, revealing traces of walls (from c1100) around an altar stone, with a (possibly pre-Christian) holy well nearby.

A sharp ascent crosses the neck of Gurnard's Head. If you have energy to spare, side-tour along an exposed footpath to explore Trereen Dinas, a dramatically located Iron Age cliff castle. Three ramparts protected sixteen roundhouses, their platforms traceable on the leeward eastern slope.

Treen Cliff is incised by the deep Zawn Duel, the top of which is seen from the path. A descent around Porthmeor Point reveals Porthmeor Cove. Here, Penwith's unique landscape is encompassed in one vista; layered upwards from the sand and boulder beach are, successively; maritime heath, Bronze Age enclosures around Bosigran Farm, gorse-covered moorland pocked by mining ruins and standing stones and, finally, the high tor-capped summits of Carn Galver and Watch Croft.

Zennor

St Senara's church dates from at least the sixth century, although the current building is twelfth century. By legend, St Senara was a banished Breton princess who founded Zennor after washing ashore in a barrel, with a newly-born child. A fifteenth-century pew is carved with a remarkable mermaid image; the Mermaid of Zennor's singing seduced Matthew Trewella into the sea at Pendour Cove and the singing can supposedly still be heard among the waves.

During the First World War, D.H. Lawrence wrote *Women in Love* at Zennor. Xenophobic locals regarded his German wife Frieda (the Red Baron's cousin!) as a spy and after three ships were torpedoed, the police forced the Lawrences to leave.

Porthmoina Mill and Commando Ridge.

The clapper bridge behind Porthmeor Cove marks the start of the St Just Mining District (page 127). Crossing above the Great Zawn, a boggy stretch (well, boggier than usual) with stepping stones leads to Bosigran Castle. This Iron Age cliff castle is perched above vertiginous granite cliffs; the clanks and shouts emanating from far below are generated by rock climbers. Peering over the brink, you'll see Porthmoina Cove, filled by razor-backed Porthmoina Island, and, rearing from the opposite side, 'Commando Ridge', a Second World War training ground and classic climb. A stone footbridge at the back of the cove leads behind mining ruins, including Porthmoina Mill, perched on a platform.

The final four kilometres remain isolated, following rugged cliffs west towards Pendeen Lighthouse. At Trevean Cliff, the air below is filled with the screeches of kittiwakes, who have colonised Whirl Pool. Morvah Cliff is lined by traces of nineteenth-century Garden Mine, including a ruined engine house; part of a complex of mines extending up the slopes of 252m Watch Croft. Above Chypraze Cliff at Carn Clough, eleven stones arranged in a circle are traces of a Bronze Age burial mound. This marks the start of a steep descent to Portheras Cove, where stepping stones cross a bubbling brook. Wear something on your feet if you explore the sheltered (north-facing) beach, as shards of metal lurk; the legacy of the botched 1981 attempt by the Royal Engineers to dynamite the wreck of the *MV Alacrity*, grounded here since 1963!

The SWCP ascends behind Portheras Cove, before zigzagging downhill again to the fisherman's huts at tiny Pendeen Cove. A track leads to Pendeen Lighthouse. The seventeen-metre-high lighthouse, perched atop the slate promontory of Pendeen Watch, was built in 1900 to counter the notable number of wrecks caused locally by fog.

📷 *The Enys, Pendeen Watch.*

24 Pendeen Watch to Sennen Cove

Distance 15.3km / 9.5 miles	**Height gain** 525m / 1,700ft	**Difficulty** ● ● ● ○ ○
Maps	OS Landranger 203 / OS Explorer 102
Start	Pendeen Lighthouse car park TR19 7ED / blogging.ketchup.cork / SW 379 358
Finish	Sennen Cove Harbour car park TR19 7DF / tracks.disputes.gobblers / SW 350 263
Public transport	Land's End Coaster bus to Pendeen village

The dark slate and basalt cliffs stretching south-west from Pendeen Lighthouse are dotted with ghostly mining ruins; this is the 'Tin Coast'. This scarred wasteland of chimneys, engine houses, levels and spoil tips is, counter-intuitively, hauntingly beautiful.

From Pendeen Watch's coastguard cottages, a path traverses through bracken, high above The Enys ('isle') stack. Trewellard Bottoms is a jarring, apocalyptic, sight; a sprawling complex of chimneys and industrial ruins amongst toxic settling ponds and earth discoloured red by iron oxide, overlooking cliffs stained blue-green by copper waste. Geevor Tin Mine extends uphill; this operated from the eighteenth century until 1990, the last to close locally. Geevor is now a museum, where visitors can venture underground into Wheal Mexico; deviate up-valley along a footpath.

Levant Mine's well-preserved engine houses are perched on a rock-hewn level overlooking a zawn; these chasms indicate the presence of vertical ore lodes. Inside the smaller engine house is a steam-powered Trevithick beam engine, constructed at Hayle foundry in 1840 and the last example still in situ. The National Trust sometimes fire it up.

Crowns engine houses, Botallack Mine.

Tin Coast miners

The St Just Mining District extends from Porthmeor Cove (section 23) to Gribba Point. Cornish mining has sometimes been mythologised, but the harsh and dangerous working conditions were far from romantic; life expectancy was under forty. Levant Mine reached 600m below sea level, with tunnels extending 2.5km under the sea. Six hundred miners worked at temperatures of 33°C, within metres of the seabed boulders, audibly moving above! An aging lift failed in 1919, killing thirty-one. In 1893, at Wheal Owles, twenty drowned when an adjacent flooded mine was accidentally breached. The owners refused to pay £4,000 for a pump to retrieve the bodies.

A granite-walled track leads between fields and scarred heath, passing walled-off mine shafts. The SWCP veers onto Roscommon Cliff, above the spectacular, airy Stamps an Jowl Zawn (Cornish: chasm of the Devil's ore-breaking machinery) which is backed by a natural arch. After a trig point and truncated chimney above Botallack Head, the SWCP briefly re-joins the track.

Bottallack Mine is famous for the twin Crowns engine houses, among Cornwall's most photographed scenes. Perched barely high enough to clear storm waves, the lower house pumped water, whilst the higher powered a winding mechanism. Alongside the SWCP are well-preserved arsenic works, built in 1906 to extract the chemical from tin ore; arsenic vapour condensed along the 'labyrinth' tunnels, after which men crawled through and scraped it off (works also survive at Trewallard Bottoms and the Kenidjack Valley). This greened-over site, with nesting choughs, is hard to reconcile with its poisonous past.

More engine houses line the path to Kenidjack Castle; Wheal Owles, site of the 1893 disaster, and Wheal Edward. Kenidjack Castle is named for the three lines of Iron Age ramparts

defending the gorse-covered hilltop, now littered with mine ruins. Enjoy the view across the Kenidjack Valley, as the going now gets harder! The valley is filled with Boswedden Mine's lushly overgrown ruins. After crossing the Tregeseal River, which once powered fifty waterwheels, the SWCP climbs sharply from the valley; first consider a side-tour to Porth Ledden, where seals sleep, overlooked by a huge waterwheel pit.

Cape Cornwall's car park, and St Helen's Chapel, are passed. The wonderfully-located thirteenth-century oratory possibly has fifth century origins; a chi-rho cross (the earliest Christian symbol) discovered here was dumped down a well by a Victorian vicar. England's only cape is unmistakeable due to 'The Sentinel', the 1864 mine chimney on top, left in situ as a daymark. This was long believed to be Britain's westernmost point (Land's End is 914m further west). A Coastwatch lookout station sits below the summit. A steep path zigzags downhill, past the houses overlooking Priest's Cove, where a wave-battered slipway serves local fishermen.

A steep track ascends Carn Gloose cliffs, where tor-like outcrops indicate that the underlying geology is now granite. Alongside the lane at the top is Ballowall Barrow, an elaborate Bronze Age burial mound, uncovered beneath mining debris in the nineteenth century. The Brisons (French *brisant*: breakers) stand a kilometre offshore, two twenty-five-metre-high rocks, where the rare storm petrel nests.

The SWCP drops into the Cot Valley; reminiscent of the Kenidjack Valley, with its luxuriant mining ruins. The valley is escaped around Hermon Hill, but first visit Porth Nanven, 'Dinosaur Egg Beach'. It's illegal to remove the beach's ovoid granite 'eggs', ever since a northern city was found to be using them for ornamentation! The boulders tumble from a 120,000-year-old raised beach uncovered in the cliffs.

Cape Cornwall.

The following three kilometres along the coastal slope utilise a path constructed to access the numerous mine shafts and adits (side-entrances) passed. A rugged climb above Gribba Point, a descent to a side-valley overlooking Maen Dower reef, steps onto Nanjulian Cliff and some final clambering around Aire Point all mean that, when the aptly-named Whitesand Bay opens up, you've earned the view. The path trudges through sand behind Gwynver, a quiet and relatively remote spot popular with surfers, and again uphill behind Carn Towan's dunes; an alternative is to follow the beach. Basking sharks are commonly spotted in Whitesand Bay, congregating in groups.

Sennen Cove occupies Whitesand Bay's sheltered southern corner. Pretender to the throne Perkin Warbeck landed here in 1497, before capture at Exeter. England's westernmost village, named for Celtic Saint Senana, remains pleasantly undeveloped. The beachfront road arcs to the Lifeboat Station (which spectacularly lost its roof during 2022's Storm Eunice) and the distinctive eighteenth-century Round House, now a gallery but still housing the capstan mechanism used to haul boats ashore. The car park overlooks the 1908-built pier.

You are now so, so close to Land's End …

Polperro (Section 37).

South Cornwall

The 250km / 155 miles of the SWCP traversing South Cornwall continue to challenge and inspire. The magnificent Penwith and Lizard peninsulas are succeeded by a series of lesser-known, but equally stunning (and strenuous) rugged headlands extending north and east to Plymouth Sound. Innumerable secluded inlets, stone-wharfed fishing harbours and sheltered anchorages don't make the going easier; they all mean more ascent! However, they add engaging layers of maritime history and mythology to your SWCP explorations; tales of shipwreck tragedy, legends of giants and 'piskies', nefarious smuggling exploits, military heritage and the novels of Daphne du Maurier.

The majority of South Cornwall's shores are within the Cornwall Area of Outstanding Natural Beauty.

📷 *Zawn Pyg, Nanjizal Bay.*

📷 *Porth Chapel.*

25 Sennen Cove to Porthcurno

Distance 9.7km / 6 miles	**Height gain** 475m / 1,550ft **Difficulty** ● ● ● ● ●
Maps	OS Landranger 203 / OS Explorer 102
Start	Sennen Cove Harbour car park TR19 7DF / tracks.disputes.gobblers / SW 350 263
Finish	Porth Curno TR19 6JS / betrayal.decay.grumbles / SW 386 223
Parking near finish	Porthcurno car park TR19 6JX / printout.diggers.fairy / SW 384 225
Public transport	Land's End Coaster bus

Land's End, England's westernmost point! Mild paths lead atop jointed granite buttresses and castellated towers, sparkling with quartz, feldspar and mica. Below, fulmars and gulls wheel above swells surging into innumerable zawns and caves. When the sun sinks into the Atlantic horizon, punctuated by offshore lighthouses, the granite is set ablaze.

The car park of Sennen Cove, mainland England's most westerly village, overlooks the 1908-built pier, which is regularly over-topped by waves. Steps ascend to a former Coastguard lookout hut on Pedn-mên-du, overlooking the pointed Irish Lady stack. For the eight kilometres to Porthgwarra, the SWCP ambles, often with a choice of paths, above sixty-metre cliffs along a maritime heath plateau. Blue, yellow and pink colour is added by spring squill, kidney vetch and thrift.

Castle Zawn is littered with remains of the *RMS Mulheim*. Carrying plastic waste under a 'flag of convenience' in 2003, she ran aground after the lone watch officer knocked himself

Longships and Wolf Rock

The Longships reef is two kilometres west of Land's End. It does resemble a Viking flotilla, imagining Longships Lighthouse on Carn Bras (Cornish: big rockpile) as a mast. The forty-three-metre tower was completed in 1873; waves regularly obscured the previous 1795 lighthouse, with one storm smashing the lantern and turning the keeper's hair white. Wolf Rock Lighthouse is visible fifteen kilometres to the south-south-west, perched on a solitary volcanic rock named for the howling noise it generated during gales. The forty-one-metre granite tower took eight years to construct, finally being lit in 1870.

📷 *Land's End.*

unconscious. Maen Castle follows, one of Cornwall's earliest cliff castles; the ditch and stone ramparts possibly date from 800BC.

Gamper Bay arcs around to Dr Syntax's Head. This promontory of tunnel-pierced buttresses, named for an obscure Georgian cartoon character, is the *actual* Land's End. The spot is marked by a flagpole and The First & Last House (a souvenir shop); tourists, however, congregate around the gaudy complex on Dr Johnson's Head, 300m south. This was named in honour of Samuel Johnson for his 1775 *Cornish Declaration of Independence*, seemingly unaware that he had been writing in jest. The SWCP squeezes between the iconic Land's End Signpost (*'New York 3174'*), fenced-off behind a kiosk, and a theme park and 'shopping village'. Make what you will of all this.

The maritime heath sloping to Carn Greeb farmstead (now a petting zoo) is badly eroded. The farm marks the end of the tourist complex; ahead, the trails are yours ... just when the really breath-taking scenery commences! Pordenack Point offers the classic viewpoint of Land's End and its massive stacks; the turreted ridge of The Armed Knight and the arch-pierced islet of Enys Dodnan. Both stacks house auks; guillemots, razorbills and the occasional puffin.

Carn Boel headland marks the entrance to Nanjizal Bay (also called Mill Bay), a contender for Cornwall's grandest. Below the northern rim, Atlantic grey seals haul out at Zawn Reeth's caves. Diamond Horse stack is named for its quartz veins, mistaken for diamonds. The path traverses the bay, overlooking waves peeling onto shallow offshore sands. The highlight is Zawn Pyg, below a footbridge and lone house. Dubbed 'The Song of the Sea', this immense cave-slot extends clean through the cliffs from a natural swimming pool, alongside the bouldery beach; the nearest thing to a cathedral alongside the SWCP. Carn Lês Boel (another cliff castle) separates Nanjizal from the perfect granite amphitheatre and vast cave entrances surrounding Pendower Coves.

A climb from Porth Loe attains Gwennap Head, the UK mainland's most south-westerly point. A Coastwatch lookout station stands above the 'Fisherman's Land's End', where the Celtic Sea and English Channel intermingle in an, *"entire disorder of the surges"* (John Ruskin). 'Chair Ladder Cliff', famous among climbers, was the seat of witch Madge Fiddy, who summoned

Pedn-mên-an-mere.

storms to steal jewels from drowned sailors. Gaze seaward; basking sharks, minke whales, dolphins and porpoise are regularly sighted. Larger fauna appear increasingly commonly: humpback and fin whales! A side-tour can be made to Tol-Pedn-Penwith (holed headland), where the Funnel Hole plunges into a collapsed cave; follow the cliff-edge path a hundred metres from the Coastwatch building.

Two conical daymarks, black / white and red, point 1.5km offshore to the Runnel Stone, marking the entrance to the English Channel; if you've trekked from Minehead, this will be a significant spot.

Porthgwarra's cottages are the first settlement reached. A narrow tunnel (currently closed) descends steeply to the beach, bored for seaweed-gathering. A second tunnel accesses 'hulleys'; these rock alcoves had wooden lids, for storing live shellfish. Now sheltered from the Atlantic's full force, the character changes; paths squeeze through dense hedges and gorse, alongside stone-walled farmland.

Over the final two kilometres, the trails are notably more rugged. As the name implies, sandy Porth Chapel has a religious past. Stone-lined St Levan's Well was named for sixth-century Saint Selevan and an archaeological project is attempting to date the cliff-edge chapel remains, suspected to be among Cornwall's earliest Christian sites.

Pedn-mên-an-mere headland is known locally as 'Wireless Point'; mast traces remain, built by Porthcurno's telegraph company to eavesdrop on Marconi's transmissions! Seats and galleries extend across Minack Point, with Porth Curno providing a stunning backdrop; the Minack Theatre is an extraordinary open-air performance space, built by Rowena Cade and opened in 1932.

The SWCP descends to Porth Curno via some alarmingly steep steps; an appropriately spectacular finale.

📷 *Mousehole.*

26 Porthcurno to Penzance

Distance 18.5km / 11.5 miles	**Height gain** 625m / 2,050ft **Difficulty** ● ● ● ● ●
Maps	OS Landranger 203 / OS Explorer 102
Start	Porthcurno TR19 6JS / betrayal.decay.grumbles / SW 386 223
Finish	Penzance Harbour car park TR18 2GB / boasted.commenced.remake / SW 475 303
Parking near start	Porthcurno car park TR19 6JX / printout.diggers.fairy / SW 384 225
Public transport	Land's End Coaster bus

The Penwith peninsula's southern fringe offers glorious granite coves and severely rugged trails in increasingly lush surrounds. Historic harbours break up the final, flat approach to Penzance.

Alongside Porthcurno car park is PK Porthcurno: Museum of Global Communications. From this former telegraph building, fourteen telegraph cables extended, beneath the beach, to the Empire.

Percella Point overlooks a stunning bay, floored by white sand gleaming through translucent water and backdropped by craggy Treryn Dinas. Porth Curno joins Pedn Vounder at low tide, fronted by a circular sandy island. Apparently, spotting a black spectre ship in the bay denotes misfortune.

Eastwards from Cribba Head, rough-going paths negotiate gorse-covered heathland atop castellated granite. Down in tiny Penberth Cove, stepping stones cross Penberth River. Fishermen land crab and lobster at the slipway using an electric winch, rather than the preserved nineteenth-century capstan. The next inlet, Porthguarnon, is uninhabited; a waterfall tumbles onto boulders as unyielding as the climb out.

The sheltered St Loy valley, shrouded with bluebell woods, boasts Britain's warmest winters, where spring arrives first! The route negotiates St Loy's Cove's rounded boulders, passing rusting ship remains. Comb for 'mermaid's purses' (skate and ray egg cases) and 'West Indian beans' (Caribbean tree seeds).

Gorse and granite return, atop Boscawen Cliff. Rusted wreck traces are visible outside Zawn Gamper at low tide, from the 1981 Penlee lifeboat disaster. Spy fiction author John Le Carré lived in the house above. Often-muddy woodland leads above Tater-du Lighthouse (Cornish: black loaf), perched on a black greenstone outcrop fifteen metres above the water, overlooking The Bucks rocks. This was the last Cornish lighthouse constructed, in 1965 after the *Juan Ferrer* was wrecked, with eleven lives lost.

The coastal slope is divided into overgrown 'quillets'; small market garden plots sheltered by stone walls or fuchsia hedges. Until the 1930s, they grew early crops of flowers and potatoes, which were sent to London. A gate at Dorminack announces that you are passing 'Derek and Jeannie Tangye Minack Chronicles Nature Reserve'. The Tangyes wrote and illustrated the nineteen-volume *Minack Chronicles*, about their life on a daffodil farm. Choughs nest hereabouts.

Treryn Dinas

By legend, giant Dan Dinas built this Iron Age cliff castle. The eighty-ton Logan Rock is perched on the central summit, a 'logan' or rocking stone. This was dislodged in 1824, for a wager, by Naval Officer Hugh Goldsmith. After tourist guides complained, he was forced to reinstate it at his expense.

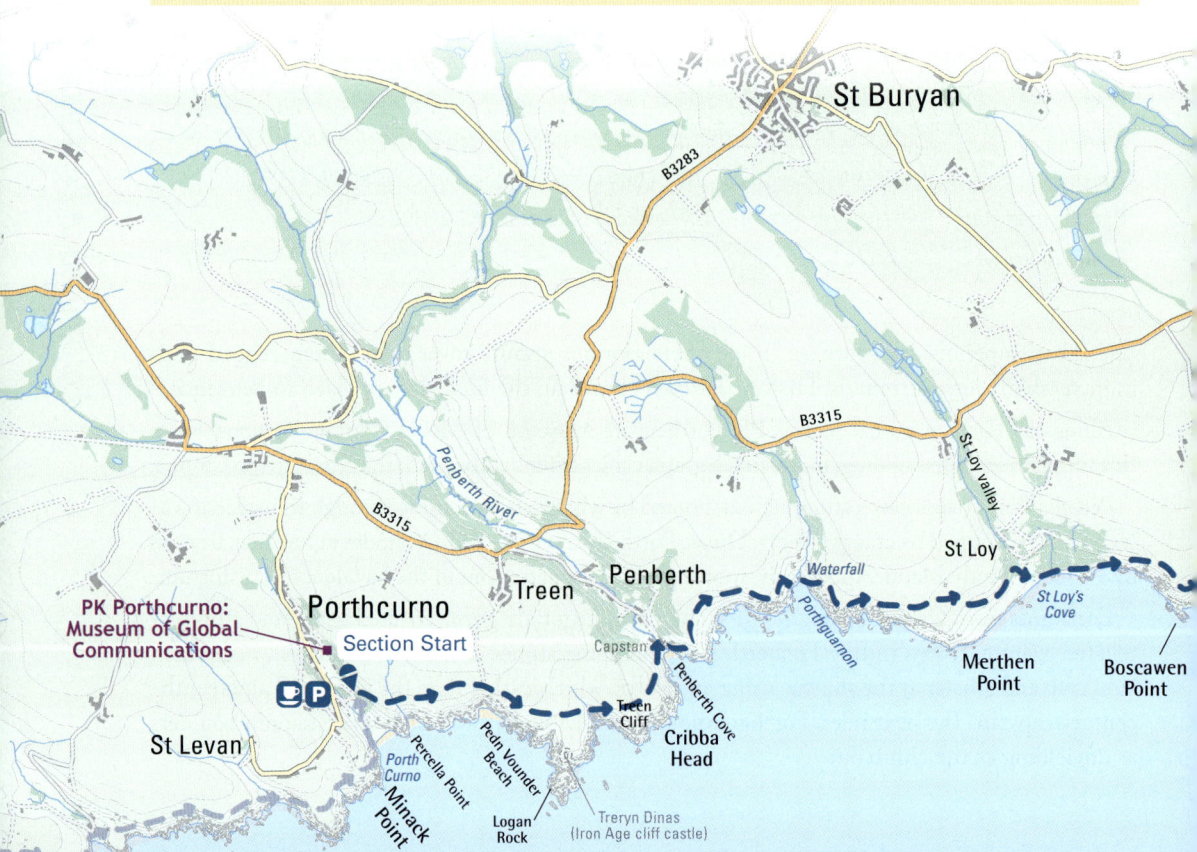

📷 *Penberth Cove.*

At Lamorna Point, a Celtic cross inscribed 'DWW 1873' marks where David Wordsworth Watson fell to his death in 1873. One of the SWCP's more rugged stretches follows, commencing with rock-clambering into Lamorna Cove. Quarrying has scarred the cove; before the quarries closed c1910, granite shipped from the quayside (now a café) constructed Wolf Rock and Longships Lighthouses.

Another rock-strewn path leads around Carn-du into Mount's Bay, where the climatic difference is obvious; the Monterey pines and cypresses of Kemyel Crease Nature Reserve, planted in the nineteenth century, envelop the path. Two kilometres of lee slope, dubbed the 'Garden of Eden' in the nineteenth century, are densely patchworked with neglected quillets. A rugged path ascends to a disused lookout hut above Penzer Point. Point Spaniard is where Spanish forces landed, in 1595; Mousehole and Newlyn were burned and Penzance bombarded.

The Wild Bird Hospital is passed on the road into Mousehole. Mousehole (pronounced 'mow-zul', referring to a cave south of the harbour), was called *'the prettiest village in England'* by Dylan Thomas. Dolly Pentreath, the last person who spoke solely in Cornish, died here in 1777; her last words were, *"Me ne vidn cewsel Sawznek!"* ("I don't want to speak English!"). Mousehole's horseshoe granite quays were Cornwall's earliest walled harbour, originating from the fourteenth century and rebuilt in the nineteenth. Outside, a cross marks the windswept St Clement's Isle.

The Solomon Browne

Mousehole's community made a dreadful sacrifice on 19th December, 1981. The *MV Union Star* had suffered engine failure, in hundred-mile-an-hour gusts. The Penlee lifeboat *Solomon Browne* launched. Coxswain Richards refused to allow one crew member to board, saying *"No more than one from any family"*. The *Solomon Browne* came alongside the *Union Star* through sixteen-metre breakers; four survivors were rescued but when the lifeboat returned for the remainder, radio contact ceased. All eight lifeboatmen of the *Solomon Browne* were lost, as well as all eight from the *Union Star*.

Newlyn Fisherman Memorial.

The remaining five kilometres follow sea front roads and tracks. Beside the disused lifeboat station at Penlee Point is a small garden commemorating the lost *Solomon Browne* lifeboatmen. The memorial plaque is headed *'Service not self'*.

Newlyn Harbour's South Pier is adorned with an 1855 cast iron lighthouse. Below is an Ordnance Datum tidal observatory; the baseline for Ordnance Survey maps. Within the harbour are over a hundred fishing boats; Newlyn is England and Wales's largest fishing port, with 14,000 tonnes landed annually. The daily landings and auction can be watched, at around 7am. At the harbour's centre, the fifteenth-century Old Quay was the *Mayflower*'s final departure point before conveying the Pilgrim Fathers to the New World; note the plaque on the adjacent house. Past the North Pier on Newlyn Green, a bronze fisherman casts his line; Tom Leaper's 2007 Newlyn Fisherman Memorial honours over twenty local men lost since 1980.

A waterfront walkway passes Bolitho Gardens and Wherry Town's supermarkets, onto Penzance Promenade. The Jubilee Pool (an outdoor lido) is followed by Penzance Harbour. The South Pier dates from 1766; the Isles of Scilly ferry departs here. The warehouse opposite was the Trinity House Depot, from 1866; Wolf Rock Lighthouse was prepared here. Ross Swing Bridge, sheltered by Albert Pier (Penzance's longer pier, constructed 1853), crosses to the Harbour car park.

📷 *St Michael's Mount.*

📷 *St Michael's Mount and Marazion.*

27 Penzance to Praa Sands

Distance	15.3km / 9.5 miles **Height gain** 475m / 1,550ft **Difficulty** ●●○○○
Maps	OS Landranger 203 / OS Explorer 102
Start	Penzance Harbour car park TR18 2GB / boasted.commenced.remake / SW 475 303
Finish	Praa Sands car park TR20 9FG / receive.workflow.seasonal / SW 576 281
Public transport	U4 bus

Flat promenade leads from Penzance to the iconic landmark of St Michael's Mount and more engaging clifftop trails.

The SWCP exits Penzance Harbour car park via the promenade path. This trail, shared with cyclists, follows the waterfront for three kilometres to Marazion. It's unexciting, all the while alongside the railway with Longrock car park being the only interruption. If the tide is out, distraction is offered by the sandy beach extending towards curlew-haunted reefs; the Cressars, Ryeman and Long Rock.

The railway peels away at Marazion Station car park and the SWCP delves into dunes. Inland across the road is Marazion Marsh, Cornwall's largest reedbed. Bitterns overwinter at this RSPB reserve and, if exceptionally lucky, you may hear this rare bird's booming call. A more predictable experience is the glorious murmurations of starlings which take place at winter sunsets.

Marazion is entered, ingloriously, via a series of waterfront car parks. This is countered by the unmistakeable looming profile of St Michael's Mount, a mainstay of postcards and tourist

brochures. A causeway leads offshore to the Mount, crossable for around four hours either side of low tide; an off-route deviation, to visit, is recommended!

A charter granted after the Norman Conquest established Marazion (Cornish *marghas byhgan*: small market) as Cornwall's first market town. Nowadays, Marazion is given over to galleries selling overpriced art of debatable quality. After Marazion's centre, the SWCP uninspiringly follows Fore Street for another kilometre. There are, at least, fine views of St Michael's Mount as the road ascends from the sea.

A track leads back down to the coast, passing among small-scale market garden plots which characterise the coastal slope hereabouts. The path around Trenow Cove is lined by pink tamarisk trees, overlooking low earthen cliffs frequented by sand martins. This unstable conglomerate causes two short diversions inland, before Basore Point and after Maen-du Point. In-between these diversions, quiet pebbly Trevelyan and Temis Coves overlook The Greeb, a ridge-like gabbro reef stretching offshore. The second diversion bypasses Perran Sands via a track from Perranuthnoe village car park.

Back above the sea at Trebarvah Cliff, the good news is that the remainder of this section boasts fine coast, and the path sticks to it! The cliffs grow in stature around Trevean Cove and then Stackhouse Cove, both overlooking wide rock-cut reefs. The latter cove is named for John Stackhouse, a botanist who built Acton Castle c1775 to indulge his study of marine algae.

The serrated promontory of Cudden Point effectively divides Mount's Bay into two. Although the SWCP cuts across, it's worth exploring this craggy highlight, which boasts grand views back towards Penzance. The adjacent headland, Little Cudden, is adorned with the remains of a 'rocket post' for coastguard training. The crag on Little Cudden is adorned with a few ruined walls, possibly an early Christian oratory. A plaque reads, *'WE HAVE A BVILDING OF GOD, AN HOVSE NOT MADE WITH HANDS, ETERNAL IN THE HEAVENS'*.

St Michael's Mount

With its church and castle spectacularly topping a ninety-metre conical rock, St Michael's Mount is Cornwall's most recognisable landmark. The Mount, supposedly built by the giant Cormoran, is possibly Ictus, a tin trading station mentioned by Greek historian Diodorus in the first century BC. There has been some form of religious site here since the fifth century, when local fishermen experienced a vision of St Michael. After Edward the Confessor granted the site to Brittany's Mont St Michel, it was a diminutive cousin of that abbey for 300 years. Various fortifications have sprung up over the past 500 years, latterly the St Aubyn family's decorative Victorian castle.

The island can be freely visited, although booked tickets are required for the gardens and castle, free to National Trust members. The latter is recommended, containing an eclectic mix of stately rooms and eccentric artefacts, from mummified cats to samurai armour.

Prussia Cove.

Quaintly-named Piskies Cove, a tiny beach backed by cave openings, sits below Little Cudden. In 1947, *HMS Warspite* ran aground on the slate reef east of the cove and spent three years stuck here and then another five being broken up beside St Michael's Mount. This was an ignominious end for a battleship which had seen action from the Battle of Jutland in the First World War to D-Day in the Second.

Piskies Cove is followed by the narrow inlet of Bessy's Cove, named for brandy-smuggler Elizabeth Burrow. The path above Bessy's Cove passes some wonderfully dilapidated fishermen's shacks and rusting winding gear, before passing behind Cliff Cottage. This sizeable house occupies the site of Burrow's 'kiddlewink' (unlicensed alehouse). A track leads from the cove, passing an impressive mansion overlooking tiny King's Cove; Porth-en-Alls House was built 1912-14, in the Arts and Crafts style.

The King of Prussia

Piskies Cove to Kenneggy Sands is collectively called Prussia Cove. The name comes from eighteenth-century local John Carter, dubbed 'King of Prussia'. He and his two brothers operated a highly successful smuggling operation, utilising the numerous caves and tunnels honeycombing the shore. Perversely, the Carters were also highly moralistic Methodists who abhorred swearing. When they mounted an audacious raid on Penzance's Custom House to retrieve a confiscated cargo, they pointedly only removed their own property.

Kenneggy Cliff overlooks Kenneggy Sand, a little-frequented strand bookended by extensive reefs. At Pestreath Cove, a footbridge is followed by a final climb onto Hoe Point. The stacks below are Lazy Bank Island, pierced by arches and tunnels. The SWCP descends around the point into Sydney Cove, the western end of Praa Sands's long and popular beach. The path drops onto the beach for a short while, before climbing to the waterfront car park.

📷 *Trewavas Head.*

28 Praa Sands to Poldhu Cove

Distance 15.6km / 9.7 miles	**Height gain** 375m / 1,250ft **Difficulty** ●●●●○
Maps	OS Landranger 203 / OS Explorer 102, 103
Start	Praa Sands car park TR20 9TG / receive.workflow.seasonal / SW 576 281
Finish	Poldhu Cove car park TR12 7JB / joyously.grazes.quoted / SW 666 199
Public transport	34 and U4 buses, change at Helston

This is Mount's Bay's quieter and less developed eastern half: rugged headlands adorned by mining heritage are followed, after Porthleven, by an easier stretch of lower cliffs and long shingle beaches.

Praa Green overlooks a platform of 2,000-year-old peat, exposed by coastal erosion. At a memorial to the crew of a Sunderland Flying Boat that 'ditched' onto the beach in 1943, the path veers inland and winds through dunes to a cluster of holiday homes. Pengersick Castle, a medieval tower converted to a fortified manor house c1530, is a 300m side-tour inland, visible from the road.

Hendra Beach is Praa Sands' eastern outlier, with a lonely pillbox stranded on the sand. Lesceave Cliff is climbed, to two successive headlands; Rinsey Head and Trewavas Head. Both rise sheer, with columns and buttresses of granite streaked by damp mosses. This geological change and a 'caution mineshaft' sign are clues that you've re-entered the Cornish Mining World Heritage Site (page 109). Rinsey Head's overhanging cliffs are home to one of Cornwall's largest kittiwake colonies. The route bypasses the large house on the headland, winding across heathery heathland via a car park.

Along the following kilometre, some of Cornwall's best-preserved mine engine houses and chimneys cling to the slope above the granite castellations of Rinsey East Cliff, Trewavas Head (look for the 'meerkat' formation, properly called Camel Rock or The Bishop), Trewavas Cliff and finally Trequean Cliff. The path goes into 'big dipper' mode as it traverses past these evocative ruins.

The World Heritage Site is departed where the cliffs lower and shift to less stable slate. A stone wall around Parc Trammel Cove steers the SWCP clear of the crumbling brink.

Just past the white house on Tregear Point is a white cross, erected in 1949, *'IN MEMORY OF THE MANY MARINERS DROWNED ON THIS PART OF THE COAST'*. The memorial references the 1808 Grylls Act (page 150). Below is a wavecut platform of potholed dark slate, with a lighter-coloured boulder revealed at low tide; the 50-tonne Giant's Rock is a glacial 'erratic' comprised of gneiss unknown in the UK.

A lane leads into Porthleven and around the perimeter of its inner and outer harbours. The cannons alongside the harbour came from *HMS Anson*. Napoleonic prisoners built the granite pier, begun in 1811. After major storms, newspapers regularly carry pictures of waves overtopping this and the twenty-one-metre clock tower alongside. Below the tower, a plaque commemorates Porthleven local Guy Gibson VC, who led the 1943 'Dambusters' raid.

Porthleven is departed via a succession of roads ascending Parc-an-als Cliff. A track contours to Bar Lodge, overlooking remarkable Loe Bar. This is a barrier beach of flint shingles, formed by rising sea levels. Estimates of Loe Bar's age range from 700 to several thousand years old. Behind, a ria (drowned river valley) was cut off forming The Loe, Cornwall's largest freshwater lake. An alternative explanation is that Loe Bar formed when the giant Tregeagle spilled sand!

After grinding across the shingle, a second white cross awaits on the grassy slopes; the *HMS Anson* memorial cross.

Wheal Prosper and Wheal Trewavas

Above Rinsey East Cliff, Wheal Prosper Mine's granite engine house and chimney have been restored by the National Trust. It failed to live up to its name; three shafts bored 130m deep to extract tin and copper only operated from 1860-66. Unusually, Trewavas Mine's two engine houses on Trewavas Cliff (Old Engine Shaft and New Engine Shaft) were located separately from their accompanying chimneys, due to the precarious terrain. They extracted over 17,000 tons of copper from 1834 until the sea breached the mine in 1846, thankfully without loss of life.

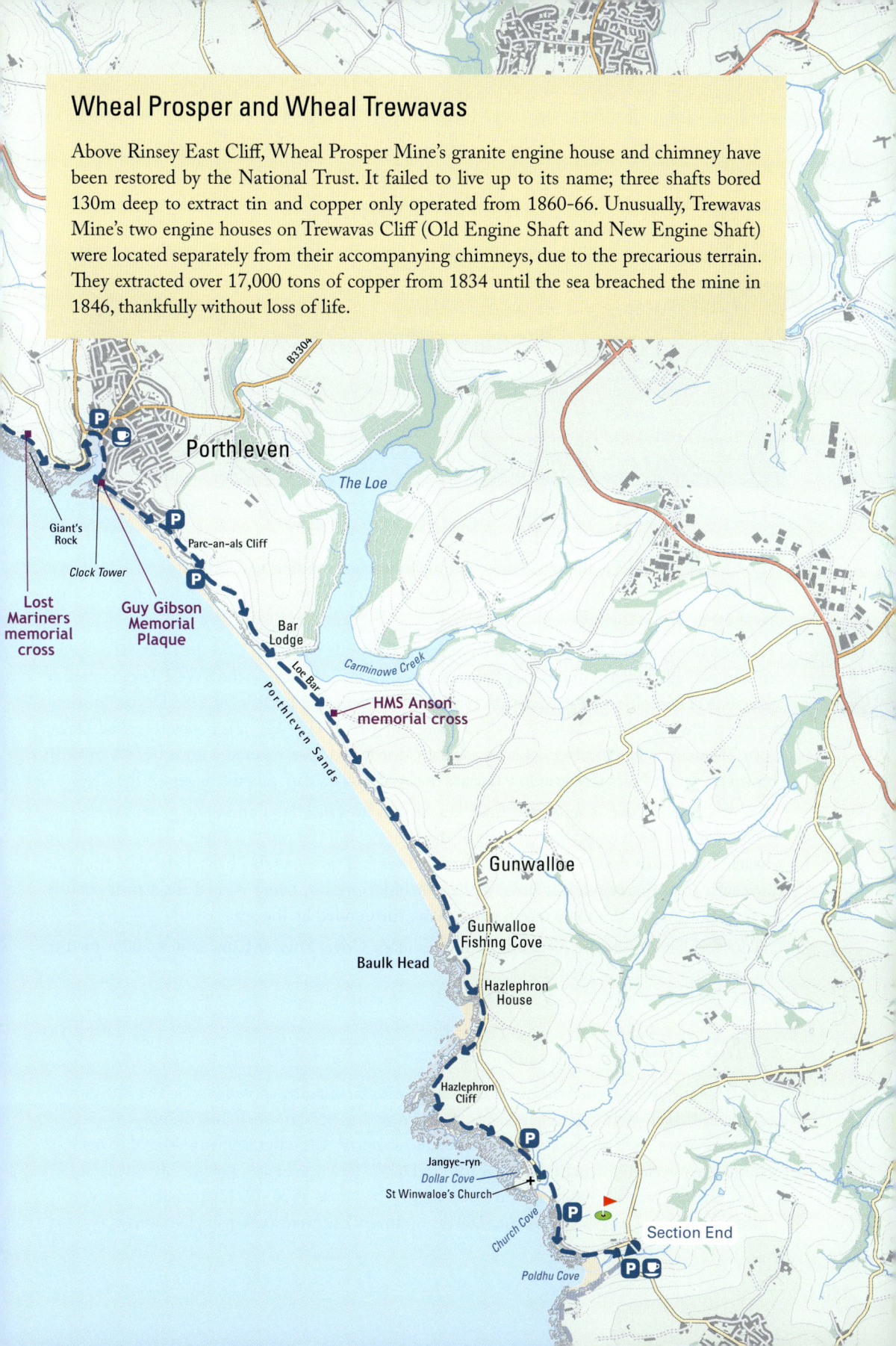

📷 *The Loe.*

Loe Bar is part of Porthleven Sands, a shingle beach extending to Gunwalloe Fishing Cove. The SWCP overlooks this long strand from low sandstone cliffs adorned with wild flowers, with one short diversion inland avoiding a cliff fall.

The few houses and rusty winding mechanisms at Gunwalloe Fishing Cove are followed by an ascent across Baulk Head. After passing battlemented Halzephron House, the SWCP leads alongside a lane onto Halzephron Cliff (Cornish: Hell's Cliff), distinctive for its contorted Devonian strata, veined with white quartz. Around this headland, reef-strewn Jangye-ryn is popularly called Dollar Cove. The name refers to silver coins occasionally discovered here, reputedly from a 1780s Spanish shipwreck; square holes visible at low tide are traces of a failed dam scheme to extract the silver.

Sandy Church Cove is separated from Jangye-ryn by a headland and dune system sheltering St Winwaloe's, the remarkable 'Church of the Storms' and the only Cornish church located on a beach. Its unusual design includes a separate tower and three parallel halls. Parts date from the thirteenth century, although it possibly has far older origins, being named for a fifth-century Breton saint. As the shoreline recedes, it is being surrounded by the sea.

A footbridge crosses the reedbeds behind Church Cove; Poldhu Cove is just 500m further, around a low eroding headland.

HMS Anson

HMS Anson was wrecked on Loe Bar in 1807, with far-ranging consequences. The 120-plus drowned sailors were buried in unconsecrated ground, as per custom. Public dismay led to the passing of the 1808 *Grylls Act*, legislating Christian burial. The trauma of witnessing the wreck led Henry Trengrouse to devote a decade (and £3,000) to developing a rocket life-saving apparatus. His 'breeches-buoy' system saved 10,000 lives from 1870-1911, remaining in service into the 1980s. Trengrouse was paid £50 for his invention, eventually dying in poverty.

📷 *Kynance Cove.*

29 Poldhu Cove to Lizard Point

Distance 14.2km / 8.8 miles	**Height gain** 500m / 1,650ft **Difficulty** ●●●●○
Maps	OS Landranger 203 / OS Explorer 103
Start	Poldhu Cove car park TR12 7JB / joyously.grazes.quoted / SW 666 199
Finish	Polpeor Cove TR12 7NU / scouts.nudge.shelter / SW 701 115
Parking near finish	Lizard Point car park TR12 7NT / bleat.start.fuzz / SW 702 116
Public transport	34 bus, from Lizard village

The Lizard, Britain's southernmost tip! The peninsula's western periphery is a plateau with few valleys, meaning that the going isn't too strenuous while you relish the wild flowers and amazing Technicolor cliffs of gabbro, gneiss, granite, schist, serpentine and slates.

Poldhu Cove (Cornish: black pool) is a lovely sandy beach, with just a café by way of development. Poldhu Care Home, and the similar Late Victorian hotels overlooking Polurrian and Mullion Coves, were built in anticipation of a railway link which never came. Tucked behind on Poldhu Point is the Marconi Centre, a wooden building used by Guglielmo Marconi for his pioneering wireless radio experiments. Four mast foundations survive. Marconi's successful 1901 transmission of the signal 'S', 3400km from Newfoundland, is commemorated by the Marconi Memorial, erected in 1937 on Angrouse Cliff; the sculpture represents the globe, but (in the author's humble opinion) resembles a cat.

Polurrian Cove sits astride a geological fault, from sedimentary sandstone to metamorphic hornblende schist, altered by heat within the earth's crust. Outside the Mullion Cove Hotel, a lone cannon marks the path into Mullion Cove.

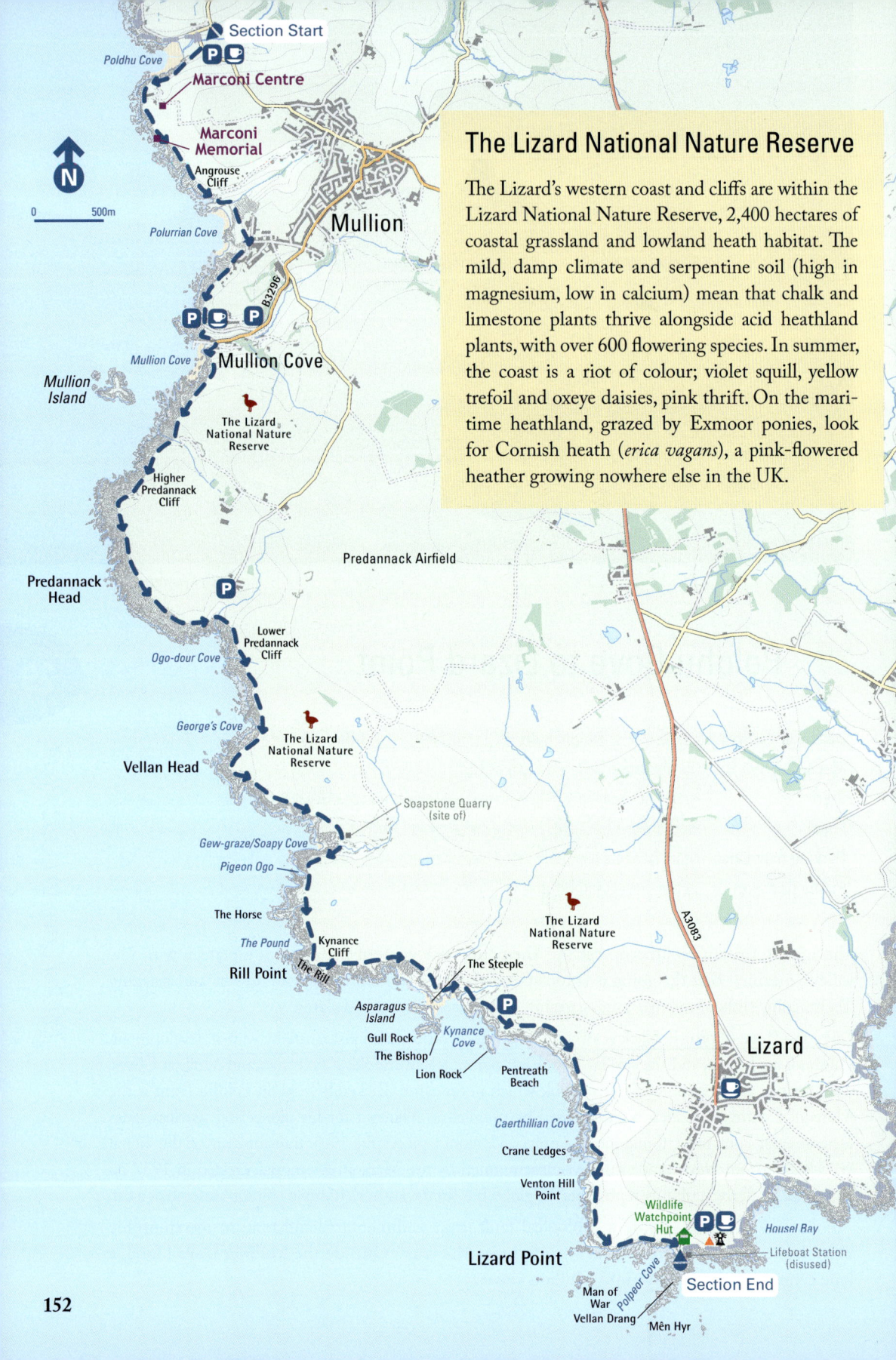

📷 *Mullion Cove.*

Mullion Cove, nestled beneath towering serpentine cliffs and stacks, might be the SWCP's most spectacular harbour. The harbour was built 1890-7 with a net store and fish cellar on the southern and western piers, respectively. The winch house above the slipway predates it. Shelter is offered by the sepulchral cliffs of Mullion Island, which teem with black-backed gulls, cormorants, guillemots, kittiwakes, razorbills and shags.

Above the harbour, you enter the Lizard National Nature Reserve.

The eight kilometres from Mullion Cove to Kynance Cove traverse an often-boggy heathland plateau, atop a magnificent seventy-metre escarpment, interrupted by three mild dips and three successive headlands. The first dip overlooks Mullion Island and leads onto the grainy-greenish schist of Higher Predannack Cliff and Predannack Head.

The second dip, at Lower Predannack Cliff above Ogo-dour Cove, marks the transition to dark red and green serpentine, followed by an airy amble around jutting Vellan Head. Predannack Airfield is close inland; expect disturbance from naval helicopter training.

The third dip is above Gew-graze, a tiny sandy beach also known as Soapy Cove. Soapstone (steatite), used in porcelain manufacture, was quarried in the ravine from 1748 to 1819. Soapstone is associated with serpentine; the site is jumbled with wonderfully colourful waste piles. The third headland is Rill Point, reached after passing above Pigeon Ogo, a sheer-sided chasm and The Horse, a spiny ridge vaguely resembling said mammal. On 29th July 1588, The Spanish Armada, an invasion fleet of 130 vessels, was first spotted from The Rill; beacons along the south coast conveyed the news to Queen Elizabeth I's Privy Council.

From Kynance Cliff, it's clear why Kynance Cove is a famous beauty spot; a cluster of dramatic stacks are linked to the shore at low tide by a tombolo (spit) of white sand. The Steeple, Asparagus Island, Gull Rock and The Bishop are composed of red-green serpentine and pinkish gneiss and adorned with wild flowers (and asparagus). The Victorians named the Ladies' Bathing Pool, Drawing Room and Parlour caves, as well as the Post Office and Devil's Bellows blowholes. All can be explored at low tide.

Lizard Point.

The SWCP escapes the tourists between the National Trust car park and Lion Rock stack, for a more undulating final three kilometres. In 1973, two local boys discovered Iron Age gold coins from Gaul below the cliff on Pentreath Beach, sparking a minor gold rush. The SWCP passes high above, before descending to cross two streams behind rocky Caerthillian Cove. Crane Ledges are the first of the treacherous reefs extending around Old Lizard Head; this coast has seen over 500 recorded shipwrecks. The base of Britain opens up; a cluster of buildings and the lighthouse mark Lizard Point, where you can go no further south!

Lizard Point's cliffs are draped with orange Hottentot fig, a South African interloper. More local is the chough, Cornwall's 'national' bird which successfully bred at the Lizard in 2001, after 50 years of absence. Choughs soar around the Point, a crow-like bird recognisable by its 'chough' cry and its curved orange bill and legs. Its Cornish name is *palores*: the digger.

Lizard geology

The Lizard's extraordinary geology is most obviously revealed in the red- or green-ish serpentine* rock, so-named because of its snakeskin-like appearance when polished. South of the Lizard Boundary Fault, between Polurrian Cove and Porthallow (section 31), is an ophiolite: a rare chunk of oceanic crust (denser than continental crust), originating around twenty kilometres beneath the surface and thrust upwards at a mid-ocean ridge, 380 million years ago. The ophiolite showcases a cross-section of the earth's crust; the serpentine represents the upper levels of the earth's mantle, the gabbro and schists around Mullion Cove and north of Coverack are the middle slice (the 'oceanic complex') and the Cambrian gneiss and schists at the peninsula's tip (the South West's oldest rocks) are the crust's 'basement'.

*Properly 'serpentinite', composed of the mineral serpentine.

📷 *Lizard Lighthouse.*

30 Lizard Point to Coverack

Distance 17.6km / 10.9 miles	**Height gain** 700m / 2,300ft **Difficulty** ●●●●
Maps	OS Landranger 203, 204 / OS Explorer 103
Start	Polpeor Cove TR12 7NU / scouts.nudge.shelter / SW 701 115
Finish	North Corner car park, Coverack TR12 6TF / worms.scooter.mentions / SW 782 185
Parking near start	Lizard Point car park TR12 7NT / bleat.start.fuzz / SW 702 116
Public transport	36 and 34 buses, change at Helston

The Lizard peninsula's quieter and more sheltered eastern side. Geologically complex cliffs of igneous schists, granite and gneiss hide a plethora of engaging natural and man-made distractions. A stunning but tough-going outing!

The smattering of shacks at Lizard Point ('Britain's Most Southerly Café!') are quite endearing; Land's End, take note. If you want to venture *further* south before setting off, a track leads past the National Trust's Wildlife Watchpoint hut to Polpeor Cove's old lifeboat station (operative 1859 to 1960) and rusting slipway.

Vellan Drang reef, extending a kilometre offshore, is composed of the SWCP's most ancient rocks; 'Man of War Gneiss' is granite metamorphosed 541 million years ago at the Cambrian Period's dawn. In 1907, the White Star Liner *SS Suevic* grounded on Mên Hyr, in fog. The RNLI saved all 456 on board (including 70 babies!), their largest ever rescue.

Lizard Point Youth Hostel is followed by Lizard Lighthouse's foghorns. Cornwall's first mainland lighthouse was erected in 1619, by Sir Thomas Killigrew; he hired dragoons after Luddite locals attempted to stop construction. The present twin octagonal towers were built in 1751 and encompass the Lizard Lighthouse Heritage Centre, however this has been closed since 2022 with no indication of when it will reopen.

Housel Bay's entrance is marked by Bumble Rock, a pointed stack. The Lion's Den is close to the path, a cave which collapsed in 1842. Look for the signal cable cut into the blue-ish schist cliffs in 1872, linking to Bilbao in Spain. The black huts alongside the footpath are the restored Lizard Wireless Station. Here in 1901, Marconi made the first 'over-horizon' radio transmission, 300km to The Needles on the Isle of Wight.

Bass Point's cubic white Lloyds Signal Station was once among the world's busiest communication hubs. A thousand ships monthly had their arrival relayed to their London owners. In 1913, the *Queen Margaret* was wrecked while awaiting an answer! Bass Point lookout station opened in 1994, the

National Coastwatch Institution's first. Turning north(!), memorials are passed to the five crew of Breton trawler *Bugaled-Breizh*; this sank mysteriously in 2004, with allegations of submarine entanglement.

The path narrows and becomes more rugged, through overgrown gorse and blackthorn hedges, with colour provided by tall pink *digitalis* (foxgloves). The Lizard Lifeboat Station clings below forty-five-metre cliffs in Kilcobben Cove, accessed by a lift ramp. Shortly after, Church Cove is a handful of buildings and a slipway with a converted capstan roundhouse. Parn Voose Cove is overlooked by an abandoned quarry, followed by a sharp ascent above The Chair natural arch. A greened-over quarry pond is passed before the Devil's Frying Pan; here, the path edges gingerly around a chasm where a vast cave collapsed, with an arch leading seaward.

Picturesque Cadgwith's thatched cottages are tucked inside an inlet with twin tiny beaches; Little Cove is separated by The Todden, a rocky promontory, from Cadgwith Cove, crammed with boathouses and fish cellars. With no harbour, the fishermen drag their boats ashore. Cadgwith Cove Inn hosts Cornish sea shanty singing on Friday nights.

Climbing from Cadgwith, the tall-chimneyed black shack is the 'Huer's Hut', a former coastguard lookout from 1869 which possibly originated for 'huers', who spotted mackerel shoals.

After passing above an old quarry at Kildown Point and over Enys Head, the SWCP descends, through woods, to another heritage treat. A footbridge crosses Poltesco Stream behind Carleon Cove's pebble beach, where the Lizard Serpentine Company processed serpentine from 1855-93, powered by an eight-metre waterwheel; preserved are the fish cellars, warehouses and rounded capstan house. Beachcombing can reveal polished examples of their work.

The cliffs fall back at Kennack Sands, fronted by the Caerverracks, a serpentine reef. Kennack Sands West is reached down a lane, then a climb over Kennack Towans (dunes) leads past a pillbox guarding Kennack Sands East's Second World War anti-tank wall. Footbridges cross reed-strewn streams behind both beaches; part of the Lizard National Nature Reserve.

📷 *Chynhalls Point.*

The climb onto Eastern Cliff commences this section's most rugged and least-frequented part, with views down into precipitous inlets. Serpentine outcrops adorn the path, coloured by the white-pink petals and reddish leaves of English stonecrop.

A slender gabbro promontory extends between Spernic and Lankidden Coves towards offshore Carrick Lûz (Cornish: grey rock). Cross the bank and ditch of this dramatically-sited (aren't they all?) Iron Age cliff castle, for careful exploration.

The Downas Valley is a strenuous interlude; an overgrown stream trickles to remote Downas Cove, sandy at low tide. An easier descent follows, crossing a footbridge above Beagles Hole, a sheer-sided inlet rearing above Meludjack rock.

Craggy Treleaver Cliff extends around Dinas Cove towards Black Head, the path leading through heathland where, due to National Trust gorse clearance, violets and orchids flourish. Black Head is adorned by a restored coastguard lookout, with displays about the flora, fauna and ships seen from this significant headland.

The cliffs now become less steep, and lose elevation. A final challenge awaits; a hand-scrawled sign recommends taking the *'much safer and easier'* path ahead to Coverack; this reaches the village via the engaging Terence Coventry Sculpture Park. However, the official SWCP route veers downhill, traversing Chynhalls Cliff. The going is indeed fairly arduous, with clambering over angular boulders followed by duckboards to Porthbeer Cove and Chynhalls Point. Across the Point (another cliff castle), a track leads past whitewashed cottages and around Dolor Point.

Coverack is a delightfully undeveloped fishing village. The serpentine harbour wall and preserved capstan are overlooked by a former lifeboat station. The Paris Hotel displays memorabilia of the 10,449-ton liner *SS Paris* which grounded on Lowland Point in 1899; locals rescued all 800 passengers and crew.

Whitewashed St Peter's Church opened in 1885, with a serpentine pulpit donated from the Poltesco factory. The B3294 takes you to Coverack's car parks.

📷 *Helford.*

31 Coverack to Helford Passage

Distance	19.6km / 12.2 miles
Height gain	675m / 2,200ft
Difficulty	● ● ● ● ●
Maps	OS Landranger 204 / OS Explorer 103
Start	North Corner car park, Coverack TR12 6TF / worms.scooter.mentions / SW 782 185
Finish	Helford Passage TR11 5LB / hires.rave.deluded / SW 763 269 or Helford Point TR12 6JX / legend.shows.youths / SW 759 264
Parking near finish	Helford Passage car park TR11 5LE / divisible.vertical.twigs / SW 763 270 or Helford Village car park TR12 6JU / budget.lawn.clincher / SW 759 260
Public transport	Numerous multi-bus options from Helford Passage or Helford Village, not Sundays

This long outing includes fine coastal stretches, two rural inland diversions and a final act exploring the Helford River's idyllic sheltered creeks. If finishing at Helford Passage, you'll need to complete the distance before the ferry closes.

Coverack's car park sits astride the 'moho', the Mohorovičić Discontinuity. The harbour end of the bay is serpentine: the earth's mantle. Northwards is gabbro, the earth's crust. This conjunction, revealing the planet's innards, only appears at the surface at a handful of locations worldwide; it's usually buried around seven kilometres underground.

Lowland Point is an expansive and unkempt raised beach, reached via a wonderful bouldery path ambling through gnarled woods, gorse and, via stepping stones, marsh and bog. Bronze Age

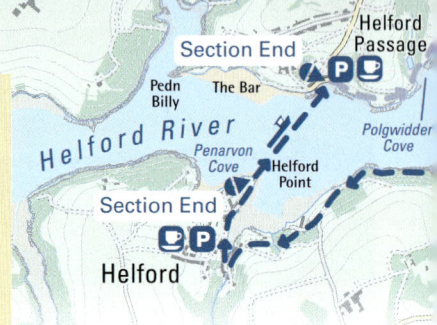

Helford Point to Helford Passage ferry

To summon the ferry, open up the yellow signal board. It operates daily between 9.30 am – 5 pm, from 1st April to 31st October, running an hour later from 7th July to 7th September. Cards or cash are accepted*, the cost was £7 in 2024. Call ahead to check details on 01326 250770.

Carrying cash to cover contingencies is recommended!

hut circles and medieval field strips are sometimes discernible. In 1933, 600 Mesolithic flints were discovered at the embayment past Pedn-myin.

Dean Quarries sprawl across Dean Point, the entrance marked by a sign and flagpole. The quarries extracted gabbro for road-building but are currently mothballed, their future use uncertain. While nature is attempting to reclaim the site, notably in the overgrown quarry pool, the quarried cliffs, waste tips and security fencing will dismay most. A beach and jetty are followed by huge concrete edifices used to grade the gabbro.

Godrevy Cove comes as a glorious relief, a little-frequented beach; although, the 'sand' is quarry spoil! The next headland is Manacle Point, scarred by West of England Quarry. St Keverne's spire is visible from the infamous Manacles rocks (Cornish *maen eglos*: church stones); buried in the churchyard are 48 of 106 who drowned when the liner *SS Mohegan* struck the rocks in 1898.

The SWCP bypasses Manacle Point, heading inland across the reed-choked lagoon behind Godrevy Cove and up-valley to the hamlet of Rosenithon. Before descending through fields to Porthoustock, make a hundred-metre side-tour to the Giant's Quoits, a granite tor moved from Manacles Point in 1967 to avoid destruction by quarrying.

Porthoustock fishing village acquired a jetty and huge loading silo, from which barges would carry gabbro to Falmouth. Enjoy this brief sea view, because a second inland stretch passes behind St Keverne Quarries to Porthallow Cove.

Porthallow is significant for two reasons; the geology becomes Devonian (100 million years younger), meaning that you're departing the Lizard Peninsula. It's also the SWCP's halfway point, monumentalised by a 2009 'Midway Marker' stone inscribed with the poem *Fading Voices* by Stephen Hall. The stone proclaims that Minehead and South Haven Point are both 315 miles / 517km away. Do the maths: one of those numbers isn't correct.

The next landmark is Nare Point, where a Coastwatch lookout station overlooks the Helford River and the nearby 'starfish bunker' is part of a Second World War decoy system, linked to that on its namesake Nare Head (section 34). However, in 2022 a bridge collapsed in Parbean Cove, blocking the SWCP; although you can still access Nare Point, the route is currently (2024) diverted inland beforehand, across to Gillan.

Stepping stones shortcut across Gillan Creek, three hours either side of low tide. Otherwise, the dogleg around this beautiful backwater involves farm- and woodland paths on its south side, and a lane hugging the north shore, lined by trees trailing or tumbled into the water. The creek mouth is Gillan Harbour, where a sprinkle of cottages comprises St Anthony-in-Meneage. The church tower is fifteenth century, but tradition dictates that the church was established c1150, by shipwrecked Normans giving thanks for their survival.

📷 *Lowland Point.*

Dennis Head divides Gillan Creek from the Helford River, with glorious views. The short optional loop explores a bracken-smothered Iron Age cliff castle (Celtic *dinas*: fort), also used by Royalists in the English Civil War.

The SWCP descends from Dennis Head alongside fields, into woods lining the shoreline. The next two kilometres are a delight, weaving through dense woodland with unchecked ferns encroaching; in damp or dewy conditions, this is the nearest thing to a Cornish rainforest outside the Eden Project. The path surfaces from the wildwood at three successive miniscule and secluded coves; Ponsence, Bosahan and Padgagarrack.

Civilisation is rediscovered; a track leads behind Helford River Sailing Club's jetties to Helford Village car park. Helford is the dictionary definition of picturesque, lining both sides of a narrow creek. The SWCP crosses the ford and bridge at the creek head and leads out to Helford Point, where the passenger ferry departs. This is claimed to be Britain's oldest ferry service, operative since at least 1023.

When the ferry is not running, the options to reach Helford Passage are; a tortuous bus journey, or an attractive twenty-one-kilometre trek (mostly lanes) via Gweek.

The Helford River

The Helford River is a ria (drowned valley) with seven secretive side-creeks. The river is so sheltered that trees grow to the water's edge, these idyllic woodlands only interrupted by the tiniest settlements. The Meneage (Cornish: 'monkish land') to the south is mainly agricultural land, whilst the north shore's granite quays give clues to an industrial past. The Helford Voluntary Marine Conservation Area was established in 1987, to protect beds of eelgrass (a seahorse habitat) and oysters.

Helford River.

32 Helford Passage to Falmouth

Distance 16.1km / 10 miles	**Height gain** 425m / 1,400ft	**Difficulty** •••••
Maps	OS Landranger 204 / OS Explorer 103, 105
Start	Helford Passage TR11 5LB / hires.rave.deluded / SW 763 269
Finish	Falmouth to St Mawes Ferry, Prince of Wales Pier, Falmouth TR11 3DF / tens.outer.garage / SW 807 329
Parking near start	Helford Passage car park TR11 5LE / divisible.vertical.twigs / SW 763 270
Parking near finish	Town Quarry car park, Falmouth TR11 2BX / epic.pasta.tricky / SW 805 329
Public transport	35 bus

The Helford River's glorious secretive beaches and sheltered havens give way to more demanding trails around Falmouth Bay, followed by a not-unpleasant perambulation of Falmouth.

A clutch of houses and the Ferry Boat Inn line the water's edge at Passage Cove. If you have just negotiated the Helford River's southern shores (section 31) then you know what to expect; the north shore is similarly idyllic, with woodlands and grassy meadows sloping to glassy waters. It is however more developed, intrusively so at Polgwidden Cove where obnoxious high walls and spiked gates obscure the beach; Trebah Garden control beach access.

The valley 500m east also boasts a sub-tropical garden, taking advantage of the mild climate; the National Trust's Glendurgan Garden can be entered from the SWCP. It was created c1826 by Quaker Albert Fox, with a wonderful cherry laurel maze. Durgan is a smattering of former fisherman's cottages and fish cellars, rented out by the NT. After a lane from Durgan, a path leads through Monterey pines fronting Bosloe House, a large Arts and Crafts-style manor house built in 1903 (also a NT property).

Relish the Helford River's last kilometres. Porth Saxon (also called Porth Sawsen) and Porthallack are successive small beaches, marked only by boathouses, and a pillbox at the former. A fifty-metre ascent through gorse and bracken reaches Toll Point (Cornish *tol*: 'hole', likely a fishing reference), with views upriver and ahead to the open sea. Steep slopes enveloped in gnarled woodland are negotiated, beneath St Mawnan Church, named for a sixth-century Breton saint.

Rosemullion Head is recognisable by its low curved profile and topping of thick gorse. Cropmarks have revealed a double bank and ditch across the headland; this was probably an Iron Age cliff castle utilising the commanding views of successive headlands on either side.

North into Falmouth Bay, low cliffs overlook submerged reefs and rocky beaches. Two wooded valleys reach Bream Cove; the latter contains the gardens of Hotel Meudon, home in the

Falmouth to St Mawes ferry

The ferry runs year-round between 8.30 am (9.15 am on Sundays) and 9.15 pm (3.15 pm in winter). Cards or cash are accepted at the ticket office, the cost was £9.50 in 2024. Check details by calling 01326 741194. The ferry departs from Prince of Wales Pier year-round, and also from Custom House Quay (600m back along the SWCP) in summer. The crossing takes about twenty minutes.

nineteenth century to the Fox family, who also owned Trebah and Glendurgan. A squeeze past private gardens reaches Maenporth, a popular beach.

A final quiet stretch, before Falmouth. The *Ben Asdale*'s remains are scattered across a wave-cut platform approaching Newporth Head. This fishing trawler grounded in a 1978 blizzard with three lives lost, despite dramatic rescue efforts. Wooded Pennance Point has a monument to the Second World War Home Guard who, *'watched a thousand dawns appear across these great waters which form our country's moat'*. The bench in front gives a good view of Pendennis Castle.

Swanpool Beach, with its multi-coloured beach huts, marks your arrival at Falmouth's suburban southern fringe. The Swan Pool is a saline lagoon where the Killigrew Family reputedly bred swans, now Swanpool Local Nature Reserve. It was three times its current size until 1862, when a drainage channel was cut through the Ice Age shingle bar.

Fields around Swanpool Point lead to lively Gyllyngvase Beach, with the exotic plants of Queen Mary Gardens behind. Cliff Road, overlooking shallow reefs, leads to Castle Drive, where the houses are left behind. Pendennis Point is the high promontory overlooking Carrick Roads's entrance (page 168). Pendennis Castle sprawls across the summit plateau, glimpsed above the trees. The headland car park overlooks 'Little Dennis' blockhouse, built in 1539 as an extension

Pendennis Castle.

of the castle's defences, and is in turn overlooked by Falmouth Coastguard Operations Centre, coordinating safety and rescue for most of Devon and Cornwall.

A woodland path along Pendennis Point's eastern flank stumbles upon Crab Quay battery, overgrown Second World War gun emplacements. It emerges on Pendennis Rise above Falmouth Docks, built 1860-67, where a viewpoint and signage allow you to absorb the scale of Carrick Roads.

Bar Road leads beneath the railway into Falmouth's centre. Arwenack House on the left is Falmouth's oldest building, dating from 1385 but rebuilt 1567-1571 by Sir John Killigrew, first Governor of Pendennis Castle and effectively Falmouth's founder. Across Bar Road is the Killigrew Monument, a tall pyramidal structure built 1738, for reasons obscure. Behind on the quayside is the National Maritime Museum Cornwall, unmistakeable with its lighthouse-style lookout.

This section's remainder ambles through Falmouth's commercial precinct, behind the Inner Harbour. Ferries link the SWCP with St Mawes from two of the piers; the 'Falmouth Packets' departed from Custom House Quay, a waterborne mail service linking Britain to its Empire, from 1688-1850. Prince of Wales Pier originated in the seventeenth century, but its current form dates from 1905.

Pendennis and St Mawes Castles

Two well-preserved four-storey 'device forts' face one another across Carrick Roads (page 168), commissioned in 1539 by Henry VIII, after his break with Rome. Pendennis Castle's circular tower and pentagonal bastions (added by 1600) were built over the Iron Age *Pen-Dinas*, 'headland fort'. St Mawes Castle is smaller, designed in concentric 'clover leaves' style. Both castles were besieged and captured by Parliament during the English Civil War, and both continued in use through to the Second World War. English Heritage manages the castles which, although not directly beside the SWCP, are well worth side-tours to explore.

📷 *St Anthony Head.*

33 St Mawes to Pendower Beach

Distance 15km / 9.3 miles	**Height gain** 425m / 1,400ft **Difficulty** ● ● ● ● ○
Maps	OS Landranger 204 / OS Explorer 105
Start	St Mawes to Place ferry, The Quay, St Mawes TR2 5DG / jets.takeovers.hurls / SW 847 330
Finish	Pendower Beach TR2 5PE / flexed.loom.brightens / SW 897 382
Parking near start	St Mawes car park TR2 5DJ / sensitive.plants.ditched / SW 847 332
Parking near finish	Pendower car park TR2 5PE / sprinkle.daunted.trouble / SW 898 383
Public transport	50 bus

This is the first of two successive sections around the Roseland Peninsula, which forms the River Fal and Carrick Roads' eastern rim. Hidden within this relatively isolated area is some of Cornwall's most beautiful, and least-frequented, coast.

The day begins with at least one ferry journey. The Falmouth to St Mawes crossing is described in section 32 and the section outlined here begins by taking the St Mawes to Place ferry.

When no ferry is running, park two kilometres from Place at the National Trust's Porth car park; public transport is four kilometres away at Gerrans. Alternatively, trek fourteen kilometres around the Percuil River from St Mawes, following Carrick Roads past St Just in Roseland, before crossing the peninsula to Gerrans.

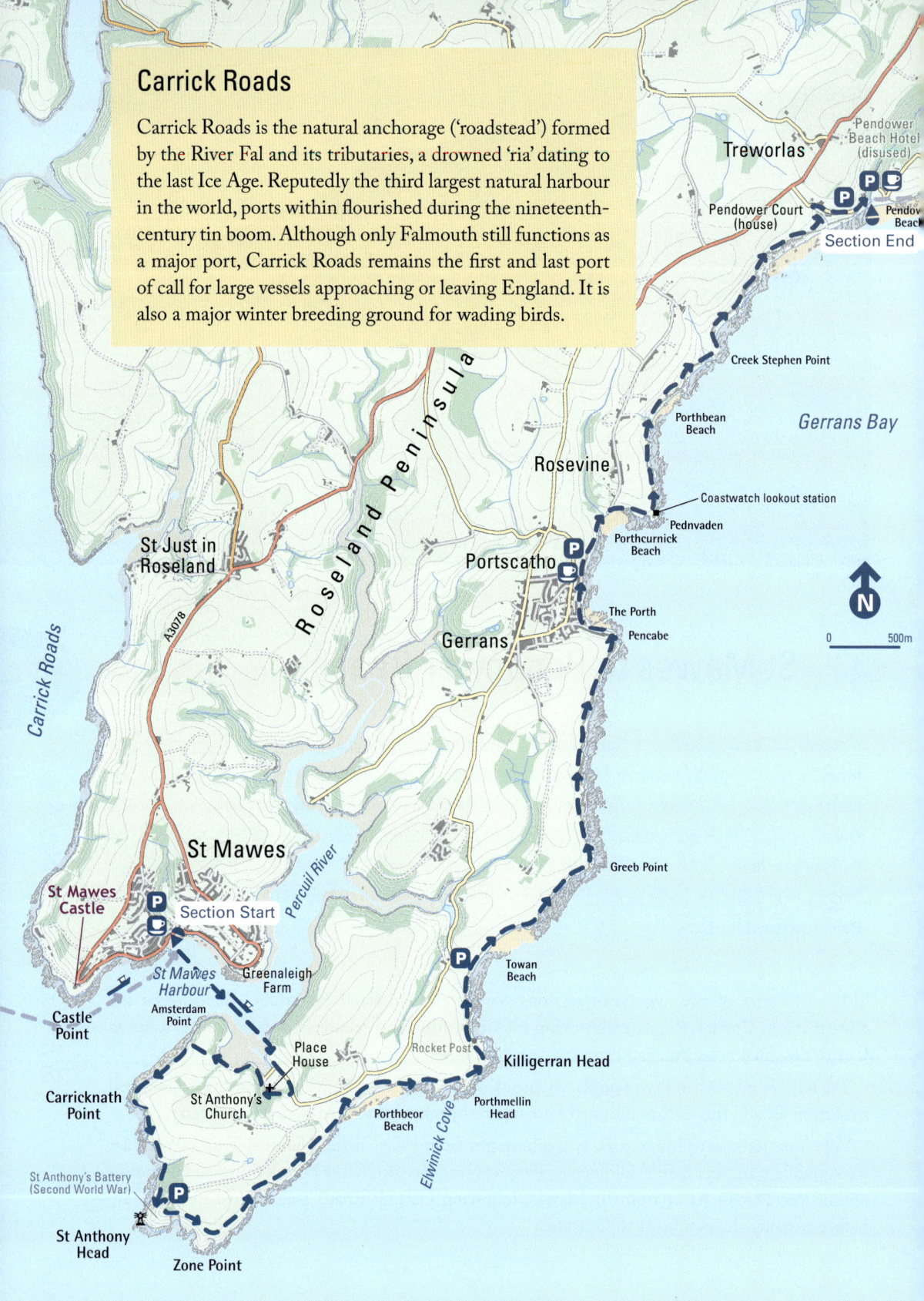

The ferry at Place.

St Mawes to Place ferry

The ferry runs April to October, half-hourly, between 9.00 am (9.30 am on Sundays) and 4.30 pm. Card payments only are accepted at the ticket office on the pier in St Mawes, the cost was £6 in 2024. Check details by calling 01326 270553.

The small ferry departs from a stone pier and takes ten minutes to cross St Mawes Harbour and the Percuil River, with views upriver. For nine months of the Second World War from 1943 to 1944, this secretive backwater was a hive of activity; Allied landing craft crews trained here until departing for the D-Day landings in Normandy. Approaching Place's floating jetty, the ferry passes the lawns of Place House, a yellow-painted mansion, built 1840; one of the two spires is actually St Anthony's Church, hidden behind.

The route ascends past Place House's gates, then contorts around the back of the house, passing the church (Pevsner: *"the best example in the county of what a parish church was like in the twelfth and thirteenth centuries"*) through a splendidly overgrown graveyard.

The tree-shaded shoreline is followed, before climbing over Amsterdam Point, revealing tremendous vistas across Carrick Roads to Falmouth. St Mawes Castle is constantly in view, guarding Castle Point at the entrance to St Mawes Harbour, as the path leads south along fields, climbing over wooded Carricknath Point.

Passing lovely meadows overlooking secret sandy coves, St Anthony Head Lighthouse becomes visible ahead. Built in 1835 by Trinity House just a few metres above the waves, it might seem familiar to those of a certain age, having featured in children's TV show *Fraggle Rock*!

Before reaching the lighthouse, a zigzagging ascent climbs from a footbridge to a road accessing St Anthony's Battery. The path winds among this overgrown complex of fortifications and gun

Porthbeor Beach.

emplacements originating from 1895 but used through both World Wars. Emerging onto Zone Point, the Roseland Peninsula's southern tip, the wave-battered cliffs (a rallying point for cormorants and seals) make it immediately obvious that you have escaped sheltered Carrick Roads.

Enjoy the path between Zone Point and Portscatho, it picks a mild but invigorating course alongside crop fields, overlooking green cliffs pitching downwards to slabs of sea-polished sandstone. Climbing above Porthbeor Beach, you are just 500m from Place House, across the peninsula. This long pristine strand belongs to the gulls, as the access path is unstable and closed.

The cliffs drastically reduce in height from Porthmellin Head, and the path comes close to the reefs which buffer the waves through this section's remainder. The wooden stump on Killigerran Head was a 'rocket post' used for coastguard rescue training. This overlooks sandy Towan Beach, which the SWCP passes close behind, en route to Greeb Point.

The village of Portscatho is entered via its delightfully time-warped sandy harbour. The garden above the quay contains a red-painted Second World War mine (a collection box for the Shipwreck Mariner's Society) and a memorial to the 26,380 missing casualties of the Burma War (1942-45), erected in 1998 by local retired veteran James Allan.

Porthcurnick Beach faces Portscatho from the bay's north end. This is guarded by the Coastwatch lookout at Pednvadan, their smallest station; when they turn the map, someone has to leave the building!

The going becomes a bit more rugged entering Gerrans Bay, the path clambering above reefs and scattered beaches. Porthbean Beach is overlooked by a hotel, otherwise these lovely shores are largely untouched. Across a footbridge onto Creek Stephen Point, you get a view of this section's final exertion; a traverse to Pendower Court House, above the beach stretching behind Gerrans Bay. A lane leads from this white building to the pink Pendower Beach Hotel, disused but being 'regenerated'. The car park is behind the beach.

📷 Nare Head.

34 Pendower Beach to Gorran Haven

Distance 21.2km / 13.2 miles	**Height gain** 575m / 1,900ft **Difficulty** ●●●●
Maps	OS Landranger 204 / OS Explorer 105
Start	Pendower Beach TR2 5PE / flexed.loom.brightens / SW 897 382
Finish	Gorran Haven PL26 6JH / rave.toolkit.ticking / SX 012 415
Parking near start	Pendower car park TR2 5PE / sprinkle.daunted.trouble / SW 898 383
Parking near finish	Gorran Haven car park PL26 6JT / shortcuts.holds.camera / SX 010 415
Public transport	23 and 51 buses, change at St Austell. Not Sundays

What a wonderful, quiet, wild coast this is! This second, far more challenging, section along the Roseland Peninsula offers imposing cliffs, formidable headlands, isolated coves and a smattering of fishing settlements.

The SWCP crosses the back of Pendower Beach, part of a long strand arcing around the back of Gerrans Bay, linked at low tide to Carne Beach. An uphill lane reaches a path onto low cliffs, reaching Carne Beach via the Nare Hotel and another lane. Before turning onto the cliff path once more, note the converted pillbox.

Gerrans Bay is guarded by Nare Head's spikily outcropped cliffs, composed from 390-million-year-old lava (the 'Roseland Breccia') and made colourful by over a hundred species of lichen. Attaining this headland starts mildly, with a traverse above the reefs at Carne Beach's eastern

end. The reef's peculiar tor-like outcrops of quartzite were apparently lobbed from Cornwall's north coast by Tregeagle, who pops up variously in Cornish folklore as a giant, or a wicked ghost escaped from Hell. He gives his name to Tregagle's Hole, a cave at rugged Paradoe Cove (also called Mallet's Cove), which the path next plunges into. The strenuous climb from the cove passes a ruined fisherman's cottage, before attaining Nare Head's eighty-metre summit (Cornish *ardh*: high place). Enjoy the well-earned views, and perhaps venture a hundred metres off-piste along the footpath to the hair-raisingly exposed brink.

Nare Head's eastern cliffs overlook Veryan Bay and Gull Rock, rearing thirty-eight metres, just 500m offshore. This guano-smeared islet is always encircled by birds, with a breeding population of cormorants, shags, razorbills, kittiwakes and the occasional puffin. The German ship *Hera* was wrecked here in 1914; fifteen of the nineteen lost were retrieved and buried (in the countries' longest grave!) at Veryan Church.

Nare Head has a hidden surprise; a bunker complex, near Rosen Cliff. The Second World War 'starfish bunker' was part of a decoy network including Nare Point (section 31), intended to lure German bombers from Falmouth. There is also a Cold War bunker, built in 1962 to observe nuclear attack.

Kiberick Cove's steep bounds are perambulated, high above the rocky shore. The Blouth headland briefly interjects, before the path descends into Parc Caragloose Cove to The Straythe's rugged reefs and boulders. The path from the bay, claustrophobically enclosed by trees and bushes, wends an eccentric and exhausting route via switchbacks, boardwalks, footbridges and rugged steps: memorable! You eventually emerge below Broom Parc, a National Trust villa.

Past Manare Point, Portloe's whitewashed buildings are spied, half-hidden within a deep inlet. This tiny fishing village has no harbour; crab and lobster boats are simply dragged onto the miniscule beach. In Portloe's 1900 heyday, a fleet of fifty seine boats were squeezed ashore. The SWCP passes between the former lifeboat house and chapel (now private homes) before a steep walkway back atop the cliffs.

The path clambers along rocky slopes shrouded in yellow gorse, with overlapping headlands ahead and behind, above pyramidal stacks glistening with sea spray. Simply magnificent! It's all tough-going, including climbs from footbridges crossing valleys near Caragloose Point and Cellar Rock. The latter climb gains a grassy ridge, which narrows into steep steps to the limekiln and fishing cellars at West Portholland. West and East Portholland are a smattering of buildings connected by a short road, gloriously undeveloped (other than a modern sea wall) since a nineteenth century attempt to develop a fishing port.

Portholland is part of the Caerhays Estate, centred on Caerhays Castle. This is reached via trails through cow fields, passing below a Coastguard hut restored as a romantic wedding venue!

173

East Portholland.

A road descends steeply through a wooded cleft into Porthluney Cove where Caerhays Castle is revealed, sitting grandly at the head of a landscaped valley behind the beach. Architect John Nash's 'castle' is actually a mansion with medieval pretensions, built 1807-10 (he later designed Buckingham Palace). The house and gardens are open to the public, February to June. After passing the castellated front wall and gatehouse, the route heads up a grassy slope and through estate woodlands overlooking both cove and castle.

The next landmark is the serrated ridge of pyroclastic rhyolite which, seemingly, bars progress after the footbridge behind Lambsowden Cove. The path climbs high to bypass this barrier, before reaching Hemmick Beach; the especially prominent stack passed en route is Black Rock.

This section's final major obstacle is Dodman Point, among the south coast's most prominent and recognisable headlands; fishermen dub it 'The Deadman', due to its coffin-like profile. Excruciatingly steep steps from the road behind Hemmick Beach access the west side's spectacular stacks and cliffs. A dip between Gell Point and High Point, and final steps among scraggy windblown trees, attain the top. Two enormous earthen ramparts (the 'Bulwark') slice 500m across the headland's twenty-hectare summit plateau, forming the South West's largest Iron Age cliff castle. Dodman's 114m apex is marked by a tall granite cross, erected as a daymark in 1896 by a local parson, *'in the firm hope of the second coming'*. The Second Coming is still on hold and the daymark didn't prevent destroyers *HMS Lynx* and *HMS Thrasher* being simultaneously wrecked below, the following year. A Napoleonic signal station, built in 1794, stands fifty metres back from the cross.

A blessedly mild path completes this section, enjoying meadows along Dodman's eastern side and a gradual descent to lovely Vault Beach, a completely undeveloped strand. Minor ups and downs round the final headland, Pen-a-maen, entering Gorran Haven above the harbour wall.

Silvermine Point.

35 Gorran Haven to Charlestown

Distance	17.2km / 10.7 miles	**Height gain** 925m / 3,050ft	**Difficulty** ● ● ● ● ●
Maps	OS Landranger 204 / OS Explorer 105		
Start	Gorran Haven PL26 6JH / rave.toolkit.ticking / SX 012 415		
Finish	Charlestown car park PL25 3NJ / seagulls.slave.damp / SX 038 516		
Parking near start	Gorran Haven car park PL26 6JT / shortcuts.holds.camera / SX 010 415		
Public transport	Multiple options changing at St Austell. Not Sundays		

This trek north around Mevagissey Bay into St Austell Bay explores a glorious stretch of lush green cliffs and isolated coves. After the historic settlements of Mevagissey and Pentewan are passed, the going becomes increasingly severe.

In the thirteenth century, seine nets were used to encircle pilchards at Gorran Haven, the earliest recorded Cornish harbour; its now-larger neighbour Mevagissey only took prominence in the eighteenth century when drift-netting became common. Gorran Haven is squeezed around small beaches, sheltered by a pier which has existed in various forms since the fifteenth century. The climb from the beach follows steep, narrow Church Street, appropriately named as alongside are the fifteenth-century St Just Church which was restored from ruin in 1885 after use as a fish cellar, and Haven Church which was built by local fishermen in 1863.

Mevagissey.

Cliff Road leads out onto fields and to a further climb above Great Perhaver Beach, reaching a mysterious earthwork at Pabyer Point. The guano-smeared rocks 900m offshore are the Gwineas, where Atlantic grey seals haul out.

The SWCP gradually descends to Turbot Point, entrance to Mevagissey Bay. A cleft here is known as 'Bodrugan's Leap'; as the Wars of the Roses waned, Sir Henry Bodrugan of nearby Bodrugan Barton supposedly rode his horse off the cliffs into a waiting boat, fleeing Henry VII's retribution. Newtonian physics had yet to be discovered, hence this story is plausible. Turbot Point overlooks Colona Beach and Chapel Point; the sandy cove is occupied solely by a white boathouse, and the low promontory by an isolated group of Arts and Crafts-style houses, built in 1936 from the Point's stone. This spot featured in Daphne Du Maurier's gothic tale, *The House on the Strand*. A road leads around Portmellon Cove and through Portmellon, effectively a suburb of Mevagissey.

Over Polkirt Hill, Mevagissey is revealed, named for Saints Meva and Issey and a contender for Cornwall's most engaging coastal town. Descending through Cliff Park above the sheltering quays of Mevagissey's Outer (1897) and Inner (1775) Harbour, you'll appreciate how active the local fishing industry is, with around sixty registered boats constantly coming and going past the cast iron Victorian Pier Head Lighthouse. Mevagissey first thrived on pilchard fishing, landing 30,000 fish a boat until the shoals were exhausted. During the Napoleonic Wars, Mevagissey's fast boats smuggled tobacco and brandy, but were also built for the Preventive Waterguard! Exploring is recommended; the small alleys behind the waterfront ('squeeze bellies') were historically choked with fish guts and from 1895, lit by electricity generated from pilchard oil. Mevagissey Museum and the (free) Aquarium face one another across the Inner Harbour.

The SWCP departs bustling Mevagissey via a steep, narrow ramp; the town is quickly obscured from view by the dramatic vertical cliffs around Penare Point. Vegetation somehow clings to these, sheltered from the prevailing winds, and rugged stacks guard their base. This is a foretaste of the coast to Charlestown, which becomes correspondingly tough-going, with numerous steep dips and climbs. The second of these drops into Portgiskey, passing behind ruined fishing cellars.

Amidst all this grand scenery, adjoining Sconhoe and Pentewan Beaches are a jarring shock; every square inch of land behind is crammed with the tents and caravans of Pentewan Sands Holiday Park. Quickly bypass the whole thing via the B3273 behind. Turning into Pentewan, your surroundings improve. This quiet village was, remarkably, a major port serving the china clay works inland via a tramway from 1829, and a railway from 1874. The harbour eventually choked with silt from the St Austell River and the last clay shipment departed in 1929.

Pentewan is escaped along The Terrace and the remainder of this section negotiates verdant cliffs, often hedged-in, with plenty of hills to overcome. The first ascent is around Polrudden Cove, where a band of golden granite lights up the mudstone cliffs; this is a dyke, a volcanic intrusion called an 'elvan' by Cornish miners.

178

Approaching Black Head.

Two more ups and downs lead to a descent through woods, with wooden statues, to Hallane. Here, a waterfall trickles to the beach fronting Hallane Mill, a rental cottage. Another harsh ascent crosses Drennick headland, to Black Head. This long promontory, in sight since Turbot Point, divides Mevagissey and St Austell Bays. The SWCP doesn't extend to this Iron Age cliff castle, but a side-tour is recommended. The junction can't be missed, marked by a massive carved block of Bodmin Moor granite commemorating A.L. Rowse (1903-1997), who lived at Trenarren. A renowned historian, Rowse was also a poet awarded the title 'Bard of Gorseth Cornwall' for championing the county's culture.

Take in the views from Gerrans Point, before the trail is enveloped by the gnarled trees of Ropehaven Cliffs, a Cornish Wildlife Trust nature reserve. Steps descend steeply through these ancient coastal woodlands; don't miss the left turn beside a bench, or you're needlessly descending all the way to sea level (mea culpa!).

Silvermine Point is a highlight; sheer cliffs enclose a beach seemingly snatched from the Mediterranean. This view is, however hard-earned, via an especially severe descent and climb. After descending (again!) from Phoebe's Point, the path to the beach at Lower Porthpean is kinder. Pass behind the sunbathers and endure another steep ascent, through the woods of Carrickhowell Point.

The path to Charlestown, atop the unstable cliffs fronting the houses of Duporth, was re-established in 2022 after being diverted tediously inland for some years. The stack of Polmear Island indicates that you have reached Charlestown's remarkable historic harbour.

📷 Polridmouth.

Charlestown.

36 Charlestown to Fowey

Distance 16.5km / 10.3 miles	**Height gain** 525m / 1,700ft **Difficulty** ●●●○○
Maps	OS Landranger 200, 204 / OS Explorer 105, 107
Start	Charlestown car park PL25 3NJ / seagulls.slave.damp / SX 038 516
Finish	Fowey to Polruan ferry, Fowey PL23 1HZ / bearings.clef.crash / SX 123 514
Parking near finish	Main car park, Fowey PL23 1EU / nicer.succeed.removal / SX 122 516
Public transport	24 or 25 bus

This eclectic section can be summarised as; an easy first half through the (often engaging) industrial landscapes around St Austell Bay, followed by a hillier second half around Gribbin Head, a headland steeped with Daphne du Maurier's legacy.

Charlestown's photogenic Georgian waterfront is a popular and buzzing place, lined in summer by cafés and stalls. Originally the village of West Polmear, it was re-named after founder Charles Rashleigh. John Smeaton (of Eddystone Lighthouse fame) designed the harbour and dock, built between 1791 and 1801. Tin, and later china clay, were shipped from St Austell's mines; the latter until the 1990s. Charlestown is now incorporated within the Cornish Mining World Heritage Site and is home to a collection of historic ships. It is regularly used as a filming location, popping up in productions as diverse as *Alice in Wonderland*, *The Eagle has Landed* and *Poldark*.

From the car park at the dock's rear, the SWCP departs Charlestown along Quay Road past the Shipwreck Treasure Museum (a huge collection of shipwreck artefacts) and above the 1885 octagonal harbourmaster's hut.

The next two kilometres lead along fields and parkland in front of houses, flats and hotels. The Coastwatch lookout station on Landrion Point and the stack of Gull Island offer some interest. The car park and road access to Carlyon Bay are then crossed. Despite being formed from silted mineral waste, Carlyon Bay is an attractive expanse of sand, punctuated by Crinnis Island, a tall isolated stack. Below the cliffs, a Benidorm-style housing development is controversially planned.

At Fishing Point, Carlyon Bay's eastern end, the cliffs lower in height and the sand is replaced by reefs. This is Carlyon Bay Golf Club, watch for flying balls! At Spit Point, the shoreline into Par is blocked by huge industrial sheds and silos. These are 'dries', where china clay pumped in slurry form from quarries was dried, before export from the small harbour. Operations largely ceased in 2007, and there are proposals to redevelop the site as housing. From the Second World War searchlight building at Spit Point, the SWCP is diverted around the dries via an alleyway, a metal footbridge across piping and following the railway to reach Par Docks' entrance. It's all rather grim: these are not the dries you are looking for.

The SWCP through Par is uninteresting; Harbour Road leads beneath the railway to Par Green Road, which passes beneath the railway again. Opposite number 61, a path escapes town, leading to Par Beach via woodland trails which intersect with the Eden Project's Clay Trails.

Crossing the length of Par Beach is a welcome change. The dunes at the rear are (unusually) growing, shifting the high-water mark a hundred metres seaward over the past century. Par Sands extend a kilometre seaward, like Carlyon Bay largely consisting of silted mineral waste. Traces of a 365m breakwater snake across the sands, built 1829-40 by mine owner Joseph Treffry.

Inland at Polmear, a car park leads to a footbridge and ascent onto the cliffs. The cliffs give a sweeping view of St Austell Bay and the incongruous industry backing the beach; the horizon is dominated by the 'Cornish Alps': green and white conical hills of china clay.

Polkerris is hidden until a sudden steep descent to the curving harbour wall. The SWCP immediately zigzags steeply out of this sheltered enclave, emerging from woods in open fields on top. Narrow winding paths, with just one steep climb, follow the coastal slope to Little Gribbin and Gribbin Head. Gribbin Head is topped by a distinctive twenty-six-metre striped square tower, an 1832 Trinity House daymark erected to distinguish 'The Gribbin' from Dodman Point.

📷 *Polkerris.*

Daphne du Maurier's novels were inspired by the indented coast of tiny coves and short steep woodland climbs which leads to Fowey. Hidden on the hill behind Polridmouth is Menabilly, her home from 1943 and *Rebecca*'s 'Manderley'. She wrote *Rebecca* at Ferryside, her home in Fowey from 1926 to 1943. Polridmouth's twin coves are negotiated via boardwalk and stepping stones respectively, with a pond behind the second. The SWCP briefly ventures onto the sand at Coombe Haven, and after passing above Penventinue Cove reaches St Catherine's Point, where St Catherine's Castle guards Fowey. Built by Edward III and enhanced by Henry VIII in 1540, this is worth a quick explore.

From Readymoney Cove, the Esplanade passes behind a ruined blockhouse. Lining the drowned valley of the River Fowey, the town's picture-postcard appearance belies its reputation in the Middle Ages as a wretched hive of scum and villainy. The 'Fowey Gallants' waged a private war against French vessels. A Royal messenger sent to remind these pirates that England wasn't at war with France had his nose and ears cut off. Later, 'free trading' was rife, with eighty-one Fowey vessels confiscated for smuggling between 1786 and 1815.

The Polruan ferry sails from Whitehouse Pier.

Fowey to Polruan ferry

The ferry runs year-round between 7.00 am and 11 pm (reduced hours at weekends and from October to April). Cards or cash are accepted, the cost was £3 in 2024. Check details by calling 01726 870232.

October to April and summer evenings, the ferry runs from Town Quay, 350m upriver along the Esplanade.

📷 *Lantic Bay.*

37 Polruan to Polperro

Distance 11.5km / 7.1 miles	**Height gain** 600m / 1,950ft **Difficulty** ● ● ● ● ○
Maps	OS Landranger 200, 201 / OS Explorer 107
Start	Fowey to Polruan ferry, Polruan PL23 1PA / develops.butternut.kettles / SX 125 510
Finish	Polperro PL13 2RA / pocketed.opera.discussed / SX 208 509
Parking near start	Vevery car park, Polruan PL23 1QL / subjects.gearbox.deeds / SX 131 507
Parking near finish	Polperro car park PL13 2PL / drift.backhand.halt / SX 205 515
Public transport	481 bus. Not possible at weekends

Between the twin picturesque harbours of Polruan and Polperro, the coast is completely undeveloped, with no facilities. The SWCP forges a path atop and across high rugged cliffs, perched above wave-cut platforms where razor-sharp serrated strata incline from the water. Locals dub this path, 'The Rollercoaster' ...

The Fowey to Polruan ferry lands at The Quay. Polruan has developed as a quieter, mirror image of Fowey, which it faces across the river. From The Quay, steps lead to West Street; turn right to follow this. The SWCP turns uphill into Battery Lane, but first continue ahead for a side-tour to the Polruan Blockhouse.

Polruan Blockhouse is one of two 'chain towers' constructed to control access to the River Fowey after a French attack in 1457. You can enter the tower, which is much better preserved

than Fowey Blockhouse, 300m across the river. The chain between the blockhouses was confiscated by Edward IV and donated to Dartmouth Castle, as punishment for unsanctioned raids on the French. The Second World War saw the chain revived, in the form of an anti-submarine boom between the towers.

The SWCP emerges from Polruan's streets at the top of St Saviour's Hill, where a Coastwatch lookout station stands alongside the ruins of St. Saviour's Chapel, which possibly originated in the eighth century. The car park alongside is claimed by locals to have the best view of any in Cornwall; they could be right!

The path loses height to traverse steep slopes; a footbridge, tucked far below Vevery car park, marks the point where Polruan is left behind. A gradual climb tops out above the cliffs at 119m, this section's highest point. Enjoy the views past Gribbin Head to Dodman Point and beyond, before turning into Lantic Bay.

Lantic Bay is quite a sight; an arc of tall green cliffs leads around to Pencarrow Head, with a string of wonderfully isolated sand and shingle beaches perched along the base. Great Lantic Beach and Little Lantic Beach are joined at low tide. Avoid the turning onto the precarious path down to Great Lantic, unless you are happy to climb all the way up again! Conversely, the SWCP heads steeply uphill directly above the beach, before a gentle ascent on less exposed paths through heath and bracken to Pencarrow Head.

Pencarrow Head marks the entrance to Lantivet Bay, a wider embayment with gentler cliffs. The only signs of civilisation are the ancient field boundaries, the occasional glimpse of St Ildierna's Church tucked inland at Lansallos and The Watch House, a lonely cottage tucked beneath the trail above Watch House Cove. This was built by the Coastguard in 1835, after one of their officers was beaten unconscious here while apprehending smugglers. The path follows a lower trajectory than previously, allowing viewing of the rock-cut platforms which absorb the surging Atlantic breakers. Both sides of Sandheap Point, it dips into and climbs out of valleys; the 'rollercoaster' has begun! At West Coombe, the trickling waterfall once powered a watermill and a cart track was hewn through the rock to transport seaweed (a fertiliser) from Lansallos Beach.

The path contours across Lansallos Cliff to East Coombe. This valley is a great spot to access the reef and explore its layered rock pools; the uppermost brim with frogspawn in spring, whilst the lowest are inhabited by hardy limpets. The rock pools sides' pink colouring is due to calcareous encrustations of *lithothamniae*, a red algae. Yellow *xanthoria* lichen adds further colour above the tideline, contrasting with black *Hydropunctaria maura* lichen directly beneath.

The harsh climb out of East Coombe, above Broad Cove, leads past a white obelisk. This was a daymark to warn offshore craft of Udder Rock, now marked by a yellow cardinal marker buoy, with a bell mounted. The path becomes increasingly exposed and exhilarating, picking a route around slopes above airy drops to crashing waves. The path dips to a footbridge overlooking

Shelter near Polperro.

Penslake Cove and then climbs, again, above Blackybale Point, before a moderately hair-raising trail around Colors Cove (another footbridge) and past Nealand Point.

After descending from Nealand Point, the going becomes easier as the path evens out and, increasingly, shelter is provided by gnarled trees and tall bushes lining the trail. Polperro is hidden from view until the last moment, but a diminutive lighthouse reveals the entrance to this sheltered inlet. Three stone shelters line the trails around Chapel Cliff, named for medieval St Peter's Chapel. The chapel was moved to Peak Rock which overlooks the entrance to Polperro. This craggy outcrop is now the site of The Loft, a nineteenth-century building used by fishermen to store their nets.

Polperro, should it need introduction, is a fishing village squeezed along a narrow inlet, the very definition of 'picturesque'! Steps lead down to the harbour.

Polperro.

38 Polperro to Seaton

Distance 14.3km / 8.9 miles	**Height gain** 500m / 1,650ft **Difficulty** ● ● ● ● ○
Maps	OS Landranger 201 / OS Explorer 107, 108
Start	Polperro PL13 2RA / pocketed.opera.discussed / SX 208 509
Finish	Seaton Park car park PL11 3JD / forget.pumpkin.presuming / SX 304 544
Parking near start	Polperro car park PL13 2PL / drift.backhand.halt / SX 205 515
Public transport	75 and 73 buses, change at Looe. Not Sundays

This section is notably easier than the previous one. The fishing village of Polperro makes for an engaging start, and there are fine views of St George's Island. After the town of Looe, the route becomes a tad dull.

Polperro is a remarkable place. Tightly packed cottages line the steep flanks of a winding inlet, crammed with fishing boats. Its charm is inevitably tempered by the hordes of tourists crowding the streets in summer; an early visit will reward you with peace and quiet (and elbow space).

At the back of Polperro harbour, a stone bridge crosses a narrow stream walled in by overhanging cottages, including the sixteenth-century House on the Props. The Warren, a similarly narrow thoroughfare, leads along the harbour's north side, past the splendidly gaudy Shell House. Polperro Heritage Museum of Smuggling and Fishing, located in a former pilchard factory, offers insights into the village's pre-tourism existence.

The Warren is also known as Reuben's Walk, after a past harbourmaster. There are tremendous final views back through the harbour and village, then you pass above the diminutive (five-metre-tall) Spy House Point Lighthouse (decommissioned in the 1950s), out onto the coast.

The path leads across a coastal scarp densely overgrown with shrubbery. Downend Point was a gift to the National Trust by Angela Brazil, prolific author of girls' boarding school stories. A tall stone cross commemorates locals who *'gave their lives'* in conflict; forty-five are listed from the World Wars, as well as a Falklands War pilot.

Approaching Talland Bay, the coast becomes less precipitous and the path descends closer to the jagged Devonian slate reefs which now pave the shore, continuing far beyond Seaton: the 'Whitsand Bay formation'. Talland Bay, historically dubbed, 'the Playground of Plymouth', huddles around a small sandy break in the reef. The boiler of the *Margueritte* is visible at low tide, a French trawler wrecked in 1922. A short lane interlude leads past Talland's café, before steps ascend into a second stretch of wonderfully empty coast, wilder and rougher-going than before with repeated climbs and descents.

St George's Island

Just 500m offshore and almost connected by reefs, it is also known as Looe Island. This was the site of a Benedictine Priory in the Middle Ages (bombed during the Second World War, mistaken for a battleship). The island was infamous for rat infestation, the nineteenth-century novelist Wilkie Collins reporting how they were, *"eaten with vindictive relish by the people of Looe"*. The Atkins sisters lived there for four decades from 1965, described in their book *We Bought an Island*. The island is now maintained by Cornwall Wildlife Trust as a sanctuary for black-backed gulls. CWT organise boat trips to explore the island, book ahead.

The only landmarks before reaching Looe are two pairs of literal landmarks (tall white markers on the hillside, measuring out a nautical mile for marine vessel testing) and the craggy path around Hore Stone headland, where the dome-like profile of St George's Island hoves into view across Portnadler Bay. The Ranneys rocks can be seen extending from the island's south-east tip, home to Atlantic grey seals.

Just before the path ends at the housing of Hannafore, Lammana Chapel is passed on the left; a side-path leads uphill to traces of the medieval chapel, which was paired with the priory on St George's Island, built on an early Christian site dated to the sixth century.

A road, sometimes pavement-less, leads around Hannafore Point into the town of Looe. Looe consists of West Looe and East Looe, facing one another across a narrow tidal river crammed with boats. After passing opposite the Banjo Pier, named on account of its shape, a ferry offers a short-cut across to West Looe. The SWCP crosses 700m upstream at the seven-arched bridge, passing a sculpture of local celebrity Nelson, the one-eyed seal (deceased 2003).

📷 *Portnadler Bay and St George's Island.*

Across in East Looe, you will unavoidably be absorbed by the horde of tourists and shoppers thronging the town's commercial centre. Escape up Castle Street (beside the Ship Inn), which leads steeply uphill onto East Cliff, with a viewpoint overlooking Looe's beach.

The route from here is often uninspiring. A mix of tarmac paths and road leads above Plaidy Beach, through terraced holiday chalets and down steps to Millendreath Beach, backed by Millendreath Beach Resort. A tidal pool on the beaches' east side offers a chance to cool off.

A steep lane from Millendreath eventually merges into a sunken trough through woods. This ascends a hundred metres to a picnic area on Bodigga Cliff, where a great section of coastal trail seems imminent … however, landslips have diverted the route inland following Looe Hill lane. The path leads through pleasant pine woods, then along the lane itself, with hedges blocking views.

Reaching a 155m summit, 400m past Wild Futures Monkey Sanctuary, the SWCP departs the lane and redeems itself with an engaging final stretch. The current route descends along fields and follows the clifftop, passing through woods to regain the lane and descend into Seaton.

Polperro smuggling

Tiny Polperro was one of Cornwall's key 'free trading' centres. Brandy, gin, tea and tobacco were illicitly landed from Guernsey, bypassing customs duties. Zephaniah Job (1749-1822), ostensibly the village schoolmaster, operated as the industry's investment banker, even issuing his own banknotes. A customs man was shot dead at Cawsands in 1798 whilst boarding the *Lottery*, a Polperro boat. This led to the stationing of one of the first Preventive Waterguard vessels at Polperro, and the trade's decline.

◉ *Whitsand Bay.*

39 Seaton to Freathy

Distance	11.5km / 7.1 miles	Height gain	450m / 1,450ft	Difficulty	● ● ● ● ●
Maps	OS Landranger 201 / OS Explorer 108
Start	Seaton Park car park PL11 3JD / forget.pumpkin.presuming / SX 304 544
Finish	Freathy long stay car park PL10 1PS / octagon.voltages.flush / SX 394 522
Public transport	70 and 75 buses, change at Anthony. Not Sundays

An uninspiring start is followed by elevated trails with fine views, taking in the lovely little harbour of Portwrinkle and an impressive Victorian fort.

The village of Seaton (not to be confused with Devon's Seaton, section 54) is fronted by a sandy beach, allegedly formed after a mermaid was spurned by a local sailor. Well, at least she didn't get shot (page 91). Nevertheless, she took rejection badly and cursed Seaton to be submerged beneath dunes.

The SWCP follows the B3247 out of Seaton and through neighbouring Downderry. The road is initially kerb-less and lined by uninteresting holiday homes; if the tide is low, take the alternative waterfront route. This involves following the sea wall out of Seaton, and the beach as far as the Inn on the Shore, before re-joining the B3247.

> ### Tregantle Range firing times
>
> Red flags (red lights at night) denote firing taking place. Firing times can be obtained beforehand by calling 01752 822516, or by Googling 'Tregantle firing times'. The range is closed on most weekends and no firing takes place in August.

The road is escaped outside Downderry; a steep zigzagging path ascends onto Battern Cliffs, a distinctive 120m-high scarp densely overgrown with fan-like formations of bushes, interspersed with exposed faces of sedimentary Devonian slate, siltstone and sandstone. There are fine views around Whitsand Bay towards Rame Head. The eighteen-metre-high stack below the cliffs is The Long Stone.

The narrow path along Battern Cliffs, initially following an overgrown stone wall, leads into a splendid but exhausting stretch of ups and downs; down Cargloth Cliffs, along, up, down and then up again following Eglarooze Cliff, steeply down to Britain Point. This finally brings you, via a lane, into Portwrinkle.

Reefs surround Portwrinkle's tiny harbour, which dries out at low tide. This is a lovely spot to rest and indulge in a bit of rock pooling (there are twenty-five species of crab in Cornwall, lest you be wondering). Finnygook Beach takes its name from Silas Finn, an eighteenth-century

smuggler who was murdered after snitching on his comrades. Now, his ghost ('gook') haunts the village: actual fact. Finnygook Lane leads through Portwrinkle and then it's another ascent, a path winding through bracken past Whitsand Bay Golf Club, onto Skinner's Ball Cliff.

For the next two kilometres, the SWCP passes along wide slopes of grass and sprawling hedges, perched above a wide sandy beach. This is the Tregantle Ranges, an active army firing range! These commence at a gate adorned with warning signs and a flag post.

If a red flag is flying, you cannot enter; you'll have to follow the signed 'Permanent' route. This leads uphill to the busy B3247 and tediously follows it around the military land's perimeter. The redeeming aspect is expansive views *inland* to Plymouth Sound and the Lynher River estuary (as well as not getting shot).

If the ranges are open, the 'permissive' route which leads through the ranges and directly in front of Tregantle Fort is hugely preferable. Assorted military buildings and rifle ranges dot the landscape along the path. Tregantle Fort itself is surprisingly vast, its daunting granite frontage looming alongside the SWCP for 300 metres. The westernmost of the Palmerstonian forts and batteries guarding Plymouth, it originally had a thousand-soldier capacity.

The 'permissive' path emerges from the military land to re-join the 'Permanent' path at the aptly-named Military Road, where there is a great view of Tregantle Fort for those who had to bypass it. The final kilometre leads alongside the road, usually off the tarmac, including some dramatic clifftop stretches. Freathy long stay car park is simply a quiet roadside spot, outside Freathy itself.

195

Tregantle Fort.

Palmerston's Follies

From Tregantle Fort to Bovisand Fort (section 42), the SWCP passes through a remarkable network of about thirty forts and batteries, defending Plymouth Sound from all directions (including inland). These 'Palmerstonian' forts, named after the then-Prime Minister, were constructed nationwide in the 1860s, around naval bases. This was in response to a perceived threat of French invasion; in 1859, the self-styled and ambitious Emperor Napoleon III launched the first armour-plated battleship. The breath-taking cost, coupled with the fact that actual invasion was never likely, led to the moniker 'Palmerston's Follies'.

📷 *Rame Head.*

40 Freathy to Cremyll

Distance 16km / 9.9 miles	**Height gain** 525m / 1700ft **Difficulty** ● ● ● ○ ○
Maps	OS Landranger 201 / OS Explorer 108
Start	Freathy long stay car park PL10 1PS / octagon.voltages.flush / SX 394 522
Finish	Cremyll to Stonehouse ferry, Cremyll PL10 1HX / units.valid.palms / SX 453 534
Parking near finish	Cremyll car park PL10 1HU / indoor.moss.cups / SX 452 532
Public transport	70 bus

This section begins with excessive tarmac, but becomes increasingly engaging as it explores Cornwall's south-east extremity, the Rame Peninsula, locally dubbed 'the forgotten corner'.

For a diversion before you've even started, a path leads 150m from the car park to the beach beside Sharrow Point, where Sharrow Grotto (below the lifeguard's hut) is a gated-off cave excavated by Lieutenant James Lugger in 1784. His poem, inscribed on the wall, reveals that this cured his gout.

Freathy, a disparate collection of holiday homes, is approached by a dramatic cliff path. A distinctly excitement-free stretch of tarmac leads along Military Road through Freathy and beyond, however the views along Whitsand Bay are pleasant and expansive. The earthworks on the left at Tregonhawke are Whitesand Bay Battery (constructed 1889 to defend Tregantle Fort), now a chalet park. The road is departed, 500m after.

Cremyll to Stonehouse ferry

A ferry has crossed the 300m-wide River Tamar since at least 705AD. The current passenger ferry crosses half hourly from 6.45 am to 9 pm (reduced hours at weekends and October to March), taking eight minutes. Cards or cash are accepted, with contactless cards preferred. The cost in 2024 was £2.50. Check for details on 01752 822105.

The path leads among private huts peppering the coastal slope, hidden behind overgrown hedges. Keep track of way markers, a labyrinth of paths zigzag around the aptly named Wiggle Cliff.

The SWCP almost re-joins Military Road, but turns away at a 'Welcome to Whitsand Bay' sign and descends towards Polhawn Cove. Steps climb behind imposing Polhawn Fort, now a wedding venue but previously Polhawn Battery, operational 1864 to 1927.

The, occasionally rocky, path ascends steep slopes extending down to slabs above Queener Point before dropping onto Ramehead Common, overlooked by a Coastwatch lookout station. Rame Head, the Rame Peninsula's conical tip, has been unmistakeably visible along the SWCP since Gribbin Head (section 36). Now that this tip is almost reached, the route turns away from it! Definitely make the short side-tour up the bare hill, crossing this Iron Age cliff

Earl's Drive.

castle's rock-cut ditch and rampart. St Michael's Chapel occupies the summit, built c1397 with a beacon light to guide mariners. Absorbing the new vista eastwards, look for the peregrine falcons which nest nearby.

The two-kilometre path to Penlee Point, the Rame Peninsula's second headland and the entrance to Plymouth Sound, traverses bracken-covered heathland where wild ponies and roe deer roam. This becomes the Earl's Drive, a scenic carriage ride from Mount Edgcumbe House which was extended in 1823 to Penlee Point, for a visit by Princess Adelaide, wife of the future William IV. Queen Adelaide's Grotto sits below Penlee Point, a chapel remarkably hewn from the rock (1826-7), with views across Plymouth Sound.

The Earl's Drive track scythes through woodland towards Cawsand, passing above the 1888 site of a torpedo station, at Pier Cellars. The road into Cawsand is overlooked by Cawsand Fort (1863), now private residences.

Cawsand and Kingsand are conjoined fishing villages of narrow streets. The one ends and the other begins where the letters *'Devon | Corn'* are mounted on the wall in Garrett Street. Until 1844 this was the county boundary, now Cornwall continues to the River Tamar. Kingsand was possibly named for Henry VII, who landed here in 1483 as plain Henry Tudor, two years prior to victory in the Battle of Bosworth. These communities, with their waterfront tunnels and cellars, were Plymouth's smuggling base; an eighteenth-century visitor encountered, "... *females, whose appearance was grotesque ... we found that they were smuggling spiritous liquors by means of bladders fastened under their petticoats.*"

A steep climb via Heavitree Road brings you to gates marked, *'Welcome to Mount Edgcumbe'*. This section's remainder passes through Mount Edgcumbe Country Park, ornamentally landscaped in the eighteenth century. The path, often sheltered by trees, crosses a lane at Hooe Lake Valley and then loops through woods above Fort Picklecombe (another Palmerstonian fort, converted to private residences). When assembled c1779 from a medieval doorway, the Picklecombe Seat had a sea view.

📷 *Cremyll.*

A landslip diverts the SWCP steeply uphill via the Zig-Zags, paths created in the 1750s and lined with rhododendron. The Zig-Zags, equally aptly named 'The Horrors' in the nineteenth century, top out at The Red Seat, a rest shelter.

While descending, note The Folly, a tower ruin. A shoreline track leads through parkland to Cremyll. Milton's Temple (1755) which stands beside a pond in Amphitheatre Valley, is inscribed with quotes from *Paradise Lost*. In 1945, Barn Pool's bay was an embarkation point for the D-Day beaches. It's guarded by both the Tudor blockhouse and Palmerstonian battery on Wilderness Point. The path leads through the beautiful gardens and fountains of an eighteenth-century Orangery, now a (tempting) café. Edgcumbe House is briefly in view, uphill (built 1547 and restored after Second World War bombing); you then arrive at the ferry landing, beside the Edgcumbe Arms.

Cremyll is Norse: fortress and *Tamar* is Celtic: great water. This is a significant spot, defined as the Cornish border by Athelstan in 936AD and, more pertinently, the end of the 478km/297-mile Cornish SWCP. If you've just completed this, congratulations!

> 'The speedy Tamar, which divides
> The Cornish and the Devonish confines'
>
> Edmund Spenser, *The Faerie Queene*

📷 *Outer Hope and Bolt Tail (Section 44).*

South and East Devon

Over the 216km / 134 miles of trail linking South Devon's fabulous wave-cut platforms and East Devon's ancient sandstone stacks, SWCP explorers will encounter huge diversity and variation. The region from Plymouth to Brixham is known as South Hams; the name derives from *Hamm* (Old English: Sheltered Place), yet the coast is anything but! Don't discount Tor Bay, with its conurbation of resorts; this is the UNESCO English Riviera Geopark. Across the River Exe, East Devon was notorious for 'free trading', i.e. smuggling, with all sections of society shamelessly profiting. The Jurassic Coast World Heritage Site then commences, characterised by unique and spectacular coastal landforms.

One distinctive feature is the numerous estuaries and rias (drowned river valleys), obstacles which must be crossed, by ferry or wading.

The East and South Devon Areas of Outstanding Natural Beauty encompass most of this coast.

Smeaton's Tower.

Royal William Yard.

41 Plymouth (Stonehouse) to Jennycliff Bay

Distance	13.9km / 8.6 miles	**Height gain** 175m / 550ft	**Difficulty** • • • • •
Maps	OS Landranger 201 / OS Explorer 108		
Start	Cremyll to Stonehouse ferry, Plymouth PL1 3RJ / deeply.allows.broken / SX 462 539		
Finish	Jennycliff Bay PL9 9SW / belts.logs.shady / SX 491 523		
Parking near start	Strand Street car park PL1 3RL / sulk.else.socket / SX 462 539		
Parking near finish	Jennycliff car park PL9 9SF / flats.popped.lamp / SX 492 523		
Public transport	2 and 34 buses, from St John's Church or Mount Batten and Barbican, Royal William Yard & Mount Edgcumbe ferry services		

There is no sugar-coating it: this section is entirely within Plymouth, confined to surfaced roads and paths passing through a city of 250,000 inhabitants. Some folk choose to bypass some, or all, of 'Ocean City's' bustling waterfront by ferry, but this would be a mistake. The convoluted route (ending 3.5km from the start point) takes in masses of maritime and naval heritage. Plymouth City Council have embraced the challenge of engaging SWCP visitors, designating 'their' section as the Plymouth Waterfront Walkway; even where the surroundings become grim, public art and eccentric way markers maintain interest.

The first part leads out and back through the district of **Stonehouse**. At Admiral's Hard, the ferry's landing pier, a stone 'doormat' reads, *'Welcome to Plymouth. Please wipe your feet'*.

The disconnected words embedded in pavements were coded telegraph messages sent from sailors overseas using Captain D. H. Bernard's 1908 *Nautical Telegraph Code Book*. To save money, one word would stand for a specific message.

Stonehouse's highlight is the grand, granite quay front buildings and preserved cranes of Royal William Yard. This was a victualling yard supplying the navy, designed and built, 1825-34 by John Rennie for William IV (there is a statue of him). The South West Coast Path Association are based here.

The old walls around Devil's Point Park are climbed by the Eric Wallis Memorial Steps. Devil's Point is a great viewpoint; across The Narrows to Cornwall (section 40) and up the River Tamar (called Hamoaze here) to *HMNB Devonport*. The UK's largest naval base originated in 1691, named Plymouth Dock until 1824. Royal Navy vessels frequently squeeze past, negotiating the fierce currents.

The route turns away from the shore at eight-sided Firestone Bay Artillery Tower, dating from the 1480s and now a restaurant overlooking a tidal swimming pool. The SWCP leads up Durnford Street, the pavement embellished with Sherlock Holmes story quotes: Arthur Conan Doyle had a medical practice at number 1 (now gone). After passing the imposing Royal Marines Barracks (home to the Marines since 1756), a right turn into Barrack Place leads towards **Millbay**.

The SWCP leads around the basins of Millbay Docks. In recent years, major redevelopment has been underway in this not-especially-attractive commercial district. Millbay Road's blue railings reveal the order given in 1564 by Sir John Hawkins, attacking the Spanish: *"Serve God daily, love one another, preserve your victuals, beware of fire, and keep good company"*. Further along, two popular features have been removed during building work, but should be restored in due course: the 'Wall of Stars' at the ferry port entrance roundabout names transatlantic luminaries such as Charlie Chaplin and Judy Garland who docked here, whilst the Gold Bullion sculpture recalls the ingots which regularly sat on the quayside during the 1930s, before shipping to Fort Knox.

Turning down West Hoe Road, note the Eddystone Lighthouse Pavement, interlocked stones revealing the lighthouse's construction technique. The lead nugget in the centre recalls Henry Hall's death (page 208). Reclaimed heritage signs line the road, the Wall of Industrial Memories.

The Royal Citadel, from Staddon Heights.

The Hoe ('high ridge') is reached at the Customs Office tower (1850), now Plymouth Lifeboat Station. The Hoe waterfront is Plymouth's centrepiece, a limestone outcrop overlooking Plymouth Sound.

The Royal Navy Millenium Wall on West Hoe is adorned with models of Devonport naval vessels. This gives the best view of Drake's Island, named after island governor Sir Francis Drake; Palmerstonian (1860s) gun emplacements dominate the east shore.

West Hoe Pier is followed by the Belvedere (1891), three levels of 'Wedding Cake' decorative steps which overlooked Plymouth's Pier (destroyed in the Blitz). The SWCP continues along the waterfront road, passing the Plymothian Heart (a sailor's tattoo sculpture) and the glorious 1935 Art Deco Tinside Lido.

A detour up the Belvedere steps accesses the Hoe Promenade where Smeaton's Tower stands, a striped lighthouse moved here from Eddystone reef. A visit to the top is recommended! Behind are statues of Nancy Astor (first female MP in parliament) and Francis Drake, marking where, in 1588, he (reputedly) played bowls before sailing to face the Spanish Armada. The Plymouth Naval Memorial's obelisk commemorates 23, 211 sailors lost in both World Wars with no known grave.

The SWCP now passes beneath the Royal Citadel's high walls; this fortress was built for Charles II after 1665, to defend against the Dutch. Across the road is the older (1490) Fisher's Nose Blockhouse, followed by the Hoe Cannons which guard Cattewater, the branch of Plymouth Sound formed by the River Plym.

The **Barbican** is Plymouth's liveliest district. Along Commercial Road, look for St James' Scallop, marking the sailing point for pilgrimages to Santiago de Compostela and the Shrine of Stella Maris, a salvaged Madonna representing the patron saint of sailors. A ferry from Commercial Wharf runs year-round to Mount Batten Point, optionally skipping this section's second half.

The Mayflower Steps are opposite Plymouth's Tourist Information Centre. A 1930s portico, plaques and US flags commemorate the 1620 departure (but not the exact spot!) of the Pilgrim

Fathers, onboard the *Mayflower*. The pilgrims docked as their second ship *Speedwell* was leaking; it was abandoned here. The site was renovated for the quadricentennial celebrations (spoiled by Covid).

The Leviathan sculpture (the 'Barbican prawn', an aquatic creature on a mast) marks Sutton Harbour's gates, crossed via a swing bridge leading to the National Marine Aquarium.

Cattedown is all housing and commercial properties. At Breakwater Hill, a cycleway leads above a former quarry, enlivened by the giant striped navigation beacon used as a SWCP marker, a Green Man sculpture, nautical portholes in the wall and a shrine to St Christopher, patron saint of travellers.

Neptune Park Industrial Estate smells unpleasant, keep moving. Cattewater is crossed via Laira Bridge, alongside the A379; a 'poem wall' tries to distract you from the heavy traffic, but it's written in the wrong direction.

Oreston is entered at Billacombe roundabout, where a rhino(!) sculpture recalls the fossils found in nearby caves. Trudge past some depressing offices and industrial units and you've cleared the worst of the entire SWCP.

After passing among housing over a small hill, The Causeway passes between Hooe and Radford Lakes, beneath Radford Castle. Hooe Lake is a tidal lagoon adorned with rotting ship timbers, the 'castle' is a dilapidated nineteenth-century folly. The route continues around Hooe Lake, past the housing of **Hooe** and then **Turnchapel**. After passing a lime kiln and the supports of a vanished bridge, the SWCP leads through brightly coloured housing, turning uphill towards **Mount Batten** at the Clovelly Bay Inn.

The Mount Batten peninsula (named after Captain Batten, who defended it for Parliament in the Civil War) is just a stone's throw across Cattewater from Plymouth's centre, and there are tremendous views of The Hoe. The path passes a marina, Mount Batten Watersports Centre and the landing point for the Barbican ferry, to reach Mount Batten Point; continuing to the breakwater's end is irresistible. Close by is a 'propellor' memorial, sculpted by Owen Cunningham (also responsible for the South West Coast Path Monument at Minehead); from 1928, this was flying boat base *RAF Mount Batten*. TE Lawrence ('Laurence of Arabia') served here anonymously, as 'Aircraftman Shaw'. Above is Mount Batten Tower, built c1652 to defend Cattewater.

After ascending behind the tower, the SWCP passes behind Mount Batten's buildings to reach the first unsurfaced path since stepping off the Cremyll ferry, following low cliffs to Jennycliff Bay.

The Eddystone lighthouses

The Eddystone Lighthouse, visible fifteen to twenty kilometres offshore from sections 40 to 42, is the fifth to mark the Eddystone reef. Henry Winstanley completed the first, in 1698: a fantastical wooden pagoda. His wish to inhabit it during, *"The greatest storm there ever was"* came true when a 1703 storm left no trace of Winstanley or his lighthouse. The second Eddystone light was completed by John Rudyerd in 1709 but burned down in 1755. Keeper Henry Hall (aged eighty-four!) battled the blaze and claimed that molten lead had poured down his throat. After he died twelve days later, a seven-ounce metal lump was removed from his stomach. John Smeaton completed the Eddystone's first stone lighthouse in 1759. 'Smeaton's Tower' survived the elements for 123 years before the underlying reef fractured: townsfolk raised funds for it to be dismantled and re-erected on Plymouth Hoe. James Douglass constructed the present forty-nine-metre lighthouse in 1882.

📷 *Wembury Point and Great Mew Stone.*

42 Jennycliff Bay to Warren Point

Distance	10.5km / 6.5 miles **Height gain** 350m / 1,150ft **Difficulty** ●●●●○
Maps	OS Landranger 201 / OS Explorer OL20
Start	Jennycliff Bay PL9 9SW / belts.logs.shady / SX 491 523
Finish	Warren Point to Noss Mayo ferry, Warren Point PL8 1DG / ledge.cools.buying / SX 538 478
Parking near start	Jennycliff car park PL9 9SF / flats.popped.lamp / SX 492 523
Parking near finish	Wembury car park PL9 0LF / bends.ladder.thick / SX 527 494
Public transport	3km walk to Wembury, 48 and 2 buses, change at Plymstock. Not Sundays

This section offers fine views of Plymouth Sound and of the Great Mew Stone, a distinctive inshore island. There are several mild ascents to contend with.

A popular grassy open space overlooks Jennycliff Bay's low cliffs ('jenny' is an archaic word for a donkey). The benches and café occupy the concrete foundations of Lord Howard's Battery, completed in 1909 and used in both World Wars. A hefty carved granite slab depicts what Plymouth Sound looked like 20,000 years ago: cold and dry, if you were wondering. Staddon Heights overlooks the bay, where Staddon Fort is the centrepiece of the 1860s Palmerstonian forts and batteries (page 196) guarding Plymouth Sound's eastern entrance. Note the dauntingly tall 'Bovisand Wall', a firing butt.

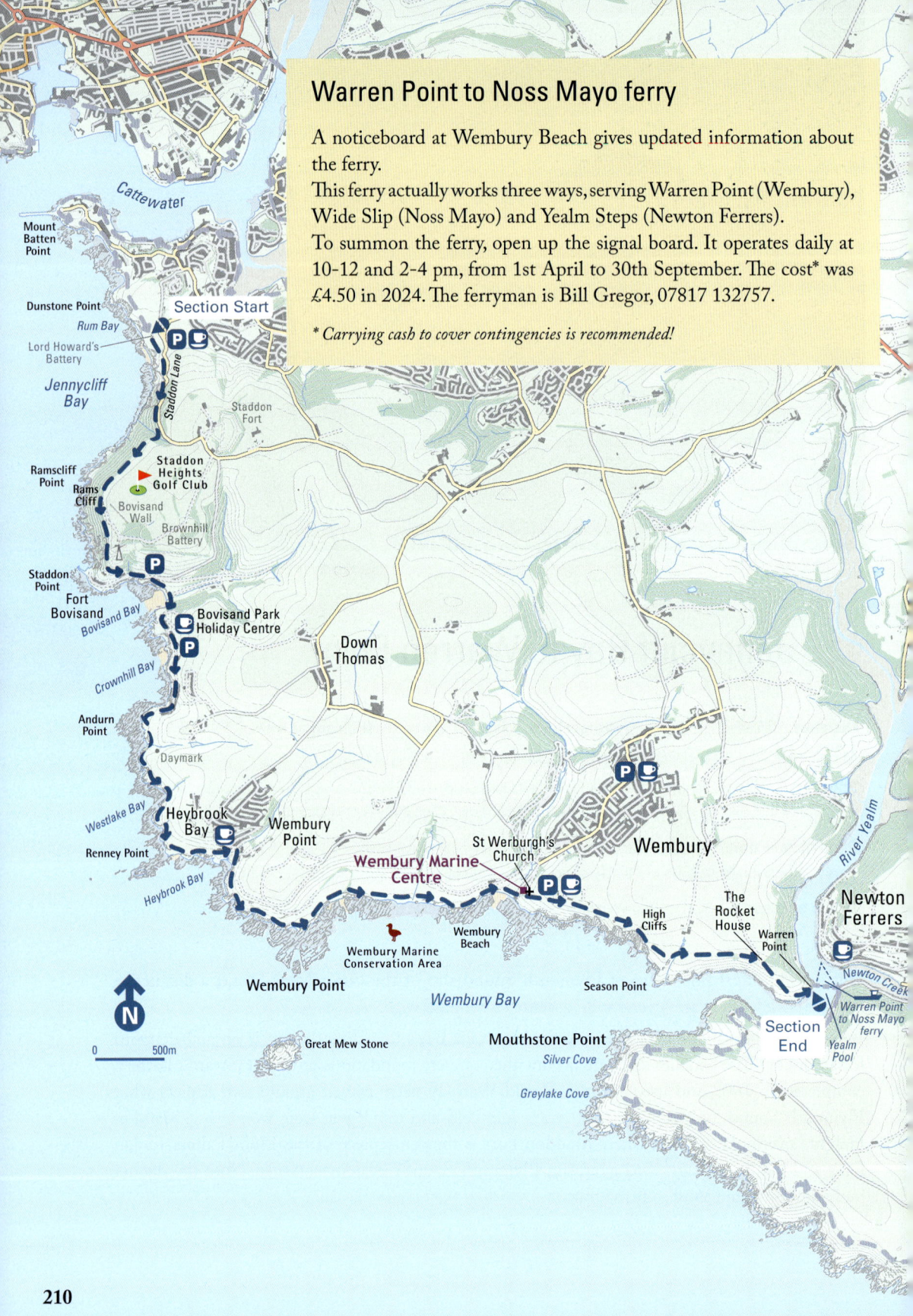

📷 *Fort Bovisand and Plymouth Breakwater.*

A gradual ascent leads past a *'Welcome to Plymouth'* mat (like that at the start of section 41) and a blue monolith announcing that Poole Harbour is only 175½ miles away (actually, it's more like 211 miles). Wooden steps and walkways divert through woods above a 2018 landslip. The route traverses alongside Staddon Lane, a hundred metres above Plymouth Sound, to a footbridge: Plymouth's actual outer limit.

The view from Rams Cliff is dominated by the 1.6km barrier of Plymouth Breakwater. Designed by engineer John Rennie, this took three decades from 1812 to complete, a gargantuan effort utilising four million tons of rock. Sheltered behind on Shovel Rock is Breakwater Fort, added in 1861.

Past a small radar tower, concrete steps descend behind Fort Bovisand. From 1869, this guarded the Sound's entrance with an imposing arc of twenty-three armoured casements (gun openings). The fort has a small harbour and is currently being developed into housing units. The manmade ditch crossed by footbridge extends uphill and right around Staddon Heights: herculean work went into all of this, given that French invasion was never likely and never happened.

Steps descend to Bovisand Bay's sandy beach. A tarmac road passes in front of Bovisand Park's holiday chalets, overlooking Crownhill Bay's beach.

As far as Wembury, the SWCP delightfully leads along the shore and around successive low headlands, following raised beaches created by sea level change. This is the Wembury Marine Conservation Area, designated in 1981 and stretching from Fort Bovisand to the River Yealm. Extending offshore to a depth of ten metres, it protects the first segment of the wonderful reefs characterising South Devon's coast as far as Start Point (section 46). As the designation implies, this is a natural treat; consider a bit of rock-pooling or even carrying a snorkel. Beneath the waves, apparently the thing to look out for is the bloody-eyed velvet swimming crab.

This foreshore path leads past a navigational beacon and around Renney Point to Heybrook Bay, where there is a pub just uphill. A few buildings around Wembury Point are traces of its status, until 2001, as *HMS Cambridge*, the Royal Naval Gunnery School. Great Mew Stone looms close inshore, a fifty-metre-high pyramidal islet.

◉ *The ferry landing at Warren Point.*

Wembury Beach is signposted by the tower of St Werburgh's Church. Behind the beach, Wembury Marine Centre offers insight into the MCA. If you've somehow tired of the SWCP, this is the start point of the Two Moors Way, Devon's coast to coast path leading 164km/ 102 miles to Lynmouth (section 3).

The path ascends steeply past the church: the pleasant waterside stretch is, sadly, finished. To emphasise the point, the path leads above the literally-nomenclatured High Cliffs. The good news is, the scenery is stunning; after crossing stepping stones at Season Point, the tree-shaded path leads along a terrace into, and far above, the River Yealm. Yealm is Celtic for 'kind'. This steep-sided narrow inlet, probably the most dramatic of South Devon's rias, is joined by Newton Creek at Yealm Pool.

A white cottage beside a junction is The Rocket House, so-named as until the 1930s the coastguard stored rescue rockets there. A right turn here leads downhill to Warren Point, where the ferry departs. If you are finishing at Wembury, you'll have to backtrack to this point and follow the track uphill, for three kilometres.

If the ferry is unavailable, the fifteen-kilometre trek around is not especially recommended: it's mostly along roads and not a straightforward route.

Great Mew Stone

Great Mew Stone is home to large numbers of shags, cormorants and herring gulls. Mew is an archaic name for gull, from their mewing sound. The isle is uninhabited but not apparently uninhabitable: spare a thought for convict Sam Wakeman who in 1744 was 'transported' to this guano-smeared slanting rock for seven years, preferring this option to Australia. When his sentence was completed, he chose to remain, paying his rent in rabbits.

📷 *Beacon Hill.*

43 Noss Mayo to Mothecombe

Distance 14.1km / 8.8 miles	**Height gain** 450m / 1,450ft **Difficulty** ● ● ● ● ○
Maps	OS Landranger 201, 202 / OS Explorer OL20
Start	Warren Point to Noss Mayo ferry, Noss Mayo PL8 1BN / clouding.suppers.soldiers / SX 540 478
Finish	Mothecombe PL8 1LB / pelted.fend.degrading / SX 614 475
Parking near start	Tennis Court car park, Noss Mayo PL8 1EH / fluffed.cobbles.forms / SX 547 474
Parking near finish	Mothecombe car park PL8 1LB / packages.scrambles.muffin / SX 611 478
Public transport	2km walk to Battisborough Cross, 94 bus. Not Sundays

This coast is absolutely gorgeous. Pink thrift and yellow kidney vetch adorn slate cliffs whilst at water level, gnarled reefs display phenomenal rock formations. This whole section is road-free and surprisingly remote. Whilst the first half is an easy, level track, the second joltingly transitions to steep inclines and some awkward path surfaces. If you plan to continue past Mothecombe by fording the River Erme (page 218), check the tides beforehand and allow extra time to avoid missing the low-tide window.

Noss Mayo, facing Newton Ferrers across Newton Creek, derives its name from *Nesse Matheu*: Matthew's nose; it was granted to Matthew Fitzjohn in 1287. This picture-postcard village is a kilometre along Passage Road from Wide Slip, the Warren Point to Noss Mayo ferry landing point; those arriving by the ferry won't see Noss Mayo unless they make a side-tour.

From Wide Slip, the SWCP follows the River Yealm's south shore to its mouth, along Passage Road, a path through Passage Wood's oaks, then a track. The track leads around the hillside, high above Cellar Beach and through the ash trees of Brakehill Plantation, emerging above Mouthstone Point. There are views of Great Mew Stone in Wembury Bay and, far further out, the Eddystone Lighthouse.

The wide and level track is the remarkable Revelstoke Drive, built in the 1880s for Edward Baring (of Barings Bank) as a clifftop carriage drive from which Lady Barings and their guests could enjoy unobstructed views. It was constructed by local fishermen, extending over fourteen kilometres around the Membland Estate. The stone walls lining precipitous stretches were built as guardrails. Revelstoke Drive contours above steep gorse-covered slopes leading down to small cliffs, home to yellowhammers, kestrels, buzzards and sparrowhawks. Fingers of vertically inclined slate protrude from the cliff base, a reef scored by wave action into countless narrow gulleys and beaches. Even the tiniest inlets are named, a clue that this wild and windswept coast was once a busy working environment.

The remains of a coastguard lookout are perched above the water's edge at the tip of Gara Point. The slopes along the following kilometre are The Warren, as the name suggests, the site of a medieval rabbit farm. This continued into the nineteenth century: the outlines of wabbit enclosures can be seen at Warren Cottage, the estate warrener's home. This isolated building was used for lunch stops by Lord Revelstoke's guests, including The Prince of Wales (the future Edward VII) and Princess Alice.

Revelstoke Drive's next landmark is the disused Gunrow Signal Station, above the track at Gunrow's Down. This dates from 1794 and was part of a chain of twenty-five towers built to warn, via semaphore, of invasion by Napoleon's *Grande Armée*; other examples survive at Dodman Head in section 34 and Steeple Cove in section 45.

Stoke Point marks the entrance to Bigbury Bay, with Burgh Island hogging the view ahead. However, the vista is temporarily obscured as Revelstoke Drive arcs inland around Stoke House and Revelstoke Park, the latter a caravan park which remains out of view until you are past. The still-consecrated ruins of St Peter the Poor Fisherman Church (1226) overlook Stoke Beach; to visit this evocative site, side-tour down the caravan park's entrance road.

Revelstoke Drive departs the SWCP with a sharp left turn at Beacon Hill, overlooked by a ruined folly; Membland Pleasure House was built in 1765 and later used as a lookout tower. The very steep, cratered and pockmarked path makes for quite a change in character! This section's remainder alternately threads through corn fields and clings to precipitous slopes above isolated beaches: glorious, but disconcerting if you are racing the clock to catch low tide at the River Erme!

After a second big descent to Carswell Cove (just to confuse, there are two Carswell Coves), the path climbs to St Anchorite's Rock, a huge igneous dolerite tor rearing from the hillside. It doesn't seem to be named for an actual saint; anchorite literally means 'hermit'.

📷 *Bugle Rocks.*

Keaton Cove, Gull Cove, Butcher's Cove and Bugle Hole are successive enclosed beaches, guarded by extraordinary reef formations. The imposing Bugle Rocks, seen up close when you descend (again) to a footbridge, are so-named because of the noise made when waves compress against their slate slabs.

Idyllic Meadowsfoot Beach (also known as, Mothecombe Beach) marks the entrance to the River Erme's estuary. The path passes before a rustic boathouse; note also the limekiln converted to a beach house. This sandy respite is short-lived: steep steps lead over wooded Owen's Hill to deposit you further up-estuary at Mothecombe Road's end. Mothecombe House and Gardens (the latter are open to the public) are 250m uphill along the road; the centrepiece of the Flete Estate, which extends along the estuary.

If you are continuing across the River Erme to enjoy more of this fabulous wild coast, then hopefully you timed your arrival correctly …

📷 *The River Erme.*

44 Mothecombe to Hope Cove

Distance	16.1km / 10 miles	**Height gain** 550m / 1,800ft	**Difficulty** ●●●●●
Maps	OS Landranger 202 / OS Explorer OL20		
Start	Mothecombe PL8 1LB / pelted.fend.degrading / SX 614 475		
Finish	Hope Cove car park TQ7 3HH / scramble.repeat.debating / SX 675 397		
Parking near start	Mothecombe car park PL8 1LB / packages.scrambles.muffin / SX 611 478		
Public transport	No options under four and a half hours!		

Bigbury Bay's shores, always attractive, start hilly and remote but become decreasingly so along the way. This section involves two very different river crossings; check the timings for these before setting out!

An information sign (with tide times) marks where the SWCP crosses the River Erme's estuary. Assuming that you've timed your arrival with low tide, you are presented with a gorgeous sandy expanse, stretching seawards and winding upriver between wooded valley sides. The river ambles through the centre of this, hopefully just a bubbling, shallow stream. This is the South West's quietest and least developed ria, enjoy.

There is no ferry, it's necessary to wade across. You are aiming for a slipway upstream on the east shore, about 600m away. The usual course is to follow Coastguards Beach, the west shore, upriver, crossing a shallow side-channel below a line of coastguard cottages, before tackling the main river channel.

Crossing the River Erme

The safe time to cross is up to an hour either side of low tide; Google 'Plymouth tides' before setting out. It may be possible to cross for an hour or more outside this window, but if the river channel is submerged by the tide, then it's a no-go.

The crossing should be ankle- to knee-deep, across a pebbly riverbed. Walking poles will help your balance and this is one of the few scenarios where 'Croc' shoes are socially acceptable.

If the river looks brown or swollen from heavy rain, the crossing should not be attempted. The alternatives are a grinding thirteen-kilometre road trek around, an expensive taxi (public transport takes all day), or starting from the east shore (very limited parking).

The east shore's slipway ascends to a lane; the route turns away from this to follow the estuary shore south. Passing Wonwell Beach (pronounced 'won-ell') look for a ruined limekiln and overgrown chimney remains, used by fishermen to boil their shellfish.

There are stunning views upriver from Muxham Point, at Erme Mouth. Just offshore at West Mary's Rock, divers recovered forty-two tin ingots from a Bronze Age shipwreck, believed to have sunk c1000BC whilst voyaging downriver from Dartmoor to Burgh Island. This and a similar site near Salcombe are Britain's oldest shipwrecks.

From Fernycombe Beach to Challaborough, the SWCP tackles a succession of steep climbs and isolated beaches, with glorious vistas along Bigbury Bay.

The Beacon is so-named as, in 1588, the hundred-metre summit was lit to warn of the Spanish Armada's approach. Thousands of locals gathered to witness the entire fleet of 130 galleons sail close by. The path dips briefly into the Freshwater valley where, in desperation during a heatwave, the author refilled water at a sheep trough. A stone bench marks Hoist Point's summit.

The slick slates, siltstones and sandstones forming Bigbury Bay's razor-edged cliffs and reefs are all Devonian, but Westcombe Beach is the geological boundary between the older Dartmouth group and younger Meadfoot group. Caves accessible from the beach at low tide reputedly have iron moorings used by smugglers (explore carefully!). The stable ruins near the footbridge were used by the Flete Estate, for seaside excursions.

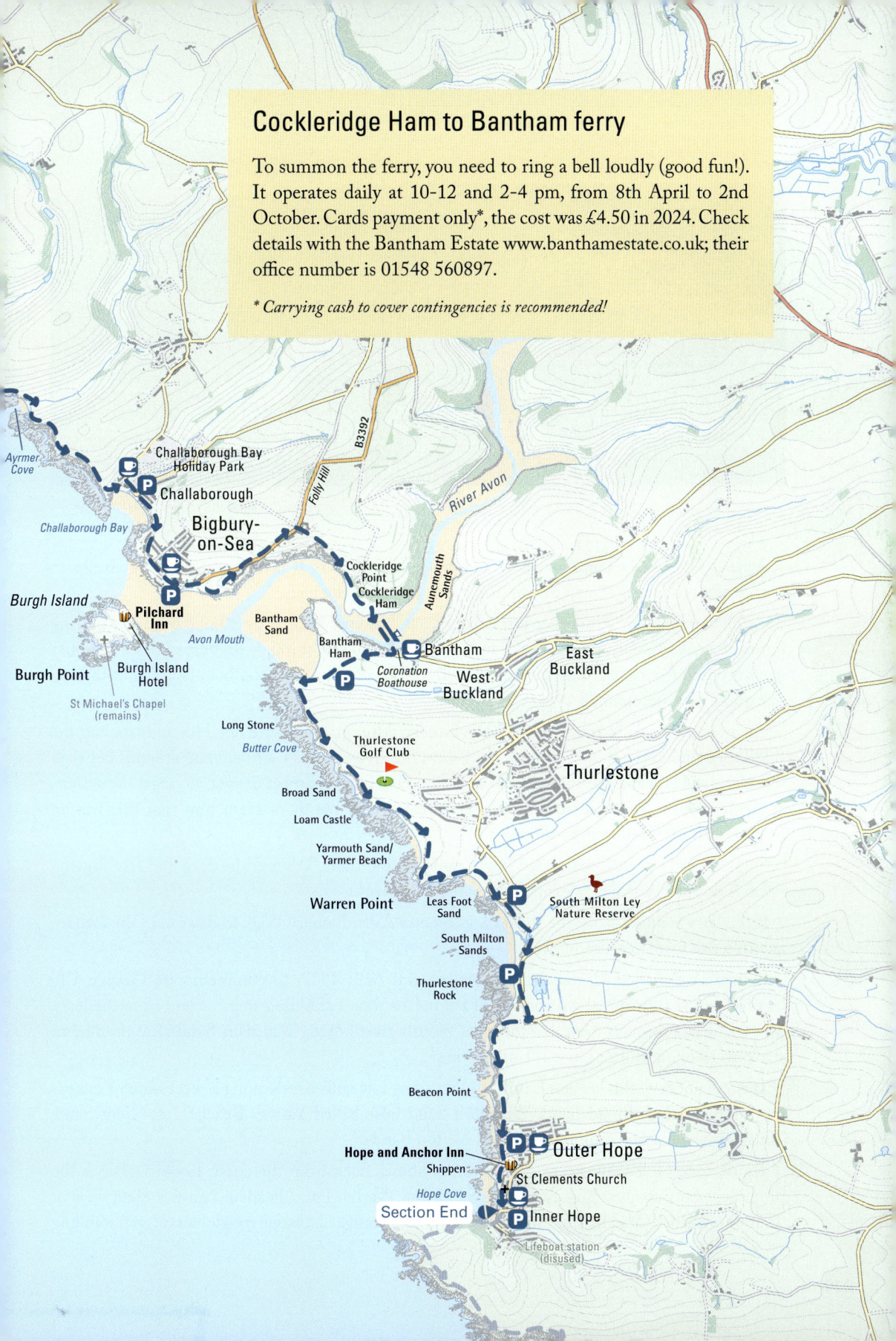

Bigbury Bay and Burgh Island.

Ayrmer Cove is a second lovely, often empty, sandy beach. It is bookended by big climbs to both reach and escape it, and by imposing slate peaks on the reefs.

Challaborough Bay is another attractive beach, however backed by a holiday park; a jarring return to civilisation. Surfaced tracks and roads lead into and through Bigbury-on-Sea. Bigbury itself is uninteresting, but it is connected to Burgh Island by a sand tombolo (spit); side-touring to explore is recommended.

The route now heads up the River Avon estuary. After grinding up Folly Hill and crossing the B3392, a wonderful panorama opens up: below, the Avon passes Bantham and s-bends between Cockleridge Ham and Bantham Ham's gorse-covered dunes to meet the sea, amongst the surfers, at Avon Mouth. North African amphorae uncovered at Bantham Ham hint that this was an important Early Medieval trading post.

Steps deposit you at Cockleridge Point, opposite Bantham. Wading the deep and fast-flowing Avon is not practical; a sign explains how the ferry works.

If the ferry is unavailable, the thirteen-kilometre Avon Estuary Walk leads around the estuary, an attractive road-free alternative.

Bantham's thatched Coronation Boathouse was built 1937, to commemorate George VI's coronation. At the time of writing, a cliff fall means that scaffolding steps ascend from the ferry. The trail leads through dunes to the river mouth, overlooking Bantham Sand. The prominent stack overlooking Butter Cove is Long Stone.

The remainder of this section is mild-going, along low cliffs overlooking a succession of tempting sandy beaches: Broad Sand, Yarmouth Sand (also called Yarmer Beach), Leas Foot Sand, Thurlstone Sand and (adjoining) South Milton Sands.

Thurlestone Golf Club keeps Thurlestone's houses back from the coast. Loam Castle is the prominent buttress guarding Yarmouth Sand, and Warren Point headland gives a great view of Thurlestone Rock (Middle English *thirl*: hole), an impressive sandstone conglomerate arch standing

📷 *Hope Cove and the Shippen.*

isolated, offshore from South Milton Sands. The latter is reached via a long footbridge, behind the dunes, crossing South Milton Ley Nature Reserve's reedbeds, a wetland habitat for warblers.

A final easy climb leads over (another) Beacon Point to Hope Cove. There are two conjoined villages, both attractive with thatched buildings. Outer Hope is the larger, with the Hope and Anchor Inn overlooking Mouthwell Sands, which is guarded by a cannon and anchor recovered from a Spanish ship, wrecked in 1630. The Shippen promontory divides Outer Hope from Inner Hope. The *San Pedro el Mayor*, the Spanish Armada's hospital ship, was wrecked on the Shippen in 1588, *"through the tempestuous weather broken in pieces and scattered on the seashore"* according to a contemporary letter. The 140 survivors were, mercifully, ransomed.

Inner Hope's beach is sheltered by a breakwater. Hope Cove car park is located past tiny St Clements Church, a 'chapel of ease' built for fishermen in 1861.

Burgh Island

At high tide, the island is reached by 'sea tractor', a trailer on stilts. Across the tombolo spit, the Pilchard Inn has been operating since 1336! Smuggler Tom Crocker was reputedly shot outside. The Burgh Island Hotel, built 1929-32, showcases classic Art Deco design, intended to resemble a white ocean liner. Luminaries such as Josephine Baker, Winston Churchill, Noel Coward and Wallis Simpson stayed here, but the most famous association is with Agatha Christie. She located her novels *And Then There Were None* and *Evil Under the Sun* at the hotel, the latter actually written there.

At the island's highest point, St Michael's Chapel (dating from at least 1411) was part of a monastery, later used as a huer's hut: a fishermen's lookout.

Sharp Tor.

📷 *Starehole Bay.*

45 Hope Cove to Salcombe

Distance 13.3km / 8.3 miles	**Height gain** 450m / 1,450ft **Difficulty** ●●●○○
Maps	OS Landranger 202 / OS Explorer OL20
Start	Hope Cove car park TQ7 3HH / scramble.repeat.debating / SX 675 397
Finish	Salcombe to East Portlemouth ferry, Salcombe TQ8 8JE / corrupted.drops.airship / SX 741 388
Parking near finish	Creek car park, Salcombe TQ8 8DU / rotation.swing.prepped / SX 739 393
Public transport	162 and 164 buses, change at South Milton. Not at weekends

This section connects two lofty headlands, Bolt Tail and Bolt Head, with the going sharply polarised between easy strolls along a grassland plateau and exhilarating rock-strewn climbs and descents.

Tiny, inoffensive-looking Hope Cove has enjoyed a long and violent association with smuggling. In 1785, a customs officer was murdered when he was thrown off a cliff. Three years later, a customs officer suffered a fractured skull, and another was crippled. In 1823, eighteen local women were sent to Exeter gaol for assaulting a coastguard.

Steps depart Hope Cove beside the old lifeboat station. A path climbs through woods above the cove and out onto open slopes approaching Bolt Tail. The route cuts across the headland's neck following a stone wall and earthwork, but it's only a short deviation out to Bolt Tail. The earthworks are the ramparts of an Iron Age cliff castle, which has been linked to the *Dumnonii*: the Iron Age tribe who gave their name to Devon.

The Salcombe lifeboat disaster

The Bar, the sand spit guarding the entrance to the Kingsbridge Estuary, was in 1916 responsible for the loss of the Salcombe lifeboat *William and Emma*. The crew rowed to aid the schooner *Western Lass*, grounded near Start Point. They arrived to find the crew already rescued. Crossing The Bar homewards, the lifeboat capsized in steep breakers. Thirteen of the fifteen lifeboatmen drowned, their names commemorated on Salcombe War Memorial.

With its unrelenting, precipitous cliffs, this section could be described purely in terms of shipwrecks: only a handful are outlined here. In 1760, the warship *HMS Ramillies* foundered on Bolt Tail after confusing it with Rame Head. Only twenty-six of 850 crew survived. A happier outcome followed the 1907 stranding of the *SS Jebba*, in fog (the same night that the *SS Suevic* was wrecked, section 30). Two local fishermen scrambled down Bolt Tail's sixty-metre cliffs to rig bosun's chairs, rescuing all seventy-six crew and seventy-nine passengers. Edward VII awarded the Albert Medal to both men.

A gradually ascending path passes intermittent clifftop crags onto 130m Bolberry Down, Second World War site of the Bolt Tail Radar Station. Hidden close to the cliff top is 'Ralph's Hole', a cave named after a smuggler who used a pitchfork to prevent customs officials from investigating within!

West Cliff also claimed a fog victim, in 1925. The tug *Joffre*'s crew were saved after the Mate swam a rope ashore, however the Captain died of exhaustion afterwards. Cathole Cliff follows; the path narrows along a ridge crest, tacking from side to side down gorse-covered outcrops to Soar Mill Cove. Twin valleys cleave into the schist strata to converge at the cove, overlooked by

the crags of Hazel Tor. Soar Mill Cove, the sole chink in this section's cliffs, is partially sheltered by the Priest and Clerk stacks. The isolated rock 400m further out is Ham Stone, which caused one of the last sailing shipwrecks; the Finnish *Herzogin Cecilie* in 1936. The wreck was towed into Starehole Bay and sunk; the outline is still discernible.

A craggy 130m ascent, including boardwalks, leads back atop the clifftop plateau, site of Second World War airfield *RAF Bolt Tail*. Look out for a square tower with a pyramidal roof, 150m north of the path: this is a rare, intact Admiralty signal station, built c1795 to warn against invasion by Bonaparte. On the opposite side of the path, far below, is the sheer-walled inlet of Steeple Cove. After the Spanish freighter *Cantabria* ran aground in 1932 (again, in fog), all twenty four crew attempted to scale the cliffs! They were fortunately discovered and retrieved by lifeboat.

The path forks, the fork ahead giving a preview of Starehole Bay. The SWCP follows the right fork, downhill along an airy path around Bolt Head's slopes, high above the Mew Stones. The horizons expand to encompass Prawle Point, Devon's southernmost tip (section 46).

Starehole Bay is a spectacular finale to this exhilarating stretch of cliffs. The path clings to steep slopes and climbs steps through Sharp Tor, a vertical array of Devonian schist spikes pierced

📷 *Kingsbridge Estuary.*

by a large 'stare hole'. Starehole could, alternatively, mean a trackway for transporting seaweed. This and the wooded track onwards towards Salcombe are the Courtenay Walk, engineered for Viscount Courtenay in the 1860s. He lived at The Moult, a pink mansion alongside South Sands.

Kingsbridge Estuary is actually a ria. The Bar guards the entrance, a shallow sand spit.

The road into Salcombe passes Overbecks, a National Trust property. Otto Overbeck, eccentric resident from 1928, became rich from his 'Rejuventor' electrotherapy machine. He bequeathed the house to the NT on the condition that they didn't convert it into a brothel! The sub-tropical gardens are well worth a visit. Sadly, since 2020 the NT have cut costs by keeping this engaging Edwardian house closed.

Two beaches lead into town: a steep road climb divides South Sands from North Sands. Fort Charles guards the latter, a Henrician fort which was among the last Royalist strongholds to surrender in the Civil War. It was then 'slighted' (blown up), explaining its current decrepitude.

Salcombe's affluent villas and yacht clubs contrast sharply with its smuggling and piracy heritage. In 1607, a magistrate described it, *"full of dissolute seafaring men who murder each other and bury the corpses in the sands at night"*.

The ferry to East Portlemouth departs from Salcombe Landing, alongside the Ferry Inn on Fore Street. In winter, it departs from Whitestrand Quay, 200m north.

Salcombe to East Portlemouth ferry

The ferry runs year-round between 8.30 am and 6.30 pm (reduced hours from November 1st). Cards or cash are accepted*, the cost was £2.30 in 2024. Check details by calling 07769 319375.

In summer, an alternative service runs from South Sands beach.

* Carrying cash to cover contingencies is recommended!

◉ *Elender Cove and Gammon Head.*

46 East Portlemouth to Hallsands

Distance 16.7km / 10.4 miles	**Height gain** 575m / 1,900ft **Difficulty** ● ● ● ● ●
Maps	OS Landranger 202 / OS Explorer OL20
Start	Salcombe to East Portlemouth ferry, East Portlemouth TQ8 8PU / denoting.hint.enacts / SX 743 387
Finish	Hallsands beach car park TQ7 2EX / oatmeal.recently.nutty / SX 817 388
Parking near start	East Portlemouth car park, East Portlemouth TQ8 8PD / dissolve.weeds.evidently / SX 746 385
Public transport	Only options are from Torcross (section 47), via Salcombe to East Portlemouth Ferry

This exceptional outing, at Devon's southernmost extremity, is one of the author's favourites. Dramatic rocky trails and short, sharp ascents are interspersed with low-lying fields, backed by ancient sea cliffs.

The ferry from Salcombe lands beside a café. The route leads south alongside the Kingsbridge Estuary to Mill Bay's popular beach, then along a woodland path behind secret beaches to Rickham Common, where views open out across the estuary's entrance. A memorial plaque at Limebury Point commemorates the 1916 Salcombe lifeboat disaster (page 224).

The SWCP traverses along the steep, craggy slopes of Portlemouth Down, with waves surging through and over reefs far below. A white tower topped with a conical thatched roof looks down on the path from Gara Rock, part of an 1847 coastguard station. Gara Rock Hotel is hidden behind.

The SWCP descends to two adjacent beaches, both (confusingly) with two names; Rickham Sand aka Abraham's Hole is followed by Seacombe Sand aka Gara Rock Beach! Bronze Age field systems can be picked out on the hillside backing the beach. More recently, Deckler's Cliff was mined for iron: the keen-eyed will identify where a tramway linked to Deckler's Island, which was served by a pier until a ship loading ore was wrecked in 1859.

A spectacular hoard of Bronze Age tin, copper and gold has been recovered from a wreck site 200m offshore of Venerick's Cove, which the path traverses above. Pig's Nose is a small headland before the spectacular stretch across Gammon Head to Prawle Point: an exposed rocky trail above hemmed-in Maceley and Elender Coves. Gammon Head's severely serrated profile reputedly resembles Queen Victoria, but a better point of reference might be Sonic the Hedgehog.

Approaching the Coastwatch lookout station atop Prawle Point's forty-metre cliffs, the path passes through a distinctive wall of upright slates; known locally as a 'shiner'. Prawle Point (Old English *præwhyll*: lookout hill) is Devon's southernmost tip.

Descending past a row of Coastguard cottages, the remarkable view eastwards is an instant geology lesson! Craggy outcrops such as Fish-in-the-Well Rock and Lobeater Rock rear behind the corn fields around Langerstone Point; these are ancient sea cliffs and the fields are raised

beaches, formed when the sea rose during an inter-glacial period 120,000 years ago and subsequently left high and dry.

The now-easier SWCP threads a path along this low shore, among thrift and sea campion, where the raised beaches give way to wave-cut ledges extending seawards. These reefs are criss-crossed by channels where surging breakers have exploited weaknesses in the Devonian strata and occasionally broken through to produce small sandy beaches. Looking back, you'll spy the angular sea arch below Prawle Point, wave-sculpted from green-tinted metamorphic hornblende schist.

This area has seen an ecological success story in encouraging the recovery of the rare cirl bunting, a striking yellow-brown farm bird. Habitat preservation by coastal farmers has led to numbers increasing tenfold, with over a thousand pairs across South Devon.

After passing in front of Maelcombe House, the once-again rocky and uneven path is shaded by trees as it passes around Woodcombe Point. There is a brief inland diversion around Woodcombe Sand (due to a rock fall) before tiny Lannacombe Beach is reached, where grinding stones lie beside a former corn mill.

Low cliffs along The Narrows reach Great Mattiscombe Sand, where a pair of peculiar 'earth pillars' on the reef have resisted erosion, due to being capped by harder rocks.

📷 *Start Point.*

The final stretch is an exposed almost-scramble around Peartree Point and across the adjacent Start Point (Old English *steort*: tail), a jutting sawtooth ridge of mica schist. Start Point Lighthouse guards the entrance to Start Bay, James Walker's 1836 design incorporating gothic battlements. The fog signal house collapsed into the sea in 1989, necessitating substantial rebuilding. Off Start Point, Black Stone harbours a colony of Atlantic grey seals.

A car park above Start Point boasts a grand viewpoint of Start Bay, arcing northwards. The SWCP makes a start on this new coastline with a gradual descent across gorse-covered slopes, into the village of Hallsands. Look for Old Hallsands viewpoint, just off the route; an information board explains that the shattered ruins clinging to rocks below were once a thriving village comprising thirty-seven homes.

The death of Old Hallsands

From 1897, sand and gravel were dredged from Start Bay for the construction of Plymouth's docks. The authorities took heed of complaints that Hallsand's beach was receding and ended dredging in 1902. On 26th January 1917, an easterly gale combined with spring tides created a storm surge; the beach was overtopped, and four houses destroyed. Hallsand's 128 residents retrieved what they could, before a second surge left just one house standing.

Blackpool Sands.

47 Hallsands to Dartmouth

Distance	20.3km / 12.6 miles **Height gain** 550m / 1,800ft **Difficulty** ●●●○○
Maps	OS Landranger 202 / OS Explorer OL20
Start	Hallsands beach car park TQ7 2EX / oatmeal.recently.nutty / SX 817 388
Finish	Dartmouth to Kingswear ferry, Dartmouth TQ6 9AP / motivate.catchers.turkeys / SX 878 510
Parking near finish	Mayor's Avenue car park, Dartmouth TQ6 9NF / highways.enveloped.duke / SX 878 514
Public transport	Only possible from Torcross: 93 bus

North from Hallsands' beach car park, you can see how this section pans out: a mostly-flat first half following Start Bay's curving shingle beach, followed by a distinctly un-flat second half.

A mild climb along fields leads over Tinsey Head to Beesands. Descending, you'll spot the hefty seawall protecting its smatter of houses and pubs, and the 1883 Mission Room, now St Andrew's Church. The small lagoon behind is Widdicombe Ley.

A track leads to Sunnydale House, behind boats drawn up on the pebbles. The SWCP ascends a narrow path, above Dun Point and past the overgrown former Beesands Quarry. The zigzagging descent into Torcross gives a sense of déjà vu: like Beesands, Torcross is a sea wall-protected beachfront village, alongside a brackish lagoon. However, Lower Ley presents a grander vista; the largest natural lake in the South West, protected by a pebble ridge formed by sea level rises, c3000 years ago.

📷 *Torcross.*

Exercise Tiger

The Sherman tank at Torcross was placed there in 1984 but had previously spent four decades underwater. In 1974, local businessman Ken Small bought the 34-ton tank from the US Government, for $50. A decade later, he raised it from the seabed.

On 27-28th April 1944, a full-scale rehearsal for the D-Day landings was held at Slapton Sands. Due to communication errors and poor planning, it was a catastrophe. Over 300 soldiers died after clambering ashore, shelled by live ammunition. German E-boats slipped into the exercise area and torpedoed three of the landing ships. At least 946 US servicemen died in Exercise Tiger, the bodies buried in mass graves on local farms. The disaster was hushed up, with participants sworn to secrecy.

A Sherman tank overlooks the lagoon and beach. This is a memorial to the forgotten US soldiers and sailors of the Second World War's Exercise Tiger.

A sandy gravel path threads, for three kilometres, alongside the reeds of Slapton Ley National Nature Reserve. The Reserve's lagoons are home to otters, great crested grebes, Cetti's warbler and the rare cirl bunting, only found in south Devon. The only interruption is a road crossing near Slapton Bridge (a good place to spot cirl bunting). The obelisk on the beach is the Slapton Monument, erected to thank the 3,000 locals evacuated from surrounding villages, to facilitate D-Day training. At time of writing, plans were afoot to relocate it near Strete Gate, due to coastal erosion.

From Strete Gate, the SWCP climbs along a woodland track, before a harsh switch-backing ascent to the A379. Strete village was Street until 1870, changed to avoid confusion with a Somerset namesake.

Back on paths, the Landcombe valley, recognisable by its lone tree, comes as a jolt: a sudden big descent followed by a steep climb over a hillside.

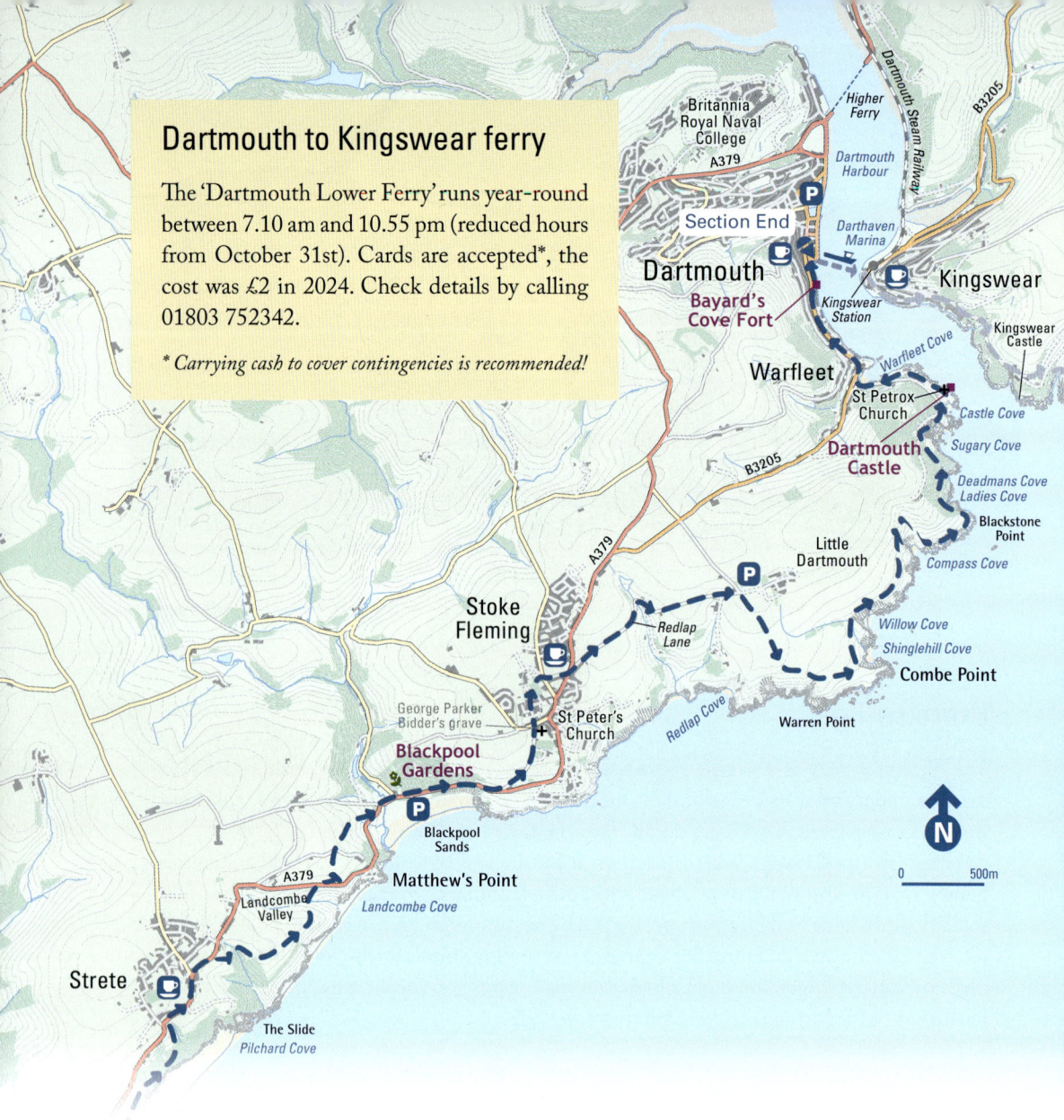

Not to be confused with the Lancashire resort, Blackpool Sands is a lovely strand (not sand), backed by woodland. In 1404, the Battle of Blackpool Sands took place here! Local peasant militia mustered by privateer John Hawley repelled William du Chastel's French force of 2,000 men, landed from 300 ships. The SWCP passes behind, but the beach is a pleasant spot to soak your toes. Across the road is the sub-tropical Blackpool Gardens.

The sea is departed for a significant distance, following unremarkable quiet lanes. A steep lane reaches Stoke Fleming village; George Parker Bidder is buried at St Peter's Church (1272), the 'calculating boy' who, alongside George Stephenson, engineered the early railways. A slog along Redlap Lane eventually reaches the National Trust's Little Dartmouth estate car park, where the SWCP thankfully veers back towards the coast.

📷 *Dartmouth.*

Warren Point, site of a nineteenth-century rabbit warren, commences a delightful clifftop stretch. Wild flowers line the path, and there are views past the River Dart's mouth to Mew Stone (section 48) and The Tower, a twenty-four-metre hexagonal daymark above Inner Froward Point, built in 1864 to welcome Royal Mail ships returning from the colonies. A succession of inaccessible coves is hemmed in by slabby silver cliffs; Shinglehill and Willow Coves are sheltered by Combe Point, Compass Cove (connected to Guernsey by telegraph cable from 1870 until the Second World War) is circumvented by a rugged path descending towards Blackstone Point. Ladies and Deadmans Coves are passed along a wooded track, and a splendid cliff-clinging walkway negotiates innumerable steps above Sugary Cove and Castle Cove, to reach Dartmouth Castle.

Dartmouth Castle originated c1388 as an artillery fort, upgraded with a chain across the Dart in 1462, with Kingswear Castle added as back-up, in 1491. It saw use in both the Civil Wars and Second World War. The SWCP passes a wall from the original *fortalice*, then descends between the English Heritage-owned castle and Dartmouth Light, a nineteenth-century tower used as a café. The unusually sited St Petrox Church, whose tall tower was added c1641, predates the surrounding fortifications.

A roadside trudge reaches Dartmouth proper. Warfleet Cove is so-named as, in 1147, c200 ships assembled here to sail for the Holy Land and Second Crusade, followed in 1190 by Richard the Lionheart's fleet bound for the Third Crusade.

Dartmouth is an attractive sight, a sheltered anchorage hemmed in by steep hillsides. Britannia Royal Naval College, opened in 1905, sprawls impressively behind; from 1863, officer training was conducted in ships on the river. Luminaries who have attended include King Charles III (the author's application, back in the '90s, failed due to eyesight issues and, possibly, insufficient royal blood). Across the River Dart, Kingswear's colourful houses rise in serried terraces.

Steps descend to Dartmouth's waterfront, through hulking Bayard's Cove Fort (1537). The Kingswear ferry departs at a protruding embankment, constructed by Napoleonic prisoners.

📷 *Pudcombe Cove.*

48 Kingswear to Brixham

Distance 18.2km / 11.3 miles	**Height gain** 900m / 2,950ft **Difficulty** ●●●●●
Maps	OS Landranger 202 / OS Explorer OL20
Start	Dartmouth to Kingswear ferry, Kingswear TQ6 0AA / general.thud.firm / SX 881 510
Finish	Freshwater car park, Brixham TQ5 8BA / plant.boils.runs / SX 923 567
Parking near start	Darthaven Marina car park, Kingswear TQ6 0SG / breed.coder.disengage / SX 884 512
Public transport	18 bus

Charles Harper's 1907 guidebook *The South Devon Coast*: *"Rocks succeed sands, and sands follow rocks; headlands alternating with bays, and ups with downs ... Not a soul will you see!"*. 'Little has changed. This section becomes wonderfully isolated, with successive testing *"ups with downs"*. There are no facilities, until Berry Head.

Kingswear ('King's weir / mill') grew in the twelfth century as a staging post for pilgrimages to Thomas Becket's tomb at Canterbury. The Free French Navy based torpedo boats here during the Second World War, now Darthaven Marina dominates the shore.

The Dartmouth to Kingswear ferries land beside Kingswear railway station. This 1864 branch line was closed in 1968, by the Beeching cuts. Enthusiasts continued operating 'Dartmouth Steam Railway', which still connects with the national network at Paignton.

Escaping Kingswear begins by passing beneath the arch beside the Post Office and ascending the Alma Steps. Roads uphill join a private lane, passing among mansions crammed along the hillside.

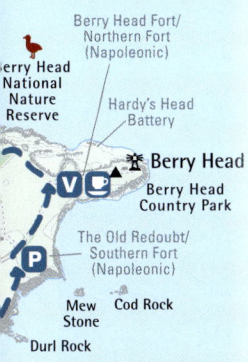

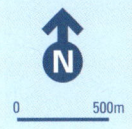

A track-side sign announces that you are entering Warren Woods, *'dedicated to the memory of Lieutenant Colonel Herbert Jones VC'*; Falklands War hero 'H' Jones grew up and lived at Kingswear. A steep descent to tiny Mill Bay Cove reaches a striking pseudo-fort; this was actually a water mill!

The SWCP ambles through pine woodlands around the headlands of The Warren and Inner Froward Point. There are glimpsed rear views of Dartmouth Castle and Kingswear Castle, facing across the River Dart's entrance. Kingswear Castle was built in 1491 as an artillery fort, but fell into disuse as cannon ranges improved. It was restored in the nineteenth century and is rented out by the Landmark Trust.

From the Coastwatch lookout station atop Inner Froward Point, the path descends through the well-preserved concrete remains of Brownstone Battery (1940), including gun emplacements, search-light positions and an inclined rail to transport shells downhill.

Between Inner Froward Point and Outer Froward Point, the woods disperse. Often-exposed paths traverse steep slopes, high above polished slabs of silvery Devonian bedrock. The views ahead are fine, but are nonetheless hijacked by the jagged bastions of Mew Stone, an igneous offshore rock surrounded by smaller siblings: Shag Stone and Shooter Rock. These are the English Channel's easternmost haul-outs for Atlantic grey seals, porpoises are also commonly spotted.

Precipitous Pudcombe Cove is shrouded by the planted woodlands (including fruit trees) of the National Trust's Coleton Fishacre estate. In the 1920s, the D'Oyly Cartes, the impresarios behind Gilbert and Sullivan operettas, constructed an Arts and Crafts Movement country house and exotic garden. The house (with café) is 300m uphill from the trail.

The toughest part ensues after Scabbacombe Head: the SWCP twice descends to remote beaches before climbing abruptly, through gorse corridors, to the 120m contour. The climb from Scabbacombe Sands summits above Long Sands, a beach which appears inaccessible but is nonetheless utilised by naturists. A calf-punishing descent drops you at (stunning) Man Sands, overlooked by a line of coastguard cottages and backed by a brackish lagoon, with a disused limekiln close to the sea. The subsequent climb rewards you with an airy traverse atop the slopes of Southdown Cliff.

Around Sharkham Point, the gradients ease. The Devonian limestone-mudstone cliffs, here and across St Mary's Bay at Berry Head, are a National Nature Reserve, hosting the south coast's largest breeding colony of cormorants. A thousand cormorants make a lot of noise, even before you factor in an additional thousand guillemots and significant numbers of razorbills, gulls, kittiwakes and fulmar. In early summer, this is a raucous place!

Golden Hind replica, Brixham.

The path around St Mary's Bay squeezes between the Riviera Bay Holiday Park and densely overgrown slopes. The view towards Berry Head's cliffs is punctuated by several offshore stacks: Durl Rock (quarried), Mew Stone (a different one) and Cod Rock. All are overlooked by The Old Redoubt, Berry Head's Southern Fort and part of Brixham's Napoleonic (1794-1804) defensive network.

Berry Head Country Park is entered past a car park. Limestone grasslands are covered, in early summer, by pink pyramidal orchids. You absolutely should make the lighthouse side-tour. The track leads through the grand walls of Berry Head Fort (also called the Northern Fort), passing a visitor centre and café. The 1906 lighthouse is an underwhelming five metres tall. It may however be England's highest, surrounded by near-vertical fifty-eight-metre cliffs. A toposcope plaque indicates that Portland Bill (sometimes visible) is forty-two miles east across Lyme Bay (almost a hundred, via the SWCP).

Descending into Tor Bay and Brixham, you'll see that Berry Head's north side has been almost entirely quarried away. The ramparts of Hardy's Head Battery are passed, built in 1779 to defend not against Napoleon, but the Americans.

The shore is reached at Shoalstone Seawater Pool, a free-to-use Victorian outdoor lido. Along Berry Head Road, the path descends to 'The Breakwater' and follows the engaging waterfront past Brixham Marina into the attractive and busy harbour, where England's highest-value catch is landed. The *Man and Boy* statue depicts two fishermen at the wheel, honouring lives lost at sea.

At the back of the harbour, there is plenty of interest. Brixham Heritage Museum is just up Fore Street. An imposing statue of William III faces inland beside a full-size replica of Sir Francis Drake's *Golden Hind* (in which he circumnavigated the globe), a tourist attraction. William of Orange is also commemorated by the Prince of Orange Monument, a granite obelisk further around the bay which pompously proclaims that he set foot ashore, *'ON THIS STONE'* in 1688. This was the so-called Glorious Revolution, when parliament invited William to sail from Holland and overthrow James II, a Catholic.

Freshwater car park is in the former Freshwater Quarry, just past the Fish market.

📷 *Paignton Pier.*

49 Brixham to Torquay

Distance 13.1km / 8.1 miles	**Height gain** 450m / 1450ft **Difficulty** ● ● ○ ○ ○
Maps	OS Landranger 202 / OS Explorer OL20
Start	Freshwater car park, Brixham TQ5 8BA / plant.boils.runs / SX 923 567
Finish	Beacon Quay car park, Torquay TQ1 2BG / goat.agents.gazed / SX 918 631
Public transport	12 bus, or Western Lady Ferry

Welcome to the English Riviera! We have the Georgians to thank for this moniker; when the Napoleonic Wars prevented continental travel, they convinced themselves that Tor Bay looked like Mediterranean France. Torquay and Paignton sprawled around the bay, boosted by the railway's arrival (in 1848 and 1859, respectively). The outcome is that this section predominantly follows concrete promenades and busy roads. Approach these with a 'glass half-full' attitude, there are plenty of points of interest.

Tor Bay's southern rim is actually rather lovely. The SWCP passes Brixham Laboratory (part of Plymouth University) to enter Battery Gardens. These aren't cultivated gardens, but an overgrown Second World War battery with gun emplacements surviving. Battery Point's defences date back to the Spanish Armada! At Fishcombe Cove, the path climbs steeply inland to Brixham Battery Heritage Centre, recognisable (or maybe not) by the camouflaged exterior; this is a great, free, museum of wartime memorabilia.

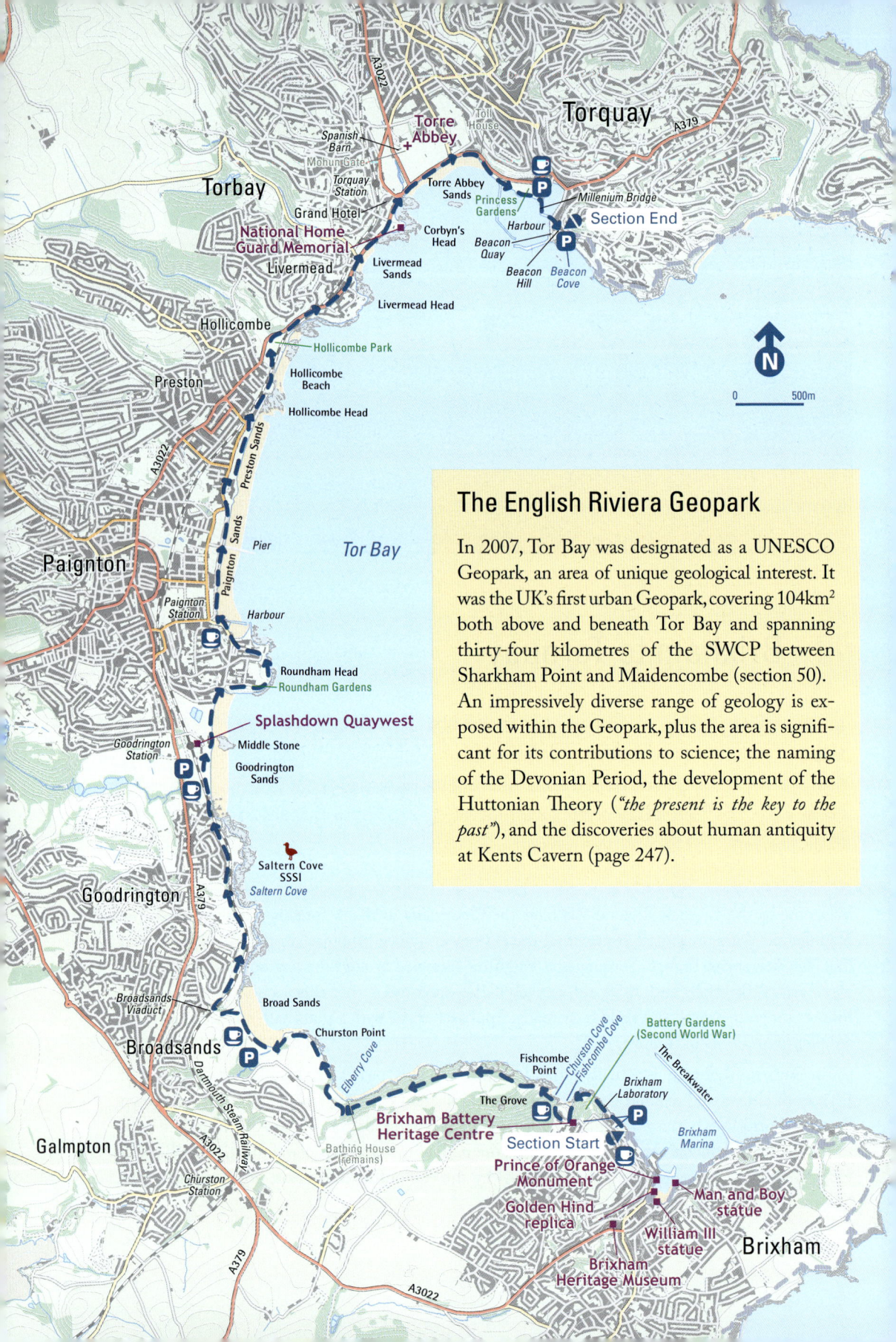

The English Riviera Geopark

In 2007, Tor Bay was designated as a UNESCO Geopark, an area of unique geological interest. It was the UK's first urban Geopark, covering 104km² both above and beneath Tor Bay and spanning thirty-four kilometres of the SWCP between Sharkham Point and Maidencombe (section 50). An impressively diverse range of geology is exposed within the Geopark, plus the area is significant for its contributions to science; the naming of the Devonian Period, the development of the Huttonian Theory (*"the present is the key to the past"*), and the discoveries about human antiquity at Kents Cavern (page 247).

📷 *Dartmouth Steam Railway at Saltern Cove.*

The path descends into Churston Cove, a tiny beach with wooded shores, sheltered by Fishcombe Point. Steep zigzagging steps ascend through The Grove woodland. The path contours, through woods, for two root-strewn kilometres, with the sea mostly obscured. Pebbly Elberry Cove is the last undeveloped beach of the day, notable for the strange fort-like ruin at its eastern end. This was Lord Churston's private bathing house! The three-storey eighteenth-century building, containing cold and hot-water pools, was in use until the 1960s.

Enjoy the grassy trail around Churston Point; from here on the coast is increasingly developed with surfaced paths. An arc of multi-coloured beach huts backs Broad Sands' beach, then the SWCP passes beneath Brunel's Broadsands Viaduct and follows the inshore side of the Dartmouth Steam Railway, with Goodrington's houses and caravan parks behind. Note rocky Saltern Cove, a SSSI which (uniquely) extends 376 metres underwater.

The path passes beneath the railway to Goodrington Sands, where the beach huts are overshadowed by Splashdown Quaywest's looping waterslides, claimed to be *'the UK's largest all outdoor waterpark'*. Presumably, no one has told them about the 'sea'.

Roundham Head is the sandstone-cliffed headland jutting out into the centre of Tor Bay. The SWCP passes beneath the pines and sycamores of pleasant Roundham Gardens, before reaching Paignton's small harbour via back streets. Paignton Sands stretch north, the promenade backed by a buffer zone of open ground (complete with amusements, such as crazy golf) separating it from the town's innumerable hotels. Paignton Pier is long (240m) and graceful. Opened in 1879, fire devastated it in 1919 but it was restored in the 1980s. This classic seaside paraphernalia has a certain charm, deserving appreciation for its heritage aspect.

The SWCP briefly diverts inland, around a hotel, between Paignton Sands and Preston Sands: alternatively, at low tide follow the beach. Preston Sands, with its colourful huts, ends at Hollicombe Head's cliffs, where the SWCP crosses the railway and leads inland through Hollicombe Park to the A3022.

📷 *Torquay.*

The trek along the busy A3022 can (fairly) be described as grim, punctuated only by the opposing 'Welcome to Torquay' and 'Welcome to Paignton' signs: the agony of choice! The A3022 passes behind Livermead Head to reach the sea again at Livermead Sands; if the tide is out, you can briefly escape the pavement. The A3022 also bypasses Corbyn's Head, but a short deviation around this grassy promontory may be welcome. Reputedly named for pirate Samuel Corbyn who was hanged here, the name simply derives from the French *courbe*, meaning a curved headland. The National Home Guard Memorial commemorates 1,206 Home Guard volunteers killed, '*by enemy action*', as well as five killed at this spot in a 1944 shell firing accident.

The twin-spired Grand Hotel marks the start of the 'Agatha Christie Mile'. Christie, the bestselling author of all time, was born in Torquay in 1890. The 'Mile' includes the seafront and nearby streets, and highlights places connected to Christie: she honeymooned at the Grand Hotel.

The A3022 is supplanted by the even busier, four-lane, A379, following Torre Abbey Sands into the heart of Torquay. Should you dare attempt to cross the road, the parkland behind leads to Torre Abbey, which gave Torquay its name. Only ruins remain of the original 1196 monastery, but attractions include the Spanish Barn (which housed Armada prisoners in 1588), the 1320 Mohun Gate and the exotic gardens.

Swanky cafés and restaurants line the road from Torre Abbey Sands to the harbour, backed by cliffs. Look for a forlorn little stone hut at the end of these modern developments: built 1840, this Toll House is a reminder that the road was cut beneath the cliffs to open up Torquay as a resort.

The promenade backing Torquay Harbour is the Princess Gardens (named for Louise, Queen Victoria's fourth daughter), lined by palm trees introduced from New Zealand in the 1820s. The SWCP crosses the harbour's centre via the Millenium Bridge, a stylish footbridge in the form of a ship's sails, to reach Beacon Quay.

◎ *Long Quarry Point and Hope's Nose.*

50 Torquay to Shaldon

Distance	18km / 11.2 miles **Height gain** 775m / 2,550ft **Difficulty** ● ● ● ● ○
Maps	OS Landranger 192, 202 / OS Explorer OL44
Start	Beacon Quay car park, Torquay TQ1 2BG / goat.agents.gazed / SX 918 631
Finish	Shaldon to Teignmouth ferry, Shaldon TQ14 0DL / doors.tells.breaches / SX 935 722
Parking near finish	The Ness car park, Shaldon TQ14 0HP / idea.acids.gazes / SX 938 718
Public transport	22 bus

This surprising section starts unpromisingly, amongst Torquay's hotels, but leads through a variety of engaging (and increasingly hilly) landscapes, with much to enjoy.

From Beacon Quay car park, Beacon Hill is ascended, past Beacon Cove where Agatha Christie swam as a teenager and on one occasion nearly drowned. The road is departed after the 1866 Imperial Hotel, which featured in several Christie novels but looks decidedly less imperial since its 1965 concrete refacing.

The path to Daddyhole Plain, known as Rock End Walk, is quite eccentric. It squeezes along the clifftop (a side-path overlooks the London Bridge natural arch), contouring up and down steps and at one point passing through an 1840s folly tower, a remnant of demolished Rock End House.

Daddyhole Plain is a grassy quarried plateau, home to a Coastwatch lookout station. The name refers to the Devil, who apparently dwelled seventy-five metres below, in a cave, at Daddyhole

Thatcher Point.

Cove. In 1815, festivals were held here celebrating Napoleon's visit! En route to exile on St Helena, Bonaparte spent seven weeks anchored in *HMS Bellerophon* off Ore Stone, never touching English soil.

Hesketh Crescent is an arc of Regency houses. A roadside trudge leads behind Meadfoot Beach (where Victorian men bathed, the women segregated at Beacon Cove) and uphill to Kilmorie. You're *still* in Torquay, but nature is beginning to reassert itself. An unsurfaced(!) path loops around Thatcher Point, permitting scrutiny of Thatcher Rock, a twin-pronged stack which is a contender for the SWCP's most spectacular island.

Back alongside the road, you pass around Hope's Nose, the headland forming Tor Bay's northern entrance. The SWCP extends out and back along this attractive, but heavily quarried, promontory. Limestone grasslands descend to raised stone beaches, showcasing early Devonian fossilised corals. Offshore are Lead Stone and Ore Stone, home to Devon's largest breeding colony of kittiwakes.

The road is escaped again, via a lane signposted for Anstey's Cove. This path, around Black Head, is known as Bishop's Walk; it was constructed in the 1840s for the Bishop of Exeter. His modest residence, Bishopstowe, was until 2017 the Palace Hotel, close to Anstey's Cove car park where the SWCP re-emerges.

Kents Cavern

Kents Cavern is 450m inland from Anstey's Cove car park. Now a tourist attraction, this is the UK's earliest known human habitation site. Flint hand axes from the caves were left by *Homo Heidelbergensis* (half a million years ago) and also Neanderthals, while a *Homo Sapiens* jawbone found here may be 44,000 years old: the oldest modern human discovered in North West Europe. John MacEnery, a local chaplain who excavated in the 1820s, discovered tools *beneath* the stalagmites and realised that this challenged the accepted date of Creation, 4004BC.

The road is left once more, to climb onto Walls Hill, site of an Iron Age hillfort overlooking the jagged remnants of Long Quarry Point, which has indeed been quarried away.

Steep lanes descend to a small pier at Babbacombe Beach. The path traverses boardwalks along and above the waterfront promenade to adjacent Oddicombe Beach, where it climbs up and passes beneath Babbacombe Cliff Railway. This funicular railway was built in 1926 astride a geological 'slip', the Sticklepath Fault. In 1884, local Emma Keys was murdered in a beach hut by John 'Babbacombe' Lee, who is remembered as 'the man they couldn't hang' after three attempts inexplicably failed.

A 2010 rockfall near Petit Tor Point diverts the SWCP inland up a grassy valley as far as the A379 in St Marychurch (a Torquay suburb), before immediately returning to the clifftop, following Petitor Road.

You've finally escaped Torquay's gravitational pull! The trails north to Shaldon now avoid settlements and also become significantly tougher-going, not least because the underlying geology has changed: the route traverses the 'Oddicombe Breccia', dark red Permian sandstone interweaved with older Devonian limestone, laid down by flash floods 250-300 million years ago.

Rocky, rooty red paths climb and descend the coastal hillside past Watcombe Beach, through overgrown jungly woodlands. The Valley of Rocks was a Victorian beauty spot, overshadowed by the fifty-metre-high Giant Rock cliff.

Maidencombe village remains out of sight, but its proximity is flagged up by the car park above Maidencombe Beach. Successive steep ascents and descents alternate between open fields and enclosed pathways, the consistent factor being that the adjacent red cliffs are obscured from view. The SWCP passes through Labrador Bay RSPB reserve, home to the rare cirl bunting. When the path, briefly, follows the A379, the end is in sight: as you descend, alongside Shaldon Approach Golf Course, to Bundle Head, there is a fine view of Teignmouth and The Ness.

The Ness (French *nez*: nose, or the Norse for headland) is the prominent wooded promontory overlooking Shaldon and the River Teign estuary. A tunnel passing through to Ness beach was reputedly used by smuggler Jack Rattenbury (page 262).

Shaldon is an attractive place, its houses crowded close along the beach. It was a centre of boat-building and fishing, until the estuary silted and industry moved cross-river to Teignmouth. On Wednesdays in summer ('1785 Days'), the locals dress up in costumes to commemorate a French attack.

If the ferry to Teignmouth is not running, the Teignmouth and Shaldon Bridge (1840) is 300m further up the estuary.

📷 *Langstone Rock from Exmouth.*

51 Teignmouth to Starcross

Distance	13km / 8.1 miles
Height gain	150m / 500ft
Difficulty	• • • •
Maps	OS Landranger 192 / OS Explorer OL44
Start	Lifeboat Lane, Teignmouth TQ14 8XZ / avoiding.overdone.twitching / SX 938 724
Finish	Starcross to Exmouth ferry, Starcross EX6 8NY / coping.booth.waters / SX 978 817
Parking near start	The Point car park, Teignmouth TQ14 8BL / bends.moral.smudges / SX 940 724
Parking near finish	The Strand car park, Starcross EX6 8PA / cherub.installs.townhouse / SX 976 821
Public transport	2 bus, or rail service

This is one of the SWCP's less inspiring sections, predominantly following straight and easy surfaced paths and roads. It is however not without interest, and if trains are your thing, then this might be your favourite section of all.

The small ferry from Shaldon hits land at Back Beach, where Teignmouth's fishing fleet is drawn up. This is the inland side of The Point, which shelters Teignmouth Harbour.

Teignmouth (pronounced 'tin-muth') was the last place in England to be invaded; the French landed in 1690, during the Nine Years' War, and burned the town.

The trek along Teignmouth's seafront commences at Teignmouth's diminutive (eleven-metre) lighthouse, built 1845. Georgian Den Crescent overlooks the slender Grand Pier. On completion in 1867, the 212m pier maintained propriety by segregating male and female bathers. It has

undergone numerous crises, including being breached to deter Nazi invaders during the Second World War and a 2014 storm-battering. However, this showpiece of Victorian heritage hangs on, the oldest of the SWCP's three surviving pleasure piers.

The remainder of this section is dominated by the South Devon Railway, which runs atop concrete sea defences and through tunnels, all the way to Starcross. Isambard Kingdom Brunel completed this feat of engineering in 1846, connecting Exeter to Plymouth and Torbay. He attempted to propel the trains quietly, installing vacuum pipes alongside the rails, but his 'Atmospheric Caper' experiment was abandoned after a year.

Reaching the sandstone cliffs where Teignmouth's seafront ends, the route splits. If the tide is high (beach covered) or if waves are breaking across the promenade, then you need to make an irritating inland diversion; turn off left at Teignmouth's Coastwatch lookout station and follow Eastcliff Walk uphill to the A379, which you follow to re-join the main route at Holcombe.

We have the Admiralty to thank for the SWCP's railway-side route, as they insisted that Brunel maintain waterfront access. The railway and SWCP are raised above a long sandy strand and overlooked by red cliffs displaying fossilised sand dunes. Newspapers regularly carry photographs of storm waves soaking passing trains; in 2014, sections of the railway were totally destroyed.

📷 *The Parson and Clerk.*

The promenade widens briefly, with a grassy picnic area at Sprey Point. Hole Head is marked by Shag Rock offshore and the Parson and Clerk formation, where a stack leans lazily against the headland. The parson and clerk were supposedly turned to stone by the Devil, for plotting to acquire the bishopric of Exeter.

The railway disappears into a tunnel; the path passes beneath the railway to reach Smugglers' Lane. The underpass floods at high tide, hence the inland diversion. The steep lane uphill to the A379 is so-named as smugglers cut contraband caves into the surrounding cliffs, later obliterated by railway construction.

The SWCP leaves the A379 and climbs over East Down, to re-join the coast. This welcome, but brief, break from surfaced promenade enjoys views of cliff-backed coves, before hitting tarmac again and zigzagging downhill to cross the railway via a footbridge into Dawlish railway station. The station's sea wall collapsed in 2014 and was rebuilt 2021-2.

Dawlish is centred on illuminated gardens alongside Dawlish Water, aka The Brook. Landscaped waterfalls are frequented by a population of black swans brought back from Western Australia by a local, in 1906. Charles Dickens made Dawlish the birthplace of Nicholas Nickleby and a stay by Jane Austen led to it featuring in *Sense and Sensibility*.

The SWCP continues alongside the railway from Dawlish, however when waves are breaking on the promenade, another inland diversion is advised: from Beach Street or the footbridge across the railway after the station, access the A379 and follow this, then a path, along the top of the cliffs. The diversion re-joins the main route at Dawlish Warren. In 2024, storm damage led to temporary closure of the main route.

The railway promenade ends at Langstone Rock, an isolated outcrop of Permian sandstone. The beaches and dunes of 204-hectare Dawlish Warren National Nature Reserve are ahead, a dune system formed at the River Exe estuary's mouth around 7,000 years ago. However, the SWCP crosses the railway and follows a winding road past dreary holiday camps.

Starcross to Exmouth ferry

The ferry runs April to October, hourly between 10.40 am and 5.40 pm (4.40 pm to mid-May and from mid-September). Only cash is accepted, the cost was £6 in 2024. Check details by calling ferryman Mark Rackley 07974 022536.

The last few kilometres follow roadside paths to Starcross along the railway's inland side, barring views of the estuary. Cockwood's harbour offers a bit of variation.

Starcross is the jumping off point for Exmouth. The ferry departs from a long jetty, accessed by crossing Starcross railway station's footbridge. The tall Italianate building alongside the station was a pumping station for Brunel's failed vacuum-propelled railway scheme, now recalled only by the Atmospheric Railway Inn, located across the road.

The 3,350-hectare Exe estuary's sand and mudflats are a Special Area of Conservation and a Ramsar site; Atlantic grey seals are commonly seen, but it especially comes alive between August and March when 30,000 migratory birds visit, including brent geese, avocets and Slavonian grebe.

If there is no ferry, the options are to travel to Exmouth by train, or to follow the Exe Estuary Trail around the estuary; the distance using the Turf Locks ferry (07778 370582, May to September) is fifteen kilometres, using the Topsham Lock ferry (07801 203338, runs April to September) is seventeen kilometres and crossing via Countess Wear Bridge is twenty-three kilometres.

📷 *Big Picket Rock.*

52 Exmouth to Sidmouth

Distance 19.6km / 12.2 miles	**Height gain** 525m / 1700ft **Difficulty** ● ● ● ● ○
Maps	OS Landranger 192 / OS Explorer 115
Start	Starcross to Exmouth ferry, Pier Head, Exmouth EX8 1ER / eyelid.voucher.incursion / SX 993 806
Finish	The Esplanade, Sidmouth EX10 8AT / powder.yards.smooth / SY 124 871
Parking near start	Pier Head car park, Exmouth EX8 1ER / trickled.prime.insist / SX 993 806
Parking near finish	Manor Road car park, Sidmouth EX10 8RR / burns.torch.sculpture / SY 120 870
Public transport	157 bus

Sandstone extravaganza! Here at the Jurassic Coast World Heritage Site's western extremity, Jurassic rocks barely feature; this section undulates atop cliffs of Triassic sandstone and mudstone, laid down in an equatorial desert 201-252 million years ago and coloured rust-red by iron minerals oxidising under hot sun. The cliff strata feature intricate patterns frozen in deep time, decipherable as dune formation, water deposition and wind erosion.

The ferry from Starcross (section 51) deposits folk at Pier Head, outside Exmouth Marina (redeveloped from the Victorian docks, which closed in 1990). Exmouth of course takes its name from the River Exe (Celtic: fish) and claims to be Devon's oldest resort, having developed in the early eighteenth century. Lady Nelson lived here, and visitors included Lady Byron and her daughter Ada Lovelace.

Exmouth's esplanade extends along the near-three-kilometres of beach, with views of Dawlish Warren. The peculiar 'dalek' dome passed is an Allan-Williams Turret, a form of Second World War coastal defence. Across the road, grassed-over dunes extend as far as the Lifeboat Station; The Maer is a local nature reserve.

The path climbs onto Rodney Point and Orcombe Point, the start of the World Heritage Site and also its oldest rocks, predating the dinosaurs. Orcombe Point is topped by the 'Geoneedle', unveiled in 2002 and layered with differing WHS rocks. The following plateau is the High Land of Orcombe, overlooking Sandy Bay's reefs.

Straight Point headland is fenced off and occupied by a Royal Marines rifle range. Its west cliffs host a colony of kittiwakes, each with their own white guano-nest glued to the sandstone. Behind Straight Point, smothering the valley and extending to the horizon, are crammed ranks of fixed caravans: Devon Cliffs Holiday Park, the largest such site along the SWCP and one of its less prepossessing vistas.

Having squeezed between the caravans and rifle range, things vastly improve. The path ascends above the crumbling cliffs of The Floors, to West Down Beacon's gorse-covered heath and its 129m trig point. The descent passes through woods beside East Devon Golf Club, and across Jubilee Park, into the charming resort of Budleigh Salterton.

Budleigh Salterton possesses Britain's highest proportion of over-65s; 45% in 2021! The beach abuts onto the esplanade road, with boats drawn up. The hard quartzite pebbles are 440

million years old, transported north from Brittany by a desert river, a relatively recent 240 million years ago. In 1870, the seafront was the location of Pre-Raphaelite John Millais' painting, *The Boyhood of Raleigh*; Sir Walter Raleigh was born several kilometres inland at Hayes Barton. A plaque identifies the wall featured in the painting! Close to the seafront, the engaging Fairlynch Museum celebrates East Devon's heritage.

The pebbles continue to the River Otter's mouth; 'The Spit' was formed by sixteenth-century storms. However, the path diverts inland, following an embankment separating fields reclaimed by Napoleonic prisoners on the left, and salt marshes on the right; medieval salt pans ('salterns') gave the town its name. In 2023, the embankment was breached to flood the reclaimed fields and the £27m Queen Elizabeth Bridge opened to span the breach. In 2024, to celebrate King Charles

📷 *Otter Estuary Nature Reserve.*

III's coronation, the Otter Estuary became a National Nature Reserve. The embankment leads alongside the estuary, with hides and viewing platforms. Otter sightings are unlikely by day, but beavers are commonly spotted, having been reintroduced upriver in 2008! The Otter is crossed at White Bridge and the estuary followed south, via gradually ascending cliffs, with pine enclosures framing the views. From Danger Point, undulating cliffs extend northwards, alongside farmland.

Brandy Head's name recalls local smuggling. Brandy Head Observation Post is a brick and concrete hut restored in 2020, used in 1940 by Sir Bennett Melvill Jones to invent gyroscopic gunsights. The view north is a SWCP highlight. At least seven isolated stacks jut from the water and beaches around Ladram Bay, with the enormous cliff of High Peak rearing behind; all, of course, hued vibrant red-orange!

Ladram Bay Holiday Park is relatively unobtrusive. Passing around Ladram Bay and Sandy Cove, you enjoy closer views of the stacks. The most prominent are Ladram Rock, Hern Point Rock and Big Picket Rock, the latter dwarfed below High Peak.

The steep, rooty ascent approaching High Peak is this section's hardest. The SWCP bypasses this Iron Age hillfort's summit; a side-tour is possible to the 157m trig point. Settlement here dates back at least to the Neolithic period.

The path regains the clifftop at a viewpoint overlooking Windgate. Peak Hill is the final climb, topped by heathland. The descent into Sidmouth winds through woodland; look for animals carved into the trees.

When the path turns from Peak Hill Road towards Jacob's Ladder Beach, Manor Road car park is just ahead on the left. 'Jacob's Ladder' is the suspended wooden steps descending from the Clock Tower, a fort-like building which originated as a limekiln in the sixteenth century and served as a battery in the Second World War. Clifton Walkway leads around the Clock Tower and Connaught Gardens, above Chit Rocks (Chit Rock was an imposing stack, destroyed in an 1824 hurricane) to Sidmouth's promenade.

📷 *High Peak and Ladram Bay.*

The Jurassic Coast World Heritage Site

In 2001, the coast between Exmouth in Devon and Studland Beach in Dorset (185km / 115 miles of the SWCP) became England's first natural UNESCO World Heritage Site. The coast's remarkable geological diversity is revealed, in cross-section; the cliffs time-travel backwards through 185 million years, spanning the entire Mesozoic Era. This was when dinosaurs roamed the earth and is divided into three 'Periods': the dark red sandstone between Exmouth and Branscombe hails from the Triassic (252-201 million years ago). The Jurassic (201-145 mya) is showcased in the cliffs, landslips and quarries from Seaton to Swanage, most famously as fossil-rich limestone. The stunning chalk scenery around Beer, Lulworth Cove and Old Harry Rocks was formed during the Cretaceous (145-66 mya).

📷 *Hooken Cliffs from Beer Head.*

◎ *Sidmouth.*

53 Sidmouth to Seaton

Distance	17.3km / 10.7 miles	**Height gain** 725m / 2,400ft	**Difficulty** ●●●●●
Maps	OS Landranger 192 / OS Explorer 115, 116		
Start	The Esplanade, Sidmouth EX10 8AT / powder.yards.smooth / SY 124 871		
Finish	Seaton Esplanade EX12 2QN / yards.twee.cleansed / SY 244 899		
Parking near start	Manor Road car park, Sidmouth EX10 8RR / burns.torch.sculpture / SY 120 870		
Parking near finish	Seaton long stay car park EX12 2WD / hero.mats.replaying / SY 247 902		
Public transport	9A bus		

Towering cliffs of red Triassic mudstone extend eastwards from Sidmouth, with a topping of lighter Jurassic and Cretaceous sandstone gradually encroaching, until white Cretaceous chalk takes over at Beer Head. What's daunting isn't the cliffs' height but that they are repeatedly interrupted by V-shaped clefts, plunging towards sea level.

Sidmouth's seafront boasts fine Georgian and Regency architecture, a legacy of its fashionable heyday when it was frequented by royalty: George III (1791) and the infant Victoria (1819), whose former home is now the Royal Glen Hotel.

Mammoth teeth have been found at the River Sid's mouth. Alma Bridge, made from shipwreck timbers and named after a Crimean War battle in the year it was built (1854) was damaged by floods in 2012. In 2020, a new footbridge replaced it.

Rockfalls on Salcombe Hill Cliff divert the first ascent through backstreets. Emerging, enjoy fine views of Sidmouth before a zigzagging woodland ascent to the grasslands topping Salcombe Hill's plateau summit. The five domes of the Norman Lockyer Observatory, a historic observatory and planetarium, occupy the hilltop 500m north.

A stone marker atop Salcombe Hill notes that in 1937, the Cornish family dedicated it as, *'a permanent open space'*. Their land bequest also included the Salcombe Regis valley's dramatic cleft, which meets the sea at Salcombe Mouth. Before descending, the Frog Stone is passed; this greensand boulder (yes, resembling a frog) was apparently deposited here by naval helicopter in 1964. The path drops almost to sea level, contouring around the final ravine, before regaining all that lost ascent, through Combe Wood, onto Higher Dunscombe Cliff.

The next deep cleft is the Lincombe valley, which the path mercifully traverses around. Nature thrives in this beautiful wooded enclave, sheltered from the prevailing wind; listen for woodpeckers! A viewpoint on Lower Dunscombe Cliff's brink is followed by a plunge through Dunscombe Coppice, into Weston Combe.

Emerging from the woods, look for the Weston Plats, under south-facing cliffs. These were sheltered plots of land fertilised with seaweed, lugged up by donkeys, to grow the celebrated 'Branscombe spuds'. The Plats fell from use and became overgrown in the 1960s, but have been cleared by the National Trust, with a 'linhay' (stone shed) restored.

Weston Mouth's beach is gloriously desolate; shingle and cliffs stretch in both directions and there is nothing other than a few huts, and a stream to jump across. You know what comes next ...

Atop the zigzagging 160m grind onto Weston Cliff, the reward is Weston Wildflower Meadow; the restored grasslands thrive with colourful butterflies and flowers, including pyramidal orchids and the rare purple gromwell.

From Coxe's Cliff, the path passes behind less sheer cliffs; you'll spy paths leading to huts on the terraces. The route passes through Berry Camp's ramparts, an Iron Age hillfort which lost its south wall to coastal erosion. The path deviates from the coast around old quarries, following a woodland track overlooking Branscombe village.

The coast is regained after descending West Cliff to Branscombe Mouth, where there is just a café and a 13,500kg anchor! The latter belonged to the *MSC Napoli*: Branscombe Mouth received international media attention in January 2007, when this sinking container ship was beached a kilometre offshore. Containers floated ashore and looters descended from across the country, even carting off motorbikes.

The stretch to Beer Head undergoes a startling change of character; instead of ascending the cliffs yet again, the route leads through Sea Shanty Holiday Park's caravans and chalets into the rugged and overgrown terrain beneath: the Hooken Undercliff. The Hooken Landslide of March 1790 saw the chalk and greensand cliffs subside eighty metres and push the shoreline 200m out, leaving crab pots high and dry. Rooty and confined paths wind through the undergrowth behind Castle Rock, the tottering chalk spires separated from the cliffs during the landslip. The Undercliff is truly spectacular, finishing with a steep and exposed ascent topping Hooken Cliffs. Looking back, note the tunnel emerging from the cliffs; this is an adit to Beer Quarry Caves, 1.5km inland, which have been worked since Roman times and supplied stone for Westminster Abbey and the Tower of London.

Approaching Beer.

Beer Head, marking the entrance to Seaton Bay, is Britain's most westerly chalk cliffs and the first encountered along the SWCP. On the brink, the outline of a Napoleonic gun battery is discernible; half has collapsed into the sea. Beneath are impressive near-vertical, cave-riddled, buttresses, best viewed from Beer.

Beer (Old English *bearu*: woods) is an attractive village, focused around its pebble beach where the fishing fleet is pulled ashore. Beer Heritage Centre tells how Beer's lace makers provided the trim for Queen Victoria's wedding dress and the 'Bomb Shelter' houses an unexploded Second World War bomb which almost destroyed the village.

Two alternative paths zigzag steeply out of Beer onto East Ebb; the more seaward option gives lovely views of the boats on the beach.

The final stretch into Seaton is anti-climactic. Landslips in 2012 diverted the SWCP inland via woodland and Beer Road. At low tide, it's possible to descend to Seaton Hole Beach (note the 'Everything's Changed' geology sculpture) and trudge along the pebble shoreline.

At Seaton Esplanade, Fisherman's Gap is bounded by twin sculptures of frothy waves: *'WAVES SHAPE THE SHORE ... SHORE SHAPES THE WAVES'*.

Smuggling at Beer

Beer was home to Jack Rattenbury, 'Rob Roy of the West' whose celebrated *Memoirs of a Smuggler* (1837) offer an entertaining insight into this murky profession, with tall tales of outwitting customs men, soldiers, press gangs and the French.

Smuggling has been heavily romanticised, but was of course organised crime. An epitaph in Branscombe churchyard reads: *"Here lieth John Hurley, Custom Officer ... He fell by some means or other from the Top of the Cliff to the Bottom."* Poor Hurley died in 1755, the only witnesses being local women who were strongly suspected of murdering him.

📷 *The Undercliff.*

54 Seaton to Lyme Regis

Distance 12.1km / 7.5 miles	**Height gain** 425m / 1,400ft **Difficulty** ● ● ● ● ○
Maps	OS Landranger 193 / OS Explorer 116
Start	Seaton Esplanade EX12 2QN / yards.twee.cleansed / SY 244 899
Finish	Charmouth Road car park, Lyme Regis DT7 3DW / flexibly.profile.minute / SY 343 926
Parking near start	Seaton long stay car park EX12 2WD / hero.mats.replaying / SY 247 902
Public transport	378 bus. Multiple buses and rail service on Sunday

Welcome to the jungle! The path traverses an inaccessible No Man's Land between cliffs and sea: the Axmouth to Lyme Regis Undercliffs National Nature Reserve. The Undercliffs are a series of huge landslips reclaimed by nature, densely covered by trees, creepers and ferns. Once you enter this wilderness, you're committed to finishing or turning back. Take extra water, the temperature and humidity can be surprising! The reward for successfully passing through is arrival at the glorious resort of Lyme Regis.

Seaton's Esplanade leads to Axmouth Old Bridge across the River Axe, alongside a larger bridge carrying the B3172. This is the oldest concrete road bridge in the country (1877), a treat for concretophiles (I may have just invented that word). The river is engaging; Axmouth, formerly known as Fleet (Old English *fléot*: estuary) was a port from Roman times, until the river mouth

The Undercliffs

The Undercliffs were formed by a succession of landslips, the best-documented occurring on Christmas Eve 1839. Geologist William Coneybeare recorded how the 1.2km long, forty-five-metre-deep and eighty-metre-wide 'Chasm' appeared, leaving a wheatfield isolated on 'Goat Island'. The shore shifted 500m seawards and a 1.5km-long limestone reef arose offshore, debated in Parliament as a potential naval base (it eroded away). Subsequent earth movements included a massive landslip at Whitlands Cliff in February 1840.

The landslips are caused by unstable geology: Cretaceous sands and chalk, topping Triassic and Jurassic clays. The sands and chalk absorb rainwater, the clays are impermeable; pressure builds and eventually something has to give.

The Undercliff has been largely untouched, since 1900, and has evolved a wilderness ecosystem of self-seeded trees (Ash, Beech, Field Maple and Sycamore), hart's tongue ferns, creepers and pyramidal orchids. Landslips continue: the SWCP was blocked from 2014 to 2016.

was blocked in the fourteenth century by successive landslips (or a mermaid's curse, depending upon which version you believe). You might spot 1950s electric trams running along the west bank: this is the Seaton Tramway which connects to Colyton, following the former railway course.

The Undercliffs are approached via a grinding climb along Squire's Lane and through Axe Cliff Golf Course. Turning right towards Haven Cliff, things improve with views of Beer Head (section 53).

The path follows the cliff's rim for a kilometre, then, after a warning sign, plunges into the Undercliffs.

Enclosed within the Undercliffs' dense woodland, the narrow path continuously contorts, climbs and falls with numerous steep steps, roots and rocks to negotiate.

The path threads a ridge above the Chasm, beneath on the left, with Bindon Cliffs rearing behind. Goat Island is ascended, an open patch of chalk grassland somehow left high and dry by the 'Great Landslip' of 1839. Before 2016, the SWCP bypassed this.

📷 *Goat Island.*

Dowlands Cliffs follow, the only landmark being the ruin of a sheepwash from c1800. Nearby are traces of Landslip Cottage; William Pritchard's cottage survived the 1839 slip and, rebuilt, served tea to sightseers until burning down in 1953.

The path opens out to a track, beside a tall chimney; this was a pumping station and engineer's house, until subsiding in 1911. It supplied fresh water to the Rousden Estate, on the cliffs above. William Henry Peek acquired the estate in 1872, introducing exotic species including rhododendron and holm oak to the Undercliffs.

Steep steps plunge back into the jungle, passing along Whitlands Cliff, Pinhay Cliffs and then Ware Cliffs, including some boardwalk. Above, Chapel Rock crag marks where non-conformists worshiped in the 1660s. A bench overlooking Pinhay Bay provides a rare sea view.

The path becomes a track and emerges from the Undercliffs at Underhill Farm. Chimney Rock rears above, accessed by a signposted side-tour. Descending into Lyme Regis, look for a fence sculpture marking the Devon-Dorset border and depicting three nineteenth-century women associated with the town and palaeontology: Mary Anning, Mary Buckland and Sarah Woodruff. The latter is fictional, the *French Lieutenant's Woman* of the novel and film.

You enter Lyme Regis behind Monmouth Beach; here in June 1685, the Duke of Monmouth, illegitimate son of Charles II, landed and proclaimed himself King. That September, a dozen of his supporters were hanged and dismembered on the beach. There is a pavement of Blue Lias limestone on the beach, with large ammonites easily found.

Lyme Regis grew around the River Lim, gaining the 'Regis' (Royal) moniker after Edward I granted it a Royal Charter in 1284. It developed into a major fishing port and became a fashionable resort from Georgian times. The central landmark is the 200m Cobb, Britain's oldest working breakwater. This sinuous thirteenth-century barrier appears indestructible, but has had to be repeatedly rebuilt. The eighteenth-century buildings at the end house a splendid tiny aquarium.

📷 *Lyme Regis.*

The beachfront promenade leads to the town centre; note the 20th Century Conflicts Clock, a war memorial. The promenade continues above the reef of Broad Ledge, below the walls of Lyme Regis Museum and the Marine Theatre to a statue of Mary Anning, unveiled in 2022 by Professor Alice Roberts (the author's single permitted adult crush!). Anning holds a geological hammer and is striding towards the fossil-rich slopes of Black Ven. Anning's grave is close by, at St Michael's Church.

Steep steps lead directly to Charmouth Road car park.

Durdle Door (Section 59).

Dorset

Dorset's coast showcases some of Britain's most stunning scenery; the SWCP is almost entirely within the Dorset Area of Outstanding Natural Beauty and is all within the Jurassic Coast World Heritage Site. The county's complex geology means that the variety of coastal landscapes explored is quite amazing, from mudstone landslips to blinding white chalk cliffs. It also ensures that the final 166km / 103 miles of the SWCP, to the finish beside Poole Harbour, are rarely easy going! The fossil haven of Lyme Regis is followed by Golden Cap, the south coast's highest point. The vast Ice Age landforms of Chesil Beach and The Fleet provide an interlude from the cliffs, before the loop around the heavily-quarried Isle of Portland. The SWCP's final sections do not disappoint; they explore the breathtaking Isle of Purbeck, with iconic landforms such as Durdle Door and Old Harry Rocks.

Near Charmouth.

📷 *Golden Cap and Seatown.*

55 Lyme Regis to West Bay

Distance 16.3km / 10.1 miles	**Height gain** 950m / 3100ft **Difficulty** ● ● ● ● ○
Maps	OS Landranger 193 / OS Explorer 116
Start	Charmouth Road car park, Lyme Regis DT7 3DW / flexibly.profile.minute / SY 343 926
Finish	East Beach car park, West Bay DT6 4EW / milder.making.raven / SY 464 903
Public transport	X53 Jurassic Coaster bus

This section explores a dramatic landscape, which is very much in flux. There are repeated tough climbs, including the highest point on the south coast. Palaeontology enthusiasts will be in raptures; on the shore, large sea-polished ammonites and belemnites are easily located. Mary Anning made her fossil discoveries here; enlightened Victorians perceived that they implied a world predating 4004BC, the generally accepted date of Creation. This is the famous Blue Lias limestone, laid down in beds, interspersed with shale layers 200-195 million years ago on the bed of warm shallow Jurassic seas.

The section begins unsatisfactorily, with landslips forcing a diversion inland. Lyme Regis Golf Club, high above atop 178m Timber Hill, is reached after a long ascent via road, fields and woodland. The 'contour lines' sculpture in Fern Hill's woods marks the Lyme Regis parish boundary. A surfaced permissive path contours around the golf course before descending into Charmouth, reaching the seafront via Higher Sea Lane.

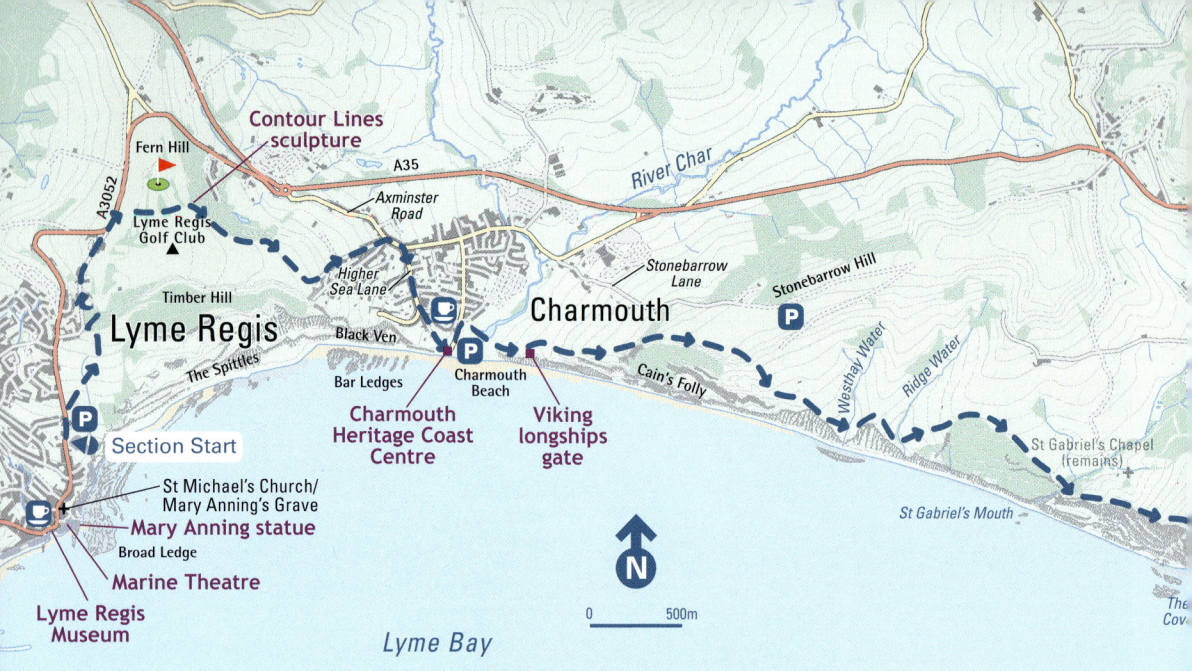

The Princess of Palaeontology

Mary Anning (1799-1847) of Lyme Regis made remarkable fossil discoveries, including the first ichthyosaurus and the first complete plesiosaur. She first sold her finds to the tourists (reputedly being the origin of, *'she sells sea shells on the seashore'*!), but gained attention from the international scientific community. Visiting academics were surprised to discover that Anning (a woman, of low status) was not just a 'fossil finder', but was better conversant with the underpinning science than almost anyone else. Anning's finds contributed to the development of the theories of extinction and evolution, although many were attributed to others and her significance was largely unacknowledged within her lifetime. *"She says the world has used her ill,"* a friend wrote, *"These men of learning have sucked her brains, and made a great deal by publishing works, of which she furnished the contents, while she derived none of the advantages."*

The reason for this irritating inland excursion is the highly dynamic cliffs between Lyme Regis and Charmouth, called The Spittles and Black Ven. At least seven massive terraces rise staircase-like from the sea. Each is subsiding, with major landslips as recent as 2008. In the 1930s, tourists came to view the 'mud glacier'! There have been blockages and diversions since 2001. An unofficial alternative is to follow the shoreline between Lyme Regis and Charmouth, at low tide; for obvious reasons, this requires great care.

The coast is regained at Charmouth Heritage Coast Centre; the cliffs directly west are a good place to start fossil hunting, but first consult the Fossil Collecting Code, introduced in 2020. The Centre overlooks Charmouth Beach, which owes much of its material to a 1979 flash flood which deposited a pebble delta (and caravans) at the River Char's mouth.

Some Ordnance Survey maps show the SWCP diverted out of Charmouth along roads. Thankfully, the coast route has reopened and you ascend 148m Stonebarrow Hill by path, above crumbling Cain's Folly cliffs. Note the splendid 'Viking longships' gate which marks the Charmouth parish boundary, recalling a Viking incursion of 836.

Golden Cap, the highest point on the south coast, dominates the skyline ahead from Stonebarrow Hill. Getting there is hard work, as the path traverses a rough and uneven ridge atop ancient landslips, dropping to cross three successive secret vales: Westhay Water, Ridge Water and St Gabriel's Mouth. A deviation up the latter valley allows you to visit ruined St Gabriel's Chapel, abandoned in the nineteenth century and used as a warehouse by smugglers.

Golden Cap is named for the band of lighter Cretaceous sandstone which tops the Jurassic cliffs. Steep steps access the summit plateau, which is marked by a 191m trig point and a stone memorial to the Earl of Antrim. Having absorbed the sweeping views, enjoy the long descent, passing another boundary sculpture (a spidery tree-seat) to reach Seatown after a short diversion inland. Seatown, despite the name, consists of a pub and car park. The River Winniford trickles into a shingle beach; another great fossil-finding spot.

📷 *Charmouth.*

Hopefully you kept something in reserve with your legs and sense of humour, because having dropped to sea level, the path immediately regains most of the lost height. The traverse around Ridge Cliff (bypassing epic 2021 and 2023 cliff falls) and across Doghouse Hill is made more than bearable by grand views of Golden Cap rearing behind. Thorncombe Beacon (along with every other south coast Beacon) is so-named as, in 1588, it was lit to announce the sighting of the Spanish Armada. The 157m summit is topped by a pole-mounted cresset (fire basket).

The route drops into and out of a basin; be mindful, a 2022 cliff fall left an alarming void in the path. Eype Mouth is down at sea level, occupied by the caravans of Eype Beach Holiday Park; Eype is Old English (*stæphlýpe*) for 'steep', but you knew that by now.

After bridging the River Eype, the final ascent is relatively easy. Fields behind West Bay's West Cliff soon bring you down into this small port, an offshoot of Bridport which is three kilometres inland. East Beach car park is located on the far side of the small harbour.

📷 *East Cliff, West Bay.*

56 West Bay to Abbotsbury

Distance 14.6km / 9.1 miles	**Height gain** 100m / 300ft **Difficulty** ● ● ○ ○ ○
Maps	OS Landranger 193, 194 / OS Explorer OL15
Start	East Beach car park, West Bay DT6 4EW / milder.making.raven / SY 464 903
Finish	Grove Lane, Abbotsbury DT3 4JJ / workouts.reminds.nerves / SY 575 848
Parking near finish	Rodden Row car park, Abbotsbury DT3 4JL / schools.weeps.lots / SY 578 852
Public transport	X53 Jurassic Coaster bus

This section offers easy cliff-top trails (if we ignore the first tough climb), followed by level paths alongside the infant Chesil Beach. The surprising twist, is the calf-burning stretches along pathless shingle.

West Bay is based around a small enclosed harbour at the mouth of the River Brit, lined by colourful food shacks. East Cliff's striated yellow sandstone may look very familiar, being a motif of the iconic TV crime drama *Broadchurch*.

East Cliff is ascended at an intimidating gradient. A 'stacked boats' sculpture marks the Bridport parish boundary and recalls the East Cliff 'spotters' who, when they spied a shoal, yelled, *"mackerel straying!"* to the fishermen below.

The sandstone cliffs are overhanging and, due to geological faults, unstable; the path has been diverted around numerous major collapses in recent years, one sadly fatal. In 2024, one such cliff

fall led to a temporary diversion inland, as far as Burton Freshwater. This is one part of the SWCP where the oft-repeated advice 'stay back from the edge' is more pertinent than usual.

After the grassy undulations of Bridport and West Dorset Golf Course, the path descends to Burton Freshwater, where the River Bride has scythed through the cliffs (but not the pebble beach, which it quietly percolates through). This lovely grassy valley is obscured beneath Freshwater Beach Holiday Park, with identikit static caravans crammed to the waterfront. The river is bridged 500m upstream, forcing an inland diversion.

Burton Cliff is a continuation of the stunning-but-unstable sandstone; cliff falls in the past have sometimes diverted the route inland along the River Bride valley and past the pleasant village of Burton Bradstock. After crossing a lane, the path leads behind a huge white clifftop villa (former home of socialist singer Billy Bragg, and a source of amusement for the redtop newspapers) overlooking Hive Beach with its café and car park.

There is a marked change in character, the cliffs diminishing in height as the path leads past Old Coastguard Holiday Park and descends to Cogden Beach. This is the nascent Chesil Beach;

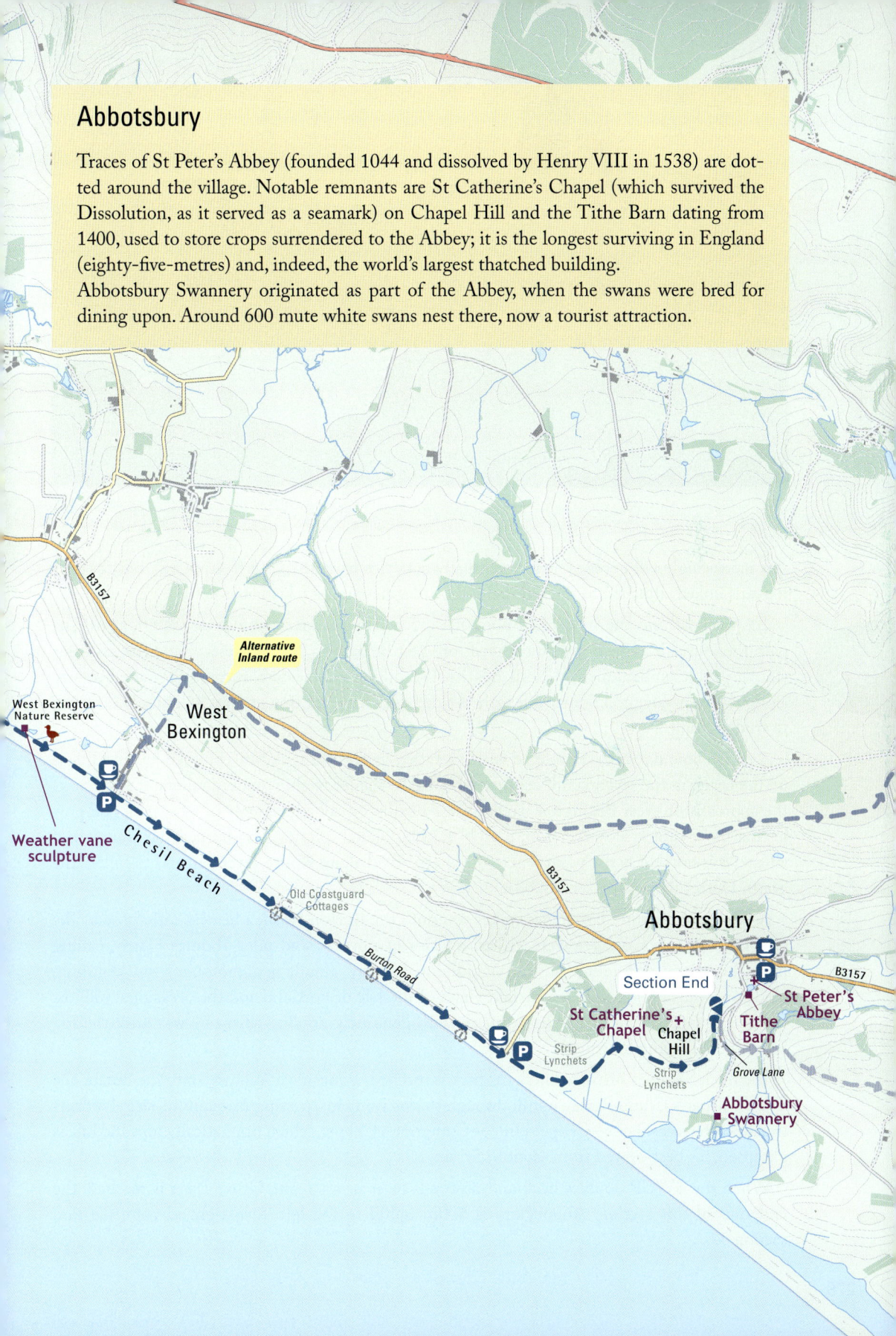

Abbotsbury

Traces of St Peter's Abbey (founded 1044 and dissolved by Henry VIII in 1538) are dotted around the village. Notable remnants are St Catherine's Chapel (which survived the Dissolution, as it served as a seamark) on Chapel Hill and the Tithe Barn dating from 1400, used to store crops surrendered to the Abbey; it is the longest surviving in England (eighty-five-metres) and, indeed, the world's largest thatched building.

Abbotsbury Swannery originated as part of the Abbey, when the swans were bred for dining upon. Around 600 mute white swans nest there, now a tourist attraction.

St Catherine's Chapel, Abbotsbury.

this increasingly tall pebble barrier eventually detaches from the land (section 57), but for now remains linked, attached to the hills behind by marshes and brackish lagoons.

The track behind the reed-filled pool of Burton Mere is often muddy or waterlogged. The path then threads a line between the reeds of West Bexington Nature Reserve and the sea kale-strewn pebble embankment. Chesil Beach's 180 billion pebbles are, incredibly, graded in size along its twenty-eight-kilometre length. At this end, they are tiny and excruciatingly draining to trudge along.

A parish boundary marker topped with a weather vane / fish sculpture commemorates a house on the beach in the seventeenth century, which gave shelter to shipwrecked sailors. It also marks the approach of West Bexington. Today, West Bexington consists largely of a car park and pub, having never quite recovered from a 1440 raid by French pirates who burned the church and village. It is notable as the point where the alternative **Inland Route** diverts inland to follow the South Dorset Ridgeway (section 63).

A final pebble grind past chalets takes you onto the Burton Road, a heavily rutted track. The Old Coastguards Cottages were visited by Dorset novelist and poet Thomas Hardy, calling in on his friend and fellow author, Middleton Murray. This is a monotonous but beguiling landscape, the landmarks being distant views of the Isle of Portland and the occasional pillbox: the author once arrived and camped here, with genuinely no clue where he was until the fog lifted the following morning!

The track becomes surfaced and a car park is reached, alongside a walkway onto the beach. The SWCP departs Chesil Beach, uphill through successive fields, passing through the strip lynchets (medieval terraces) below Chapel Hill. St Catherine's Chapel, which dramatically tops the hill, is glimpsed; it's best viewed from sections 57 and 63.

When the SWCP doubles back and descends to cross a stream, Grove Lane is reached, the endpoint of this section. Abbotsbury is 500m uphill to the left, turn right to continue into section 57...

📷 *Linton Hill.*

57 Abbotsbury to Weymouth

Distance	17.6km / 10.9 miles **Height gain** 300m / 1,000ft **Difficulty** ●●○○○
Maps	OS Landranger 194 / OS Explorer OL15
Start	Grove Lane, Abbotsbury DT3 4JJ / workouts.reminds.nerves / SY 575 848
Finish	Ferry Bridge, Weymouth DT4 9JZ / yummy.salad.edge / SY 667 760
Parking near start	Rodden Row car park, Abbotsbury DT3 4JL / schools.weeps.lots / SY 578 852
Parking near finish	Fine Foundation Chesil Beach Centre DT4 9XE / weary.watch.decimal / SY 668 756
Public transport	X52 / X53 Jurassic Coaster and 1 Portland Link buses, change at Weymouth

This is a unique and remarkable landscape; there is nothing like Chesil Beach or the Fleet elsewhere along the SWCP or, indeed, nationally! The route is remote from roads, yet 'inland' from the sea, alongside England's largest lagoon. The going is mostly easy; a mildly hilly start is followed by level paths alongside farmland pasture and crops. Heavy rain, coupled with exceptional tides, occasionally inundates parts of the path, making for an arduous experience.

From Abbotsbury, the SWCP is reached by following signs for 'The Swannery'. The SWCP ascends seventy metres from a lane onto the ridge of Linton Hill, with great views allowing you to get your head around this amazing landscape. Back west, St Catherine's Chapel stands proud above Chapel Hill's distinctive strip lynchets (medieval terraces). To the south, the Fleet lagoon begins, hemmed in by Chesil Beach.

Chesil Beach and the Fleet

Chesil Beach (Old English *sæceosel*: shingle) is a monumental landform: twenty-eight kilometres long, twelve metres high and 160m wide, consisting of 180 billion pebbles from the cliffs of Lyme Bay, deposited around c7,000 years ago by rising sea levels and graded in size along its length. Reciting bare statistics barely does it justice; seeing is believing!

The Fleet (Old English *fléot*: estuary) is around 480 hectares of salt or brackish water, thirteen kilometres in length and rarely deeper than three metres. This sheltered lagoon is home to 150 species of seaweed, as well as seagrass and seahorses. Birds attracted to the lagoon include brent geese, ducks, herons, egrets and of course swans. Little terns and ringed plovers nest, undisturbed, on Chesil Beach.

At Merry Hill, the SWCP veers off the ridge and descends steeply, crossing a lane and small hill before crossing a parish boundary sculpture footbridge, to reach the Fleet at Rodden Hive. The route now follows the lagoon's, surprisingly lonely, shores along and around a succession of bays and headlands; farms and houses are perched away from the water, uphill. Occasional small cliffs offer loftier perspectives of looming Chesil Beach.

The West or 'Upper' Fleet narrows at Langton Hive Point, where Coastguard Road reaches a slipway. The Mid Fleet begins at Herbury 'Island', where the path cuts across the (sometimes marshy) neck of a peninsula, to Gore Cove. It was also known as 'Donkey' Island, being the winter grazing spot of Weymouth's beach donkeys! In 1749 the Dutch vessel *Hope* was grounded on Chesil Beach, across from Herbury. After news spread that she was carrying gold, the army were called to disperse a crowd of 10,000!

📷 *Royal Engineers Bridging Hard and Chesil Beach.*

A parish boundary in Gore Cove is marked by both an inscribed stone and a gate featuring a contour map of the locality; the blue line denotes the predicted sea level rise. Moonfleet Manor Hotel is the largest building encountered along the Fleet. This sprawling Georgian house was imagined as 'Fleet Manor' in John Meade Falkner's 1898 children's smuggling tale, *Moonfleet*.

The following stretch leads alongside a 'gallop', for exercising horses, to Butterstreet Cove and the East Fleet's start. Pillboxes are a reminder that this area was heavily militarised during the Second World War, with Moonfleet Manor stationing US troops preparing for the D-Day landings on Omaha Beach, and Barnes Wallis' 'bouncing bomb' tested extensively on the West Fleet before use in the famous Dambusters air raid.

The tiny chapel in Butterstreet Cove is the chancel of a larger church, destroyed by the storm surge from the Great Gale of 1824. East Fleet Farm Touring Park is shortly after.

Chickerell Hive Point has another landing stage, followed by Cuttcleeves Bay, where the carved information board is yet another boundary marker. Tidmoor Point is occupied by the Chickerell Range, an MOD rifle range. If red flags are flying, you'll be redirected inland for a short diversion. Tidmoor Point's clay cliffs offer a fine view of the Fleet at its widest part, and are popular with fossil collectors.

Lynch Cove is overlooked by Littlesea Holiday Park's chalets. The Fleet then changes character, with the tide visibly squeezed through The Narrows, a fifty-metre-wide 'river'. This is overlooked by Royal Engineers Bridging Hard, where the Army train to cross water obstacles. Following the perimeter barbed wire fence is irritating, but it's an engaging site to observe.

The path descends onto the beach at Pirate's Cove, with the risk of wet feet during higher tides. In the final stretch, the Isle of Portland looms ominously above Chesil Beach. Interest is provided by a flooded pillbox and also the complex of ramshackle huts occupying the far shore, only accessible by boat.

The Chesil Beach Holiday Park and then the Crab House Café intrude, indicating that Weymouth has crept up; the A354 is reached and the Isle of Portland awaits.

In 2024, path erosion led to a temporary inland diversion, after Pirate's Cove.

◎ *Portland Bill Lighthouse.*

58 The Isle of Portland

Distance 21km / 13 miles	**Height gain** 325m / 1,050ft **Difficulty** ●●●●●
Maps	OS Landranger 194 / OS Explorer OL15
Start / Finish	Ferry Bridge, Weymouth DT4 9JZ / yummy.salad.edge / SY 667 760
Parking	Fine Foundation Chesil Beach Centre DT4 9XE / weary.watch.decimal / SY 668 756

Resist any temptation to bypass the Isle of Portland perambulation; this Brobdingnagian slab of 140-million-year-old limestone is unlike anything else on the SWCP. Victorian fortifications, a vast harbour, abandoned quarries returning to nature and an iconic lighthouse make for a constantly engaging outing. There are several rugged, steep or mildly exposed stretches.

The concrete Ferry Bridge has spanned the Fleet's powerful currents since 1985; until 1839 there was only a precarious ferry. The Fine Foundation Chesil Beach Centre is across the bridge; a walkway from the Centre ascends onto Chesil Beach, revealing how Portland is actually a 'tied' island, attached to the mainland by the enormous pebble tombolo.

The three-kilometre causeway forming the start (and finish) of this section gives an imposing view of the Isle, rising 140m behind. The embankment of a former railway follows Portland Harbour's shores, frequented by kite surfers. Constructed between 1849-1906, this was the world's largest manmade harbour. The immense breakwaters extend 4.6km; six million tons of Portland stone were laid down from scaffolding piers, carrying five railway lines, a testament to Victorian engineering, imperial confidence and the use of convict labour.

Blacknor.

A roundabout, a cycle path and dull industrial units reach the sea front at Chesil Cove. A 2014 storm overtopped the twelve-metre-high beach and smashed the Cove House Inn's windows; further back, in 1853, a fishing boat was deposited on a hotel roof and the Great Gale of 1824 killed twenty-seven and destroyed eighty homes.

The hundred-metre climb onto West Cliff is the day's toughest ascent; the upside is the tremendous view which emerges of the harbour and Chesil Beach, curving to the horizon. The route now follows the brink of sheer cliffs extending along the Isle's west coast. The Isle is tilted towards its southern tip at Portland Bill, so the six kilometres trend downhill.

The SWCP has been diverted inland at two points since 2013, avoiding collapsing cliffs: the first diversion leads through Tout Quarry Sculpture Park and Nature Reserve. Since 1983, limestone waste has been used to produce dozens of engaging sculptures, including a work by Anthony Gormley; take time to explore this magnificently unkempt site. Back atop the cliffs, high above Hallelujah Bay, the path follows a quarry tramway beneath a grand limestone block arch. The second diversion briefly arcs inland through Bowers Quarries, re-joining the clifftop at an exposed path around Blacknor Fort (built 1902), now a private home.

The hulking buildings at Southwell were previously the top-secret Admiralty *Underwater Weapons Establishment*, infiltrated in the 1950s by Soviet agents: the infamous 'Portland Spy Ring'. The Old Higher Lighthouse is the first of two decommissioned lighthouses flanking Portland Bill; it was previously home to birth control and women's rights advocate Marie Stopes. Stopes also, notoriously, promoted racist eugenic ideas. The Old Lower Lighthouse can be seen to the south-east and is home to Portland Bird Observatory.

The path veers around the *MOD Magnetic Range*'s wire fences, to reach Portland Bill. Pick your way through rubble to locate Pulpit Rock, a small stack known as the 'White Arch' before quarrying reduced it. At Dorset's southernmost extremity, a white obelisk inscribed 'TH 1844' (Trinity House) stands watch over the incessant tidal currents of the Portland Race, which is regularly whipped into a frenzy of white water. Portland Bill Lighthouse is unmistakeable, with its classic tapering form and red stripe. It was opened in 1906, after a 1901 storm destroyed fourteen ships. Alongside, the lighthouse keeper's cottages host a visitor centre.

Commencing Portland's east coast, low cliffs are followed past huts. The medieval field systems behind are known as 'lawnsheds'. The Red Crane is a wooden derrick for loading stone onto barges, later utilised for launching fishing boats; the first of several encountered. Pom Pom Rock, an eight-metre stack, reared offshore until felled by a January 2014 storm. Cave Hole is a grille-covered opening in the limestone, forming a blowhole when waves crash beneath!

The remainder of the east coast sees the SWCP weave through successive abandoned quarries, a no man's land between cliffs and scree-like limestone spoil on both sides. After a short road interlude, steps descend into Church Ope Cove. The beach huts splendidly have 'gardens', sculpted from pebbles. The bay takes its name from St Andrew's Church, whose ruins are located on the cliffs behind. Just behind is Pennsylvania Castle, a mansion built in 1800 for Portland's last governor, John Penn (grandson of the founder of Pennsylvania and Philadelphia). This shouldn't be confused with Rufus Castle, the crumbling medieval ruin tottering above the steep steps from the cove. Portland Museum is a worthwhile side-tour, just inland.

The route now follows the dramatic course of the Portland Branch Railway, which linked Easton's quarries with Weymouth. This traverses above the boulder scrublands of Penn's Weare and Grove Cliff, beneath quarried walls popular with climbers. Descending seawards, a sharp left veers up the cliffs. The enormous stone barrier to the north of these zigzagging steps was a Victorian firing range butt.

Back on top, the dauntingly high walls of *HMP/YOI Portland*, a Young Offender's Institution, confront you. The penal theme continues with the Verne Citadel, now *HMP The Verne*. This sombre Victorian fortress (1857) occupies the Isle's highest point, surrounded by a deep, dry moat, quarried by convicts.

The descent to Portland Harbour follows the Merchant's Incline, a tramway which initially loses height gradually as it arcs below The Verne, but then plunges down a steep chute hidden within Fortuneswell's housing estates, emerging alongside Portland Castle. This is one of Henry VIII's fan-shaped artillery forts; the last along the SWCP was at St Mawes (section 33). English Heritage now manage it.

Osprey Quay was redeveloped following the Navy's closure of *HMS Osprey* in 1999. Portland Marina and the National Sailing Academy reinvigorated the waterfront, hosting the 2012 Olympic sailing event.

Back on the causeway, retrace your steps to the Ferry Bridge.

📷 *Swyre Head and Durdle Door.*

59 Weymouth to Lulworth Cove

Distance 23.2km / 14.4 miles	**Height gain** 725m / 2,400ft **Difficulty** ●●●●●
Maps	OS Landranger 194 / OS Explorer OL15
Start	Ferry Bridge, Weymouth DT4 9JZ / yummy.salad.edge / SY 667 760
Finish	Lulworth Cove BH20 5RQ / quietest.sleep.ruby / SY 824 799
Parking near start	Fine Foundation Chesil Beach Centre DT4 9XE / weary.watch.decimal / SY 668 756
Parking near finish	Lulworth Cove car park BH20 5RJ / tidal.woke.blues / SY 821 800
Public transport	1 Portland Link and X54 Jurassic Coaster buses, change at Weymouth

This outing starts easy, through Weymouth. It builds to a stretch of intense calf-burning ascents and descents where the SWCP crests above dazzling white arches, coves and stacks which feel misplaced in gloomy Britain, seeming more suited to the Mediterranean.

Just north of Ferry Bridge, the SWCP departs the A354 to follow the Rodwell Trail, a former railway line, along Portland Harbour's shore. A succession of suburban roads pass Sandsfoot Castle and bypass a landslip at Western Ledges. The castle was completed in 1539 for Henry VIII, utilising stone from recently-dissolved Bindon Abbey (section 60). It's currently in a parlous state, crumbling seawards and fenced-off.

After Bincleaves Green, a park with a memorial to Weymouth MP and abolitionist Thomas Fowell Buxton, a stone footbridge at Newton's Cove crosses to Nothe Gardens. Several routes

(with tame squirrels!) reach Nothe Fort. The SWCP descends steps to Weymouth Harbour, but first consider visiting this well-preserved Palmerstonian edifice, built 1860.

Weymouth Harbour is bustling and vibrant. The Weymouth Town Bridge lifts, allowing large vessels through; you may have to wait, or use the tiny ferry. Along Customs House Quay, look for the sign sheepishly admitting that the Black Death first reached England here, in 1348; *'It killed 30%-50% of the country's total population'*.

Weymouth Beach arcs away from the Pavilion Theatre, golden sands backed by a sweep of Georgian buildings. Along the esplanade are; a fairground, sand sculptures, a grand 1809 statue of George III, said monarch's bathing machine (overlooked by the Gloucester Hotel, previously his summer residence), war memorials and the colourful Jubilee Clock Tower (built 1888 in honour of Queen Victoria).

Past the Sea Life Aquarium, a causeway departs Weymouth, alongside the B3155. Across the road is Lodmoor Nature Reserve, an RSPB-managed wetland. Bowleaze Coveway leads to a path over Furzy Cliff. Jordan Hill, a 150m side-tour, has traces of a fourth-century Romano-British temple, where offerings and over eighty burials were excavated.

Bowleaze Cove is smothered by holiday park amusements. Across the River Jordan(!), is the attractive, modernist Riviera Hotel (1937), the last significant coastal development until Swanage. A contrastingly quiet stretch now follows, punctuated only by Osmington Mills and Ringstead villages.

The path veers around active landslips approaching Redcliff Point before dipping, fenced-in, past PGL Osmington Bay. Boardwalks then negotiate boggy woodland, inland of Black Head's terraced landslips. Emerging above Osmington Mills, note Goggin's Barrow on the right, a prominent Bronze Age burial mound. Just before the village, the South Dorset Ridgeway (section 63) joins on the left.

Osmington Mills is simply a line of cottages, leading to the Smuggler's Inn overlooking Hannah's Ledge reef. The path squeezes around the inn and then closely follows the clifftop to Ringstead, via three successive wooded enclaves. Two Second World War emplacements are reminders that this was *RAF Ringstead* radar station, active into the 1970s. The fields approaching Ringstead also bear traces of West Ringstead, a village abandoned following the Black Death.

Ringstead Bay curves towards the chalk headland of White Nothe, indicating that exceptional scenery awaits ahead. A track veers inland behind Ringstead's villas and ascends above the Burning Cliff, terraces named after bituminous shale caught fire and burned for several years from 1826. Past the 1906 wooden Church of St Catherine-by-the-Sea and then Holworth House, you emerge atop precipitous White Nothe, with a commanding view of Weymouth Bay, and pass a line of coastguard cottages overlooking a Second World War observation tower. The path tops out at 169m: don't fall off.

A nineteenth-century stone obelisk, erected as a navigation beacon, marks the start of a truly amazing, and truly strenuous, four kilometres. Firstly, the oft-rugged path contours dramatic inclined slopes to reach the platform of Middle Bottom, perched twenty-five metres above the beach. An immediate steep climb along the rim of vertical cliffs utilises rough-cut footprints to gain purchase to the ninety-metre summit. An equally steep descent passes a small promontory jutting seaward; this is Bat's Head. Venturing onto this exposed perch, with care, is recommended; the vista in either direction is quite something.

Completing the descent (again, to the twenty-five-metre contour) note the isolated stack in the cove below, and Bat's Hole, a tunnel piercing Bat's Head. A few metres of flat terrain, then another ridiculous incline summits Swyre Head, overlooking the wonderfully-named dry valley of Scratchy Bottom.

The climb from Scratchy Bottom reaches fabulous Durdle Door. This huge but slender limestone arch, from certain angles, resembles a Brontosaurus. The name derives from Middle English *thirl*: holed rock. Crowds throng to Durdle Door; to enjoy this iconic landmark by yourself, arrive early or late.

📷 *Stair Hole and Lulworth Cove.*

Man o' War Cove is sheltered by both Durdle Door's 'rear end' and The Man o' War, rocks extending into St Oswald's Bay. A 2013 landslip diverted the SWCP uphill to Durdle Door car park, and across slopes to Hambury Tout (Old English *tōtian*: lookout), the hill overlooking Lulworth Cove; consider a side-tour to the summit burial mound.

A wide path descends into Lulworth Cove car park. Behind the Visitor Centre, the SWCP deviates uphill to visit Stair Hole, a cluster of archways and caves where the sea has broken through the limestone, revealing erratic folds in the strata. The circular formations are traces of fossilised tree trunks. Stair Hole's eastern end is overlooked by the World Heritage Site stone, unveiled by Prince Charles in 2002.

Finish at the water's edge in Lulworth Cove.

The geology of Lulworth Cove

Lulworth Cove's perfect horseshoe curve is a geologist's delight. The narrow entrance gap was formed by glacial floodwater breaching a wall of durable Portland and Purbeck limestone, deposited 210-150 million years ago in the warm tropical seas of the late Jurassic period and forced into an upright position by the same tectonic forces which formed the Alps.

The cove's unique outline is due to the softer Wealden Beds behind the entrance; once exposed to the sea, they were scoured at a faster rate than the limestone. At the cove's rear, 50 million years forward in time, the harder Cretaceous greensand and chalk are eroding more slowly.

Stair Hole gives an idea of how Lulworth Cove may have looked 10,000 years ago, at the onset of its formation. Man o' War Cove and rocks hint to the future of Lulworth Cove, once the limestone beds finally succumb to the sea. Durdle Door is also formed from these same beds.

📷 Mupe Rocks.

📷 *Arish Mell and Bindon Hill.*

60 Lulworth Cove to Kimmeridge Bay

Distance 11.6km / 7.2 miles	**Height gain** 600m / 1,950ft **Difficulty** ●●●●●
Maps	OS Landranger 194, 195 / OS Explorer OL15
Start	Lulworth Cove BH20 5RQ / quietest.sleep.ruby / SY 824 799
Finish	Kimmeridge Bay car park BH20 5PF / subplot.swept.blinking / SY 908 790
Parking near start	Lulworth Cove car park BH20 5RJ / tidal.woke.blues / SY 821 800
Public transport	Not possible

This section compensates for its relative shortness with both phenomenally varied scenery and intense gradients. There are no facilities along the route, which passes through the British Army's *Lulworth Camp Armour Centre*, a tank firing range. Plan ahead to ensure that the Range Walks are open and that your day won't be rudely aborted by incoming ordnance.

If the Range Walks are closed, there are no official alternatives. The inland options to Kimmeridge are a nineteen-kilometre road trudge or attractive but longer possibilities linking up paths, via Holme Bridge.

Lulworth Cove is among the UK's most popular scenic attractions. Waves passing through a gap through the limestone cliffs have sculpted a perfect arc from the softer rock behind. Despite the hordes of sightseers, traces of the cove's heritage survive; early starters may see the two remaining fishing boats return with the day's catch.

Lulworth Ranges access

Lulworth Ranges are closed from Monday to Friday and on around half a dozen weekends annually. Google 'Lulworth firing times' for dates and times. The Range Walks are open for a minimum of 143 days annually, including weekdays through most of the school holidays. On weekends when the ranges are open, the gates are unlocked around 1630 on Friday and closed around 0900 on the following Monday. Changes can be made at short notice, announced via answering machine on 01929 404714.

Trudge along the chalk pebble beach to steps at the cove's far side. If the tide is particularly high or the sea exceptionally rough, an alternative route leads 750m inland alongside the B3070; turn onto Bindon Road and through a gate, to a path ascending and contouring high above the cove. Steep steps re-join the main route.

The densely overgrown woodland above Lulworth Cove's eastern rim is Little Bindon, site of Bindon Abbey. This Cistercian monastery was founded in 1149, but soon (1172) relocated to nearby Wool as the terrain was too severe. A memorial stone at Pepler's Point, overlooking the cove's entrance, is named for Little Bindon tenant George Pepler (1882-1959) who established the 1947 *Town and Country Planning Act*, protecting Britain's 'green belt' from housing.

Lulworth Ranges are entered through a severe-looking gate. Henceforth, yellow posts mark the route. Just inside, steps and railings descend to the clifftop Fossil Forest. Here, circular mounds (known as thrombolites) in the limestone pavement reveal the outlines of 145-million-year-old tree trunks. Jurassic cypresses and tree-ferns were preserved after being submerged by a swamp and coated in algae, which hardened to tufa. Smuggled goods were once landed here by locals, who dubbed it the 'Vairy Vances' (Fairy Dances).

Along the clifftop, passing a radar hut, look for the Lulworth Skipper, a tiny brown-black butterfly only found hereabouts. Reaching a concrete pillbox, a contender for the SWCP's finest view opens before you. The stacks of Mupe Rocks extend out into Mupe Bay and Worbarrow Bay, encircled by soaring cliffs of dramatically diverse geology; a vastly scaled-up Lulworth Cove.

A murderous climb, possibly the SWCP's steepest, ends atop Bindon Hill, where there are traces of an Iron Age enclosure. The hill is eroded into a narrow ridge at its eastern end, sensationally plunging 120m sheer to the sea. The path picks a route along the inland dip slope, with views across the tank ranges to seventeenth-century Lulworth Castle, before descending sharply to sea level. Arish Mell's beach is closed due to the risk of live munitions; the burned-out tanks overlooking it are a sobering sight. This land was requisitioned in 1917 for trialling the very first 'tanks', an invention so secret that local farmers were instructed to stand behind wicker screens whenever they drove past.

The escape from Arish Mell is a long steep grind, following the rim of Halcombe Vale to the multivallate ramparts of Flower's Barrow. This Iron Age hillfort of the *Durotriges* tribe, who gave their name to Dorset, has half eroded into the sea, 160m below. The place is supposedly haunted by Roman soldiers who captured it; two Second World War lookout huts, inside and downhill from the hillfort, are more 'concrete' reminders of the past.

A plummeting descent reaches the beach at Worbarrow Bay's eastern end, where there is a steel Allan-Williams Turret (similar to that at Exmouth, section 52) and a ruined coastguard station.

📷 *Kimmeridge Bay.*

The promontory of Worbarrow Tout rears behind the beach, disconcertingly marked by a dayglo target. Across its neck, Pondfield Cove is protected by well-preserved 'dragon's teeth': Second World War anti-tank obstacles.

A track leads off the main SWCP, 1.5km up-valley, to the 'ghost' village of Tyneham; a side-tour is highly recommended.

The final ascent of this section scales the daunting Gad Cliff, where enormous limestone blocks overhang the void and peregrine falcons nest far above a shoreline of smashed cliff remnants. The clifftop ridge ascends towards the summit of Tyneham Cap; before this is reached, the SWCP veers off downhill, overlooking Brandy Bay and Hobarrow Bay.

Long fingers of dark rock, forming reefs, indicate another geological shift – this is Kimmeridge Clay. Broad Bench reef marks Kimmeridge Bay's western end, and the end of the Lulworth Ranges. The 1950s 'nodding donkey' oil well still yields about sixty-five barrels daily. At Gaulter Gap, a pillbox and dragon's teeth guard the beach below the miners' cottages, before Kimmeridge Bay car park is reached.

Tyneham village

Tyneham was forcibly evacuated for military use, in 1943. Following the Second World War, the Army reneged on their promise to return the village. Today the cottages remain empty and ruinous, within an idyllic valley; ironically, preserved by military use. Only the Church and school are intact. Displays outline the stories of the residents who departed, never to return.

📷 *View from St Alban's Head.*

61 Kimmeridge Bay to Swanage

Distance 22.3km / 13.9 miles	**Height gain** 700m / 2,300ft **Difficulty** ●●●●○
Maps	OS Landranger 195 / OS Explorer OL15
Start	Kimmeridge Bay car park BH20 5PF / subplot.swept.blinking / SY 908 790
Finish	Mowlem Theatre, Swanage BH19 1BT / aboard.spends.chair / SZ 031 788
Parking near finish	Main Beach car park, Swanage BH19 1AP / freezers.disband.cuts / SZ 026 791
Public transport	Not possible

The Isle of Purbeck is a peninsula, bounded to the north by Poole Harbour, where the SWCP ends. This long(ish) outing explores Purbeck's cliff-lined southern rim, centred on the dramatic St Alban's Head. There are no facilities, unless you divert inland to Worth Matravers.

Kimmeridge Bay is accessed via a toll road from Kimmeridge. The bay is notable for its shallow reefs, the Kimmeridge Ledges, which extend seaward from sombre grey-black cliffs, continuing five kilometres eastwards. Jurassic creatures fossilised in the crumbling Kimmeridge Clay include plesiosaurs and ichthyosaurs; the Etches Collection Museum in Kimmeridge displays numerous remarkable specimens collected, over four decades, by local plumber Steve Etches. Beside the bay, the Fine Foundation Wild Seas Centre, marked by a fin whale skull from a 2012 stranding, highlights the Ledges' underwater life, whilst the remains of a breakwater recall Sir William Clavell's 1605 alum works.

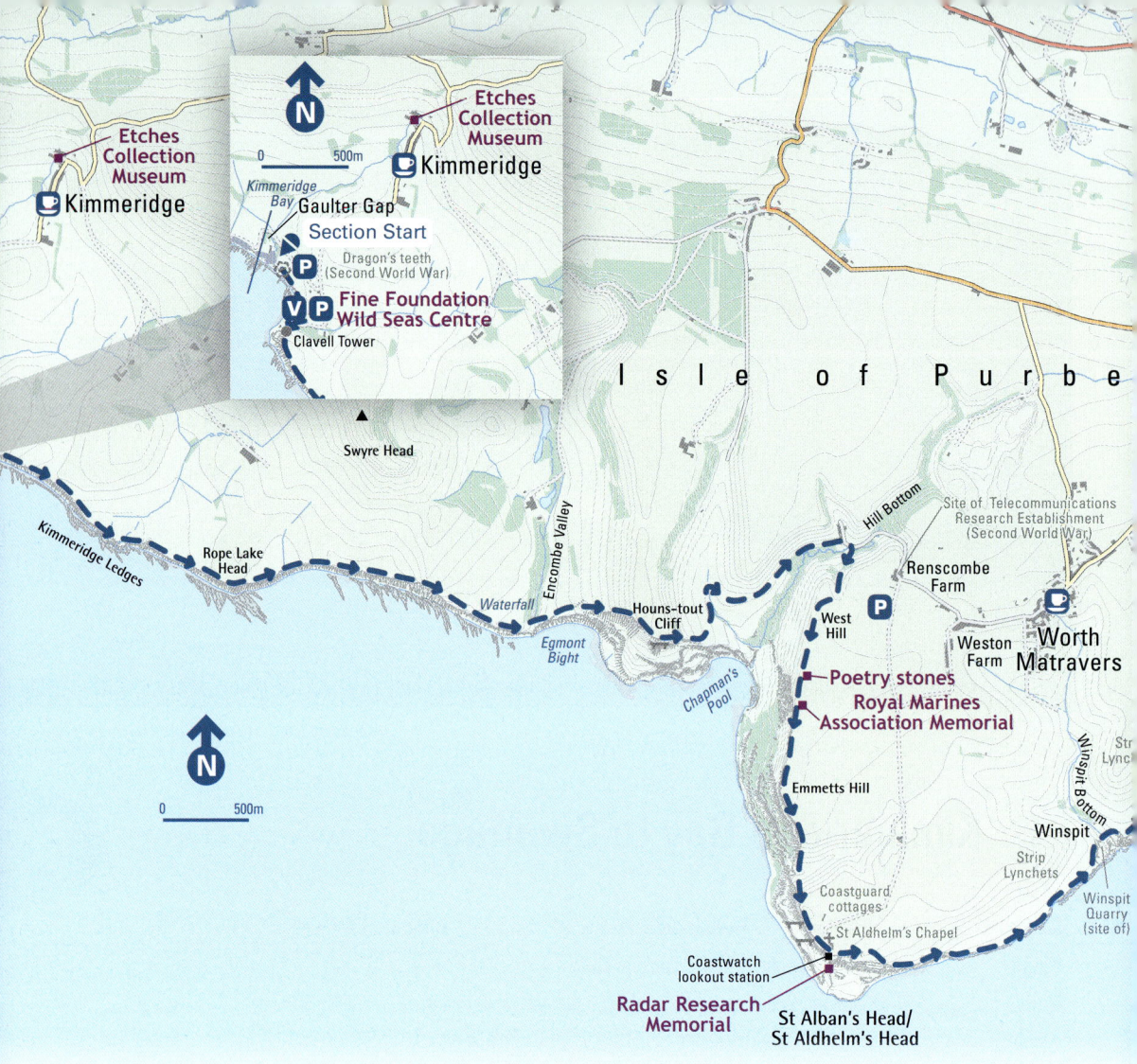

Steps ascend to the Clavell Tower, built in 1830 for Reverend John Clavell. In 2008, this eleven-metre Tuscan-style folly was dismantled and rebuilt, twenty-five metres back from the cliff. The SWCP follows a fairly level clifftop path, with occasional footbridges. Enjoy the surf breaks formed by the reef; at Rope Lake Head, refracting waves form criss-cross patterns! Across the shoulder of 208m Swyre Head, Purbeck's highest point, a jungly copse hides a waterfall spilling from the Encombe valley.

This section's middle third is harder-going, commencing with the short sharp ascent of Houns-tout Cliff. The stone summit bench, overlooking limestone crags, 140m above an undercliff wilderness of overgrown landslips, feels like a well-deserved throne! The descent negotiates severely inclined steps along the precariously eroding rim. In 2024, a landslip led to a temporary inland diversion avoiding this descent via the village of Kingston, adding five kilometres to the distance. The sheer-sided cove of Chapman's Pool awaits below, but the SWCP deviates inland around Hill Bottom valley, bypassing a deep ravine.

Following a milder ascent, onto West Hill, the path leads south atop limestone crags onto Emmetts Hill and towards St Alban's Head. The drystone wall alongside features six 'poetry stones' inscribed with quotations from local poet Paul Hyland. Also built into the wall is the Royal Marines Association Memorial, a garden and bench commemorating Marines who have lost their lives since 1945.

The headland seems so close; however, a hidden surprise is revealed! An epic staircase plummets die-straight into a valley, then a mirror-image flight of steps immediately ascends again. Having negotiated this chasm, carved stone thrones offer a final chance to soak up the stunning view westward.

St Alban's Head, also known as St Aldhelm's, is named for a seventh-century Bishop of Sherborne, possibly the first Anglo-Saxon to write in Latin. Perched atop the headland are a row of coastguard cottages, St Aldhelm's Chapel, a Coastwatch lookout station and the Radar Research

St Aldhelm's Chapel, St Alban's Head.

Memorial. The beautifully vaulted twelfth-century chapel sits amongst earthworks of a far older Christian site. The memorial sculpture, erected among the concrete foundations of a Chain Home radar mast, commemorates the top-secret Telecommunications Research Establishment based at Renscombe Farm during the Second World War. These sites are perched alongside a small quarry, a hundred metres above a tidal rapid surging around shattered cliff remnants.

Past the headland, an almost-unbroken eight-kilometre wall of limestone cliffs extends to Anvil Point Lighthouse, with quarrying scars visible. 'Purbeck Marble' helped build most of southern England's cathedrals. The cliffs were worked far into the twentieth century, with hewn limestone blocks craned onto ships. Today, the quarries are eerie open ledges, backed by extensive caves. Exploration is possible, with care.

After descending beside the headland's looming cliffs, the path is henceforth mostly easy, along wildflower-strewn limestone grasslands sloping to the cliff edge. The path deviates above and behind the first two large quarries; Winspit and Seacombe are located where side-valleys ('Bottom's) meet the sea, overlooked by strip lynchets (medieval terraces) on the hillside above. Winspit's caves and ruined buildings featured in a recent Sci-Fi TV show (set a long time ago, in a galaxy far, far away) and Seacombe's caves are notable for their daunting extent. During a 1786 snowstorm, the East Indiaman *Halsewell* was driven into a cave between Winspit and Seacombe; only seventy-four of the 240 on board survived until dawn, when crew members climbed to seek help.

Large numbers of guillemots, razorbills and kittiwakes nest on ledges along the cliffs. Pay close attention to the sea's surface after Seacombe; a sea cave, hidden from view, houses a small puffin population.

Dancing Ledge is the fourth large quarry passed. Steps and a short climb access a sloping reef, where a miniature swimming pool was blasted out in the early twentieth century for a nearby boy's school. Bond author Ian Fleming learned to swim here. The water is invariably frigid!

After a 'Mile Indicator' pylon, used pre-GPS for ship trials, Durlston Country Park and National Nature Reserve is entered. This extends around the headlands of Anvil Point and Durlston Head,

Anvil Point.

into Durlston Bay and Swanage's outskirts. Anvil Point Lighthouse was opened in 1881, a stubby twelve-metre tower reaching forty-five metres above where a dry valley meets the sea. Lookout points give views of the cliffs and their noisy guillemots, whilst a shelter offers a spot to scan for the dolphins regularly spotted here. The Hades-like entrance to Tilly Whim Caves (whim: a crane for lowering stone) was gated off in 1976; these were previously a visitor attraction, opened by George Burt. Burt was a philanthropic Swanage businessman who created the Durlston Estate, constructing the 'castle' folly and eccentric paraphernalia surrounding it. Durlston Castle now houses a visitor centre and the Fine Foundation Gallery. Outside, Burt's impressive Great Globe maps the world in 1887, via the medium of forty tons of Portland Stone. The surrounding walls are inscribed with Biblical and Shakespearean quotes aimed at 'improving' Victorian visitors.

Around Durlston Head, the SWCP dips below the castle, with views across Poole Bay to the Isle of Wight. A sculpture timeline of the earth is passed through, then woodlands lead above Durlston Bay's unstable slopes. There are only intermittent sea views and the SWCP veers inland to avoid landslips, departing the Country Park at Durlston Road.

The cliffs are regained via Belle Vue Road. The Downs grasslands slope towards Swanage Bay, ending at Peveril Point which divides Durlston Bay from Swanage Bay. This low promontory, marked by a Coastwatch lookout station, tapers to a reef, over which the tide incessantly pours. One possible route shortcuts to Swanage Pier along a lane. Most will continue to Peveril Point and follow the shoreline path; this passes Swanage Lifeboat Station and the Wellington Clock Tower, an ornate memorial to the eponymous Duke, which was relocated from London Bridge by George Burt.

Swanage Pier is a pleasant 200m walkway with preserved Victorian decor, built 1895 alongside an earlier pier whose piles are still visible. A stone quay, with promenade and preserved tram lines, leads past Swanage Museum and Heritage Centre to the Mowlem Theatre, overlooking Swanage Beach.

📷 *The Pinnacles.*

Swanage Bay.

62 Swanage to South Haven Point

Distance	11.7km / 7.3 miles
Height gain	150m / 500ft
Difficulty	● ● ○ ○ ○
Maps	OS Landranger 195 / OS Explorer OL15
Start	Mowlem Theatre, Swanage BH19 1BT / aboard.spends.chair / SZ 031 788
Finish	South Haven Point BH19 3BA / regard.props.hung / SZ 036 866
Parking near start	Main Beach car park, Swanage BH19 1AP / freezers.disband.cuts / SZ 026 791
Parking near finish	Shell Bay car park BH19 3BA / sleeps.bond.speeds / SZ 035 863
Public transport	50 Purbeck Breezer bus

This final (or very first?) outing along the SWCP is easy, yet beautiful and engaging.

The Mowlem Theatre is 250m from Swanage railway station, where steam trains lug passengers to Corfe Castle. Alongside the theatre is the King Alfred Memorial: a Tuscan column topped with Russian cannon balls fired in the Crimean War commemorates, *'A GREAT NAVAL BATTLE FOUGHT WITH THE DANES IN SWANAGE BAY BY ALFRED THE GREAT AD 877'*. The battle probably never happened (it's more likely that the Viking ships were shipwrecked), but stonemason John Mowlem, who had it erected in 1862, clearly felt that Swanage deserved some military glory.

Shore Road follows Swanage Beach past traditional tourist paraphernalia such as beach huts, folding deckchairs and a Punch and Judy show. The photogenic Banjo Pier, with its Victorian clock tower shelter, is actually Swanage's storm water outflow – perhaps avoid swimming here.

Old Harry Rocks.

The SWCP departs Swanage uninspiringly, via an inland diversion up Ulwell Road and through the Ballard Estate, a private chalet park. At low tide, it is possible to bypass this by negotiating groyne obstacles along Swanage Beach, as far as a set of steps after 900m. The paths re-join atop crumbling cliffs overlooking Swanage Beach's quiet northern end.

A short, but stiff, climb ascends above Ballard Cliff onto Ballard Down, a hulking chalk ridge. The plus-side is fine views of Swanage and, once you round the corner at Ballard Point, a tremendous vista ahead: sheer chalk cliffs and stacks, backed by Studland Beach curving towards the SWCP's finish.

The cliffs which you follow downhill from Ballard Down towards Handfast Point are a cross-section sliced through the same band of vertically-folded Cretaceous chalk exposed at Durdle Door and Lulworth Cove (section 60); the 'Purbeck Monocline'. The chalk is composed of the remnants of marine algae known as coccoliths, with around six billion per cubic centimetre! Gazing across Poole Bay, you will spot the gleaming chalk cliffs behind The Needles rocks, twenty-four kilometres east on the Isle of Wight; you could have walked there along the chalk ridge, until the sea breached it around 50,000 years ago.

The cliffs are particularly spectacular at their downhill end, known as Old Nick's Ground. The sea has eroded a succession of sheer-sided bays which allow viewing of The Pinnacles and Old Harry Rocks; be careful! The Pinnacles are a pair of stacks, the first (pointy) one called The Pinnacle and the second (truncated) one given various names, including Little Pinnacle and Haystack. The wonderful stacks and caves of Old Harry Rocks jut from Handfast Point. 'Old Harry' is the stack at the seaward end; it's an archaic name for Satan, or, possibly, comes from thirteenth-century Poole pirate Harry Paye. Harry had a wife in the nineteenth century, but he was widowed when this accompanying stack collapsed in 1896.

A track leads west towards Studland village, emerging near the Bankes Arms pub before heading back to the coast. Fort Henry perches above Redend Point's low sandstone cliffs. This sizeable and well-preserved concrete bunker was built in 1943, overlooking the length of Studland Beach.

Fort Henry, Studland Bay.

In April 1944, it was used by King George VI, President Eisenhower and Winston Churchill to observe Exercise Smash, a series of rehearsals for the D-Day landings (these were followed by the catastrophic Exercise Tiger, page 233). Outside, a memorial honours six soldiers who drowned when their experimental amphibious 'DD tanks' sank.

The path descends from Middle Beach car park. The remainder of the SWCP is, splendidly, a 4.5km trek along the sand! The first 600m passes beach huts behind an eroded and retreating shoreline, with trees and bushes sinking towards the water. Knoll Beach is recognisable by its large car park and National Trust paraphernalia. Henceforth, this glorious arc of east-facing dunes and shoreline, a National Nature Reserve, is largely yours, if you don't mind the occasional naturist. Follow the firm sand at the water's edge, or trudge arduously amongst the dunes.

A rocky spit, where the beach bends left, marks the entrance to Shell Bay. It's just a kilometre to where the SWCP reaches the road … and ends. South Haven Point is the entrance to Poole Harbour; Brownsea Island is visible a short distance within, marked by Brownsea Castle. In 1907, the island was the site of Lord Baden Powell's first Scout camp.

What will you experience at this, the terminus of a 630 mile / 1014km path? The screeching of Poole Harbour's terns is a constant, as is the metal clanking of the 'chain ferry' from Poole. David Mayne's 2003 Marker Post sculpture, mounted on a compass rose, depicts a mast and sails decorated with images that will activate memories from along the path. Whether you have reached South Haven Point via a morning's stroll, or via a far longer exploration, savour this moment.

St Catherine's Chapel and The Fleet from the South Dorset Ridgeway.

63 West Bexington to Osmington Mills

Distance	27.5km / 17.1 miles	Height gain 700m / 2,300ft	Difficulty ●●●●●
Maps	OS Landranger 194 / OS Explorer OL15		
Start	The Beach car park, West Bexington DT2 9DG / digit.device.scrubber / SY 531 864		
Finish	The Smuggler's Inn car park, Osmington Mills DT3 6HE / begins.certainly.apples / SY 735 817		
Public transport	X54 and X53 / X52 Jurassic Coaster buses, change at Weymouth. 2km walk from Swyre village		

This alternative official section, called the South Dorset Ridgeway, links sections 57 and 59 and was the SWCP's original route until the incorporation, in 2003, of the Isle of Portland. Although it veers far inland, it follows the high ground with phenomenal vistas, meaning that the sea is almost always in sight. There are no facilities or refreshments along this long outing.

Why might you select this alternative? It offers a shortcut, shaving about thirty kilometres off the overall total. However, anyone who has come this far is unlikely to be fussed about that! The real reasons to follow the SDR are; for the aforementioned views, to enjoy a fine landscape of chalk downlands and, above all, for the evocative ancient monuments.

The author's best advice is to complete this section, *in addition* to the SWCP's coastal route. Tackle it in isolation, or take a day out from the main route (having reached Weymouth?), utilising the excellent bus links.

The SDR commences with a grinding straight-line ascent, following Beach Road and then a track to the crest of Limekiln Hill. The rewards are the views westward, to Golden Cap and beyond, and the chalk grasslands which are now the order of the day, habitat to orchids and the Adonis blue butterfly. The limekiln remains are a young addition to this landscape; eastwards along the ridge towards Tulk's Hill, the first of countless burial mounds are encountered and after the B3157 is crossed, Abbotsbury Castle hillfort looms ahead. Steps ascend through earthwork walls to a 215m trig point. Boasting expansive views eastwards, along The Fleet (page 280) to the Isle of Portland, this later became the site of a Roman signal station.

Across a lane to Wears Hill's fire cresset, the SDR hugs the sea-facing scarp overlooking Abbotsbury and the strip lynchets around St Catherine's Chapel (section 56). At White Hill, the ridgetop widens to a plateau. After a fifty-metre road interlude and a traverse above a dry valley, keep your eyes open for the unassuming Hampton Stone Circle, constructed c2,000BC. Ten stones lie, easily missed, beside a gate, to the right of the track.

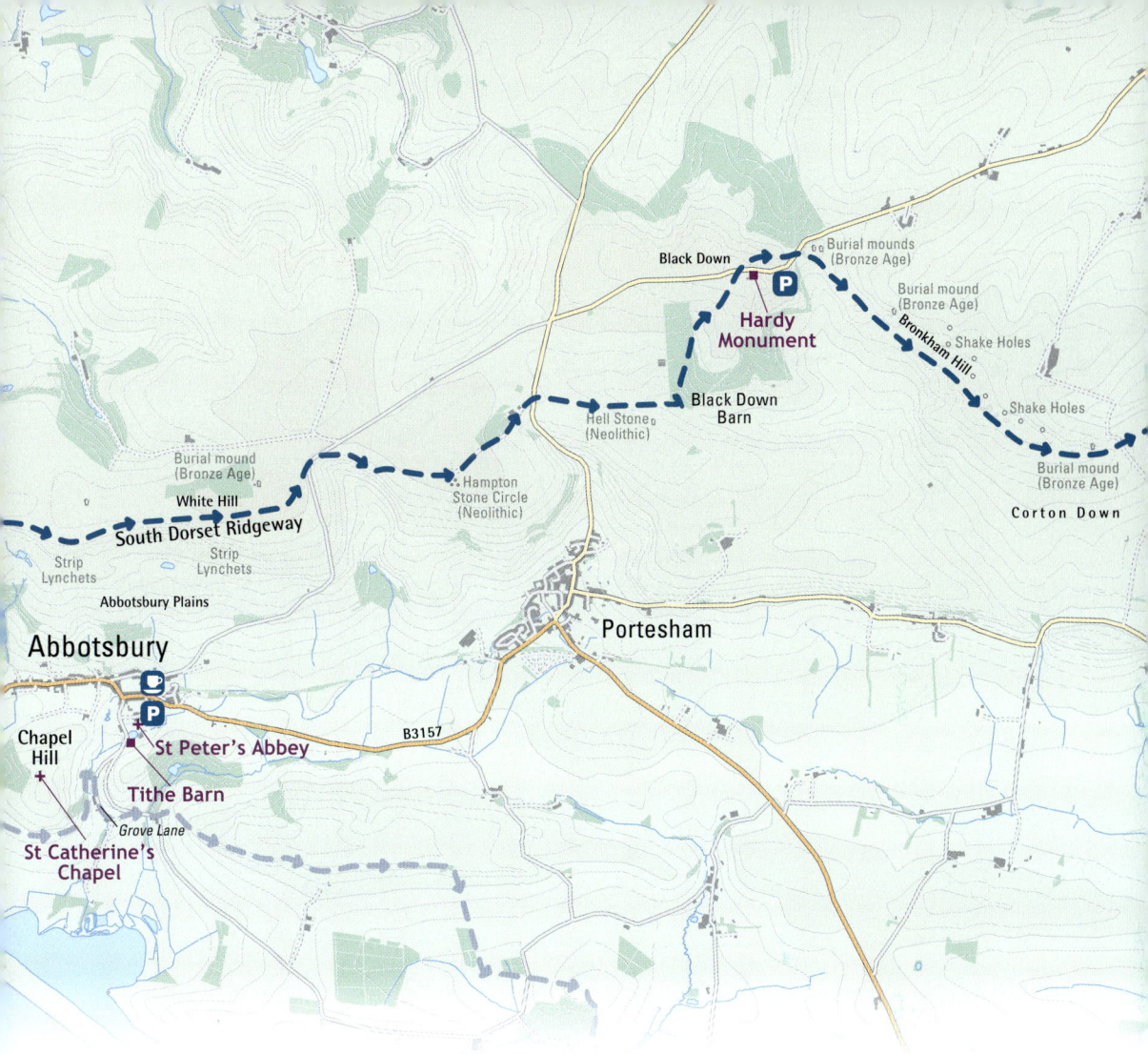

Another road interlude reaches the forestry-adorned slopes of Black Down. Before the woods, look for a stone stile on the right; this is a side-path to the Hell Stone, a 6,000-year-old long barrow. The impressive dolmen configuration, with a raised capstone, is actually the result of a haphazard 1866 'restoration'.

Within the woods, a sharp left turn before Black Down Barn veers uphill. This trail emerges above the trees at Black Down's 239m summit, where a gravel layer topping the chalk gives rise to heathland of heather, gorse and bilberry. The unsettlingly phallic Hardy Monument rears above the SDR's highest point. This 1844 tower commemorates Thomas Hardy; not the Dorset writer, but actually the *HMS Victory* captain immortalised by Nelson's dying words, *"Kiss me Hardy"*.

Across the lane, behind the monument, a path descends steeply and crosses the lane again. Bronkham Hill curves ahead, a well-defined ridge pockmarked with dozens of burial mounds and 'shake holes'; the latter are sink holes, where chalk has dissolved underneath the surface gravel layer.

Corton Down was blighted by unsightly pylons, removed in 2023. Ridge Hill is wider, with burial mounds leading to a radar tower and the B3159 crossing. The immense chalk walls of Maiden Castle, Britain's largest hillfort, can be seen northwards.

A bridge crosses the A354 Weymouth relief road, where 2009 roadworks sensationally uncovered the 'Viking Pit of Death', containing fifty decapitated Scandinavians, executed at some point between 970 and 1025. After looping around Bincombe Down's crest, a ridgetop road is followed for 500m. To escape this road, the SDR makes a convoluted deviation south of the ridge.

A descent through Bincombe hamlet, as far as twelfth-century Holy Trinity Church, is followed by an ascent to Combe Valley Road. Here, a choice of routes lead either side of diminutive Green Hill. The right-hand route gives fine views of Chalbury Hillfort's defensive embankments;

Prehistory along the South Dorset Ridgeway

The SDR has possibly Britain's densest concentration of prehistoric monuments, with over a thousand identified. The oldest are the stone circles and burial chambers erected by our earliest farmers in the Neolithic period (4,000BC-2,500BC). The c400 burial mounds (also known as tumuli or barrows), populating the high ground, mostly date from the Bronze Age (2,500BC-800BC). The hillforts are relatively youthful, their monumental walls constructed in the Iron Age (800BC-1st century AD).

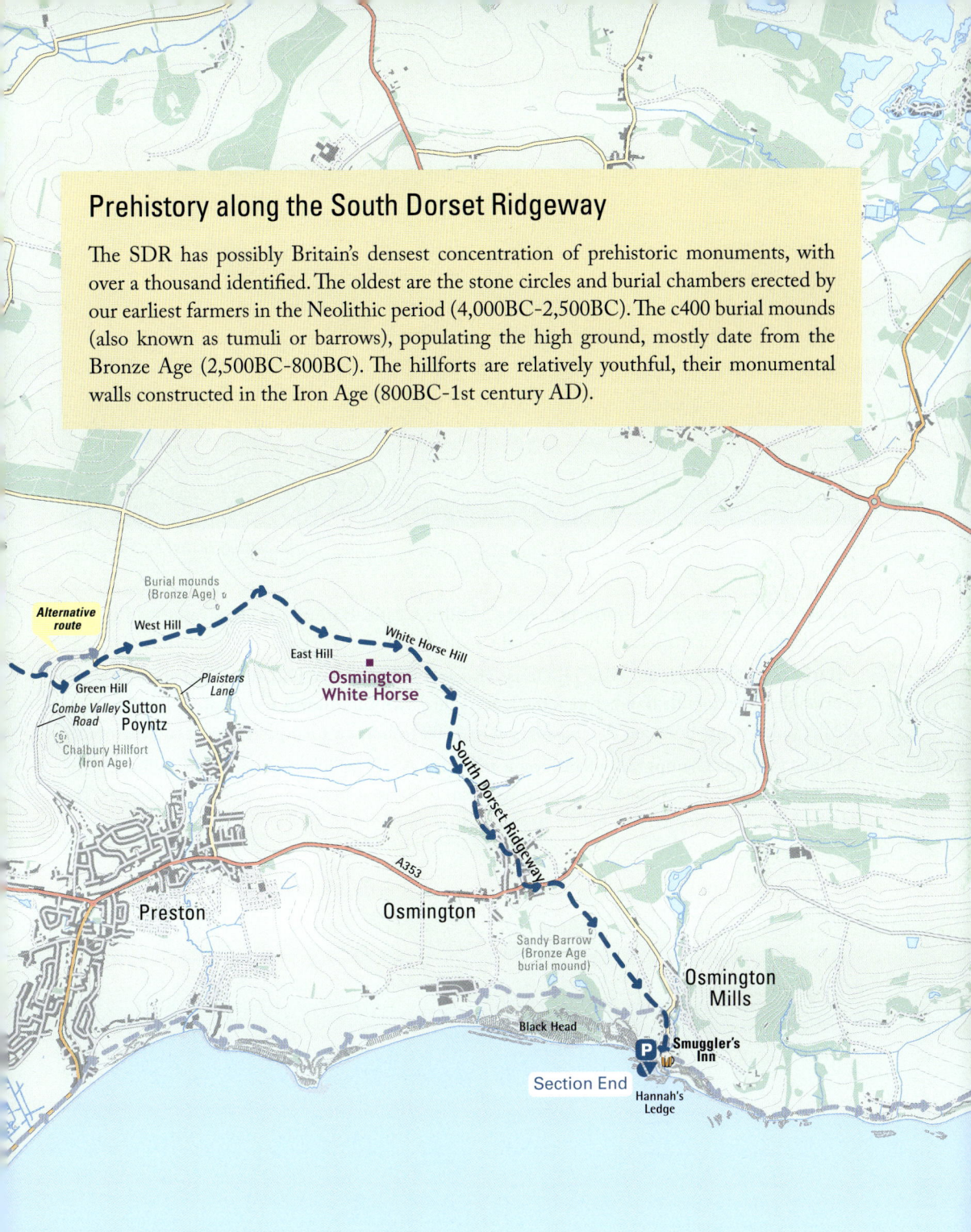

Chalbury Hillfort from West Hill.

this is one of the earliest hillforts, predating Maiden Castle. Both routes reconverge on Plaisters Lane, from where a track leads back atop the main ridge.

Burial mounds punctuate West Hill, East Hill and White Horse Hill, with final glorious views overlooking Weymouth Bay, before a track veers off downhill towards Osmington. Look back to see the faded white horse on the hillside, cut in 1808 to honour George III's visit to Weymouth.

Lanes through Osmington village reach the busy A353, which is crossed and followed. The path crests a final hill, topped by Bronze Age Sandy Barrow, before a long seaward descent. The coastal SWCP is rejoined just before the lane into Osmington Mills.

The Hardy Monument.

South West Coast Path Marker Post, South Haven Point.

Index of Place Names

A

Abbotsbury 275, 277, 278, 279
Abbotsbury Castle 308
Alma Bridge, Sidmouth 259
Anvil Point Lighthouse 301
Appledore 51
Appledore Shipyard 51
Arish Mell 295
Armed Knight, The 135
Ashley Combe House 20
Ashley Combe Lodge 19
Axmouth 263

B

Babbacombe Beach 248
Baggy Erratic 39
Baggy House 40
Baggy Point 39
Ballard Point 305
Ballowall Barrow 128
Bantham 219, 220
Barbican 207
Barnstaple 41, 44, 45
Barras Nose 77
Barrett's Zawn 82
Bar, The 224, 226
Basset's Cove 114
Bass Point 156
Bat's Head 290
Battery Gardens 241
Bayard's Cove Fort 235
Beacon Point, Ilfracombe 31
Bedruthan Steps 94
Beeny Sisters 74
Beer 262
Beer Head 262
Beesands 231
Benoath Cove 77
Berry Camp 261
Berry Head 239, 240
Berry Head Fort 240
Berryl's Point 95
Bideford 45, 48, 49
Bideford Bay 52
Bigbury Bay 215, 218
Bigbury-on-Sea 220
Bincombe 310
Bindon Abbey 294
Bindon Hill 295
Bishop, The 148
Blackchurch Rock 58
Black Down 309
Black Head, Mevagissey Bay 179
Black Humphrey Rock 95
Blackpool Sands 234
Black Rock beach 71
Blegberry Cliff 59
Bodrugan's Leap 177
Bolt Head 225
Bolt Tail 223
Booby's Bay 90
Boscastle 75, 76
Bosigran Castle 124
Bossiney Castle 77
Bossiney Haven 77
Bossington 17
Bossington Hill 17
Boswedden Mine 128
Bottallack Mine 127
Bounds Cliff 82
Bovisand Bay 211
Bowers Quarries 285
Brandy Head 256
Branscombe 261
Braunton 44
Braunton Burrows 43
Brea Hill 86
Bridport 274
Britannia Royal Naval College 235
Brixham 237, 240, 241
Broadsands Beach, Combe Martin 30
Broadsands, Paignton 243
Brownstone Battery 239
Buck's Mills 56
Bude 61, 65, 69
Bude Canal 69, 70
Bude Castle 69
Budleigh Salterton 254
Bugle Rocks 216
Bull Point Lighthouse 35
Burgh Island 220, 221
Burgundy Chapel 16
Burton Bradstock 276
Butter Hill 23

C

Cabin, The, Buck's Mills 56
Cabin, The, Clovelly 57
Cadgwith 157
Caerhays Castle 173, 174
Cambeak 73
Camel Rock 148
Cape Cornwall 128
Capstone Hill 32
Capstone Point 32
Carbis Bay 118
Carleon Cove 157
Carlyon Bay 182
Carn Clough 124
Carnewas Mine 94
Carn Naun Point 120
Carnweather Point 85
Caroline Quarry 81
Carracks, The 120
Carrick Roads 168
Carter's Rocks 102, 103
Castle Bungalow 54
Castle Point 72
Castle Rock 26
Cataclews Point 90
Cathedral of North Devon 60
Cattewater 208
Cawsand 200
Cawsand Fort 200
Chair Ladder Cliff 135
Chalbury Hillfort 310
Challaborough 220
Chapel Jane 123
Chapel of St Nicholas 31
Chapel Porth 108
Charlestown 175, 179, 181
Charmouth 271, 272
Chesil Beach 276, 278, 280, 281, 283
Chesil Cliff House 40
Chickerell Range 282
Chipman Point 71
Church of the Storms 150
Chynhalls Point 158
Clavell Tower 298
Cligga Head 106
Clovelly 53, 55, 56, 57
Clovelly Court mansion 56, 57
Cockleridge Ham 219
Coleton Fishacre 239
Combe Martin 25, 28, 29, 31
Combesgate Valley 36
Com Head 85
Commando Ridge 124
Compass Point 71
Constantine Bay 90
Coombe Valley 65
Cornish Mining World Heritage Site 109, 147
Countisbury 23

Countisbury Castle 22
Coverack 155, 158, 159
Cow and Calf, The 27
Crab Quay battery 166
Crackington Haven 69, 72, 73
Crane Castle 114
Crane Islands 114
Cremyll 197, 198, 201, 205
Cribba Head 137
Crock Point 26
Crooklets Beach 65
Crowns engine houses 127
Crow Point 43
Croyde 40
Croyde Bay 39
Croyde Sand 40
Cudden Point 144
Cuddycleave Wood 26
Culbone Combe 19
Culver Cliff Sand 16

D

Daddyhole Plain 245
Damage Cliffs 34
Dancing Ledge 300
Dartmouth 231, 234, 235
Dartmouth Castle 235
Dawlish 251
Dawlish Warren National Nature Reserve 251
Deadman, The 174
Dean Quarries 160
Delabole Point 82
Dennis Head 162
Dennis Point 81
Desolation Point 22
Devil's Bellows 76
Devil's Point 206
Dinas Head 90
Dinosaur Egg Beach 128
Dizzard Point 71
Dodman Point 174
Dollar Rock 95
Dolor Point 158
Donkey Hole 82
Donkey Island 281
Doom Bar 87, 89, 91
Dowlands Cliffs 266
Downderry 193
Down End 40
Doyden Point 85
Dripping Well 45
Dr Johnson's Head 135
Droskyn Point 105
Dr Syntax's Head 135
Duckpool beach 65
Dunderhole Point 81

Duporth 179
Durdle Door 290
Durgan 164
Durlston Castle 301
Durlston Country Park and National Nature Reserve 300
Durlston Head 301

E

Earl's Drive 200
East Cliff, West Bay 275
East Coombe 187
Eastern Brockholes 17
East Looe 191
East Portholland 173
East Portlemouth 226, 227
East-the-Water 48
Eddystone Lighthouse 208
Efford Beacon 71
Efford Cottage 69
Eldern Point 58
Elephant Rock 77
Embury Beacon 63
Enys Dodnan 135
Exmansworthy Cliff 58
Exmouth 252, 253, 257
Eype Mouth 274

F

Falmouth 163, 165, 166
Falmouth Bay 164
Fern Pit Café 101
Fire Beacon Point 74
First & Last House, The 135
Fistral Beach 99
Fleet, The 280, 281, 282
Flory Island 95
Flower's Barrow 295
Foreland Point 23
Fort Bovisand 211
Fort Charles 226
Fort Henry 305
Fort Picklecombe 200
Fowey 181, 184
Fox Cove 91
Freathy 193, 197
Fremington Quay 47
Frog Stone 260

G

Gallantry Bower 58
Gammon Head 228
Gannel, The 99, 101, 102
Gara Point 214
Gara Rock 227
GCHQ Bude 65
Geevor Tin Mine 125
Geoneedle 254

Gerrans 167
Gerrans Bay 170
Giant's Quoits 160
Gillan Harbour 160
Gilson's Cove Mine 85
Glebe Cliff 79
Glendurgan Garden 163
Glenthorne House 21
Goat Island 265
Godrevy 111, 114, 115
Godrevy Island 114
Godrevy Lighthouse 113
Godrevy Point 114
Goggin's Barrow 289
Golden Cap 273
Golden Cove 30
Gooden Heane Point 112
Goodrington Sands 243
Gore, The 56
Gorran Haven 171, 174, 175
Great Burland Rocks 27
Great Hangman 27, 28
Great Hangman Gut 28
Great Mew Stone 212
Great Red 23
Greenaleigh Point 16
Gribbin Head 183
Griffin's Point 95
Gull Rocks 102
Gull Rock, Veryan Bay 172
Gullyn Rock 111, 112
Gunrow Signal Station 215
Gunver Head 89
Gurnard's Head 122, 123
Gurnard's Head Mine 123
Gwennap Head 135
Gwithian Beach 115
Gyllyngvase Beach 165

H

Hallane 179
Hallsands 227, 230, 231
Hambury Tout 291
Hampton Stone Circle 308
Hannafore 191
Hanover Cove 107
Hardy Monument 309
Hartland Abbey 60
Hartland Point 59, 60
Hartland Point Lighthouse 59
Hartland Quay 57, 60, 61
Haven, The 83
Hawker's Cove 89
Hawker's Hut 65
Hayle 116
Hayle Bay 86
Hayle Estuary Nature Reserve 118

Heddon's Mouth Cleave 27
Hele 31
Helford 162
Helford Passage 159, 160, 162, 163
Helford Point 160, 162
Helford River 160, 162, 163
Hell Stone 309
Herbury Island 281
Heybrook Bay 211
High Cliff 74
Higher Longbeak 71
Higher Penhallic Point 81
Higher Sharpnose Point 65
High Peak, Sidmouth 256
Highveer Point 27
Hillsborough 31
Hive Beach 276
HMP The Verne 286
HMP / YOI Portland 286
Hobby Drive 56
Hoe, The 207
Holcombe 250
Holdstone Hill 27
Hole Head 251
Holnicote Estate 17
Holywell 102
Holywell Bay 102
Hooe 208
Hooken Undercliff 261
Hope Cove 217, 221, 223
Hope's Nose 247
Horrors, The 201
Horsey Island 44
House on the Props 189
Huer's House 97
Hurlstone Combe 17
Hurlstone Point 17

I

Ilfracombe 29, 31, 33
Inner Froward Point 239
Inner Hope 221
Inner Stone 30
Instow 48
Instow Barton Marsh 47
Instow Sands 48
Iron Coast, The 60
Island, The, Tintagel 77, 78
Isle of Portland 283
Isle of Purbeck 297
Isley Marsh 47

J

Jacket's Point 82
Jennycliff Bay 205, 209
Jericho Valley 107
Jurassic Coast World Heritage Site 253, 257

K

Kellan Head 85
Kelsey Head 102
Kemyel Crease Nature Reserve 140
Kenidjack Castle 127
Kennack Sands 157
Kents Cavern 247
Killigerran Head 170
Kimmeridge Bay 293, 296, 297
Kimmeridge Ledges 297
Kingsand 200
Kingsbridge Estuary 224, 226, 227
Kingswear 234, 237
Kingswear Castle 239
Kite's Shaft 111
Knap Head 63
Knoll Beach 306
Kynance Cove 153

L

Labrador Bay RSPB reserve 248
Ladies' Window 76
Lammana Chapel 191
Lamorna Point 140
Land's End 135
Langerstone Point 228
Langstone Rock 251
Lanterdan Quarry 81
Lantern Hill 31
Lantic Bay 186
Lee Abbey 26
Lee Bay 34
Lester Point 28, 29
Levant Mine 125, 127
Ligger Point 103
Limebury Point 227
Little Bindon 294
Little Cudden 144
Little Dartmouth 234
Little Hangman 28
Lizard Lighthouse 155
Lizard National Nature Reserve 152, 157
Lizard Point 151, 154, 155
Lizard Wireless Station 156
Lobber Point 83
Loe Bar 148, 150
Logan Rock 138
Long Bridge, Barnstaple 44, 45
Long Bridge, Bideford 48
Looe 191
Looe Island 191
Lower Ley 231
Lower Longbeak 71
Lower Penhallic Point 81
Lower Sharpnose Point 65
Lowland Point 159
Lulworth Cove 287, 291, 293

Lulworth Ranges 294
Lundy Hole 85
Lusty Glaze 97
Lye Rock 77
Lyme Bay 280
Lyme Regis 263, 266, 267, 271
Lynmouth 19, 23, 25
Lynton 25

M

Maen Castle 135
Maenporth 165
Maer Down 65
Maiden Castle 310
Maidencombe Beach 248
Manacles, The 160
Man o' War, The 291
Marazion 143, 144
Marble Cliff 90
Marsland Mouth 63
Marsland Water 63
Mawgan Porth 95
Meadowsfoot Beach 216
Menachurch Point 65
Merlin's Cave 77
Mermaid's Pool 54
Merope Islands 89
Mevagissey 177
Mevagissey Bay 177
Mew Stones 225
Milford Common 63
Milford Water 63
Millbay 206
Millendreath 192
Millook 71
Millook Haven 71
Milton's Temple 201
Minack Point 136
Minehead 15
Minnows Islands 91
Morte Bay 39
Mortehoe 36
Morte Point 35, 36
Morwenstow 63
Mothecombe 213, 217
Mothecombe Beach 216
Mothecombe House and Gardens 216
Mother Ivey's Bay 88, 90
Mountain, The 82
Mount Batten 208
Mount Edgcumbe Country Park 200
Mount's Bay 144, 147
Mousehole 140
Mouth Mill 58
Mullion Cove 153
Mupe Rocks 295

N

Nanjizal Bay 135
Nanny Moore's Bridge 69
Nare Head 171, 173
Nare Point 160
Navax Point 114
Ness, The 248
Newberry Beach 29
Newlyn 141
Newquay 93, 96, 97, 99
Newton Ferrers 210, 213
Northam Burrows Country Park 51, 52
Northcott Mouth 65
Northern Door 74
Noss Mayo 210, 213
Nothe Fort 289

O

Old Harry Rocks 305
Old Nick's Ground 305
Old Quay, Newlyn 141
Old Redoubt, The 240
Oreston 208
Osmington 312
Osmington Mills 289, 290, 307, 312
Outer Hope 221
Outer Stone 30
Overbecks 226

P

Padstow 84, 87
Padstow Lifeboat Station 90
Padstow War Memorial 87
Paignton 243
Palmerston's Follies 196
Par 182
Park Head 94
Par Sands 183
Parson and Clerk, The 251
Pebble Ridge 52
Pedn-mên-an-mere 136
Pednvadan 170
Pen a Gader 107
Penally Point 76
Penare Point 177
Penberth Cove 137
Pencannow Point 72
Pencarrow Head 186
Pencil Rock 39
Pendarves Point 94
Pendeen Lighthouse 124
Pendeen Watch 119, 124, 125
Pendennis Castle 165, 166
Pendennis Point 165
Pendinas 120
Pendower Beach 167, 170, 171
Penhale Point 103
Penhale Sands 103
Penhalt Cliff 71
Penhill Point 47
Penlee Point, Newlyn 141
Penlee Point, Plymouth 200
Pennance Point 165
Penpol Creek 101, 102
Pentargon 76
Pentewan 178
Pentire Point 86
Pentire Point West 102
Pentreath Beach 154
Penzance 137, 141, 143
Peppercombe valley 54
Pepper Cove 91
Pepperpot (daymark tower) 112
Pepperpot, The (Storm Tower) 71
Percuil River 169
Perran Beach 103
Perranporth 99, 103, 105
Perranuthnoe 144
Peveril Point 301
Phillip's Point Nature Reserve 71
Pinnacles, The 305
Piskies Cove 146
Place 167, 169
Pleasure House, The 60
Plymouth 205
Plymouth Breakwater 211
Point Perilous 23
Point Spaniard 140
Poldhu Cove 147, 150, 151
Polkerris 183
Polmear 183
Polperro 185, 188, 189, 192
Polridmouth 184
Polruan 184, 185
Polrudden Cove 178
Polzeath 86
Pordenack Point 135
Porlock Bay 17
Porlock Weir 15, 18, 19
Port Gaverne 82
Portgiskey 177
Porthallow 160
Porth Beach 97
Porth-cadjack Cove 114
Porthcothan 87, 91, 93
Porthcurno 133, 136, 137
Portheras Cove 124
Porthgwarra 136
Porth Kidney Sands 118
Porthleven 148
Porthleven Sands 150
Porthmeor Beach 120, 121
Porthmeor Point 123
Porthmoina Mill 124
Porth Nanven 128
Portholland 173
Porthoustock 160
Porthtowan 105, 108, 111
Port Isaac 79, 83
Portland Bill 285
Portland Bill Lighthouse 285
Portland Castle 286
Portland, Isle of 283
Portloe 173
Portmellon 177
Port Quin 85
Portreath 112
Portscatho 170
Port William 81
Portwrinkle 194
Praa Sands 143, 146, 147
Prawle Point 228
Predannack Head 153
Prince of Wales Engine House 81
Prussia Cove 146
Purbeck Heaths National Nature Reserve 306
Purbeck, Isle of 297
Putsborough Sand 39

Q

Queen Adelaide's Grotto 200

R

RAF Bolt Tail 225
Ralph's Cupboard 114
Rame Head 199
Range Walks 293, 294
Ranie Point 82
Rapparee Cove 31, 32
Redcliff Castle 94
Reedy Cliff 85
Renscombe Farm 300
Revelstoke Drive 214, 215
Richmond dry dock 51
Rillage Point 31
Rill Point 153
Ringstead 289, 290
Rinsey Head 147
River Avon 220
River Axe 263
River Camel 86
River Dart 235
River Erme 216, 217, 218
River Exe 251
River Fowey 184
River Gannel 99, 101
River Tamar 198
River Taw 43, 44, 45, 47

River Torridge 43, 47, 48, 51
River Yealm 212
Rock 83, 84, 86
Rock End Walk 245
Rockham Bay 35
Rocky Valley 76
Ronald Duncan's Hut 63
Rope Lake Head 298
Roscarrock Hill 83
Roseland Peninsula 167
Rosemullion Head 164
Rosenithon 160
Roundham Head 243
Roundhole Point 90
Royal Citadel 207
Royal Engineers Bridging Hard 282
Royal North Devon Golf Course 52
Royal William Yard 206
RRH Portreath 112
Rugged Jack 26
Rumps Point 85
Rumps, The 85
Runnel Stone 136
Rusey Cliff 74

S

Salcombe 223, 226
Salcombe Hill 260
Sally's Bottom 111
Samphire Rock 74
Sandsfoot Castle 287
Sandymere 52
Sandy Mouth 65
Saunton 37, 40, 41
Saunton Court 41
Saunton Down 40, 41
Saunton Sands 43
Scabbacombe Head 239
Scarnor Point 85
Seacombe Quarry 300
Seals Hole 74
Seaton, South Cornwall 189, 192, 193
Seaton, South Devon 259, 262, 263
Seatown 273
Selworthy Beacon 16
Sennen Cove 125, 129, 133
Sentinel, The 128
Shaldon 245, 246, 248
Sharkham Point 239
Sharp Tor 225
Sherrycombe 27
Sidmouth 253, 256, 259
Silvermine Point 179
Sister's Fountain 22

Skern 51
Slapton Ley 233
Slapton Sands 233
Smeaton's Tower 207
Soar Mill Cove 224
Song of the Sea, The 135
South Dorset Ridgeway 307, 311
South Haven Point 303, 306
South Milton Sands 221
Southwell 285
South West Coast Path Monument 15
Sparkhayes Marsh 18
Speke's Mill Mouth 63
Spy House Point Lighthouse 190
Stackhouse Cove 144
Staddon Heights 209
St Agnes 108
St Agnes Head 108
Stair Hole 291
St Alban's Head 299
St Aldhelm's Chapel 299
St Aldhelm's Head 299
St Anchorite's Rock 215
St Anthony Head Lighthouse 169
St Anthony-in-Meneage 160
St Anthony's Church 169
Starcross 249, 252
Starehole Bay 225
Starfish bunker 173
Start Point Lighthouse 230
St Austell Bay 179, 181
St Catherine's Castle 184
St Catherine's Chapel 277, 278
St Catherine's Tor 61
St Clement's Isle 140
St Cuthbert's Well 102
Steeple Point 65
Stem Point 95
St Enodoc's Church 86
Stepper Poin 89
St Gennys Church 72
St George's Island 191
St George's Well 87
St Gothian Sands Local Nature Reserve 115
St Helen's Chapel 128
St Ia's Church 118
St Ives 115, 118, 119
St Ives Bay 114, 115
St Ives Head 120
St Levan's Well 136
St Loy's Cove 138
St Materiana's Church 81
St Mawes 165, 167, 169
St Mawes Castle 166, 169
St Michael's Chapel 200

St Michael's Mount 143, 144, 145
St Morwenna's Church 65
St Morwenna's Well 63
St Nectan's Church 60
St Nectan's Glen 76
St Nicholas, Chapel of 31
Stoke Fleming 234
Stoke Point 215
Stonehouse 198, 205, 206
Storm Tower, The 69
St Peter's Church 158
St Peter the Poor Fisherman Church 215
St Piran's Oratory 103, 104
Strangles, The 74
Strete Gate 233
St Senara's church 123
St Symphorian's Church 76
Studland 305
Studland Beach 305
St Winwaloe Church 150
Swanage 297, 301, 303
Swanage Bay 301
Swanage Beach 305
Swanpool Beach 165
Swyre Head 290, 298

T

Tarka Trail 44
Tater-du Lighthouse 138
Tate St Ives gallery 121
Tea Caverns 97
Teignmouth 246, 249
Telecommunications Research Establishment 300
Terence Coventry Sculpture Park 158
Thatcher Point 247
Thorncombe Beacon 274
Thurlestone Rock 220
Tinner's Point 95
Tintagel 73, 79
Tintagel Castle 77, 78
Tintagel Haven 77, 78
Tobban Horse 111
Tolcarne Beach 97
Tor Bay 240, 241, 242
Torcross 231, 233
Torquay 241, 244, 245
Torre Abbey 244
Torrs Walk 33
Tout Quarry Sculpture Park and Nature Reserve 285
Towan Beach 97
Towan Head 95
Towanroath engine house 108
Towans, The 116

Trebarwith Strand 81
Trebetherick Point, 86
Treen 122
Tregantle Fort 195, 196
Tregantle Ranges 194, 195
Tregardock Cliff 82
Tregear Point 148
Tregudda Gorge 90
Tregurrian 95
Treligga Cliff 82
Tremoutha Haven 73
Trenance Point 95
Trentishoe Down 27
Trereen Dinas 123
Treryn Dinas 138
Trescore Islands 93
Tresungers Point 82
Trethias Island 91
Trevalga Cliff 76
Trevalgan Cliff 120
Trevan Point 85
Trevaunance Cove 108
Trevelgue Head 95
Trevellas Coombe 107
Trevemper 101
Trevose Head 90
Trewavas Head 148
Trewavas Mine 149
Trewellard Bottoms 125
Treyarnon Point 90
Tubby's Head 108
Tulk's Hill 308
Tunnels Beaches 33, 35
Turbot Point 177
Turnchapel 208
Tyneham 296

U
Undercliffs, The 264, 265, 266
Upton 71

V
Valley of the Rocks, The 26
Varley Head 83
Velator Quay 44
Verity 31
Verne Citadel 286
Vicarage Cliff 65
Vicarage, The, Morwenstow 65

W, X
Walls Hill 248
Warren Cliff, Hartland Quay 60
Warren Point, Bude 65
Warren Point, Wembury 209, 210, 212
Watcombe Beach 248
Watergate Beach 95
Watermouth Harbour 30
Welcombe Mouth 63
Wembury 212
Wembury Point 211
West Bay 271, 274, 275
West Bexington 278, 307
Westcombe Beach 218
West Looe 191
Weston Plats 260
Weston Wildflower Meadow 261
West Portholland 173
West Quarry 81
Westward Ho! 49, 52, 53
Weymouth 279, 282, 283, 287, 289
Wheal Charlotte Moor 108
Wheal Coates mine 108
Wheal Edward 127
Wheal Owles 127
Wheal Prosper Mine 149
Whipsiderry Beach 95
White Nothe 290
Whitesand Bay 129
Whitsand Bay 197
Widemouth Bay 71
Wide Slip, Noss Mayo 210, 213
Widmouth Head 30
Wilderness Point 201
Willapark, Boscastle 76
Willapark, Tintagel 77
Will's Rock 91
Windbury Head 58
Wine Cove 91
Winspit Quarry 300
Wireless Point 136
Woolacombe 33, 36, 37
Woolacombe Sand 37
Woolacombe Warren 37
Worbarrow Bay 295
Worbarrow Tout 296
Wringapeak 27
Wringcliff Bay 26

Y
Yealm Pool 212
Yenworthy Wood 21
Yeolmouth Cliff 63

Z
Zawn Gamper 138
Zawn Pyg 135
Zennor 122, 123
Zennor Head 122
Zig-Zags 201
Zulu Bank 51